NG 20

CARDIOLOGY
AT THE LIMITS IV

CARDIOLOGY
AT THE LIMITS IV

edited by

LIONEL H OPIE
DEREK M YELLON

Based on a Symposium held in Cape Town
to celebrate the ongoing collaboration between
the Hatter Institutes of the
University of Cape Town
and
University College London

University of Cape Town
and
University College London

Stanford Writers, Cape Town
2001

In no case can the institutions with which the authors are affiliated or the publisher be held responsible for the views expressed in the book, which reflect the opinions of the authors. Please call any errors to the attention of the authors.

CARDIOLOGY AT THE LIMITS IV

Edited by
Lionel H Opie, MD, DPhil, DSc, FRCP
Director, Heart Research Unit of the
Hatter Institute for Cardiology Research
Co-Director, Cape Heart Centre
University of Cape Town
Cape Town, South Africa

Derek M Yellon, PhD, BSc, Hon. MRCP, FACC, FESC
Director of Institute and Head of Division of Cardiology
The Hatter Institute and Centre for Cardiology
University College Hospital and Medical School
London, United Kingdom

With a preface by
Professor Wieland Gevers, MBChB, MA, DPhil (Oxon)
DSc h.c. (Cape Town), DSc h.c. (UPE)
Senior Deputy Vice-Chancellor
University of Cape Town
Cape Town, South Africa

CONTENTS

PRINCIPAL CONTRIBUTING AUTHORS

Professor Martin R Bennett MB, BCh, PhD, MRCP
British Heart Foundation Professor of
Cardiovascular Sciences
Unit of Cardiovascular Medicine
Addenbrooke's Centre for Clinical Investigation
Addenbrooke's Hospital
Cambridge
United Kingdom

Victor J Dzau, MD
Chairman, Department of Medicine
Physician-in-Chief, Director of Research
Brigham and Women's Hospital
Harvard Medical School
Boston
USA

Jeffrey M Isner, MD
Professor of Medicine and Pathology
Tufts University School of Medicine
Chief, Vascular Medicine and Cardiovascular Research
St Elizabeth Medical Center
Boston, MA 02135
USA

Arnold M Katz, MD, DMed (Hon), FACC, FACP
Professor of Medicine
Cardiology Division, Chief Emeritus
University of Connecticut School of Medicine
Farmington, Connecticut
Visiting Professor of Medicine
Dartmouth Medical School
Lebanon, New Hampshire
USA

Michael Marber, FRCP, PhD, FACC
Professor of Cardiology and Head of
Department of Cardiology
King's College, London
Honorary Consultant Cardiologist
Guy's and St Thomas' Hospitals NHS Trust
London SE1 7EH
United Kingdom

Tim D Noakes, MB ChB, MD, FACSM
Discovery Health Chair of Exercise and Sports Science and
Director MRC/UCT Research Unit for Exercise Science and
Sports Medicine
University of Cape Town
Sports Science Institute of South Africa
Cape Town
South Africa

Philip A Poole-Wilson, MD, FRCP, FACP, FESC
British Heart Foundation Simon Marks Chair of Cardiac Medicine and
Head, National Heart and Lung Institute Division
Imperial College School of Medicine
Dovehouse Street
London SW3 6LY
United Kingdom

Harvey D White, DSc, FRACP, FACC, FESC, MRSNZ
Honorary Clinical Professor of Medicine
University of Auckland
Director of Coronary Care and Cardiovascular Research
Green Lane Hospital
Auckland, 1003
New Zealand

Salim Yusuf, DPhil, MBBS, DPhil, FRCP, FRCP (C)
Professor of Medicine
Director, Division of Cardiology and
Director, Population Health Research Institute
McMaster University
Hamilton, Ontario L8L 2X2
Canada

AUTHORS' FOREWORD

We are delighted to present this our 4th book in the series *Cardiology at the Limits*. The chapters presented in this edition, yet again, represent knowledge at the "limits" of cardiology. Each is written by an acknowledged and internationally respected expert. Each represents a highly selected distillate, of clear interest to cardiologists and physicians, from the vast flood of new and current cardiological information.

The subjects of each chapter of this book have evolved from the 4th Cardiology at the Limits symposium, which was held in Cape Town in October 2000. To allow us the freedom we have to select our speakers from the very best in the world requires several strong support bases. First, our annual meeting takes place under the auspices of both University College London and the University of Cape Town. As in previous years, the meeting was opened with a welcome from the University of Cape Town, represented by the Senior Deputy Vice-Chancellor, Professor Wieland Gevers. Secondly, the meeting reflects the close collaboration between the two Hatter Institutes, one sited at each Institution. Thirdly, we warmly acknowledge the crucial support of Aventis pharmaceuticals, a new venture for them, allowing us to continue this unique meeting that does so much to enhance education in cardiology.

As in previous years, the aim of both the meeting, and the book that evolves from it, is to highlight a range of differing, yet equally important, topics in cardiology. It is our further intended aim to avoid maintaining any specific cardiovascular theme, thereby allowing the reader to indulge themselves in the very latest opinions selected from a range of equally important topics. This year's topics include the opportunities and limits of cardiovascular genetic manipulation, signalling in heart failure, the acute coronary syndromes, the global epidemic of cardiovascular disease, mortality in heart failure, apoptosis, the limits of exercise and two chapters on angiogenesis.

An innovation is the Hatter Award for the Advancement of Cardiovascular Science, given to Dr Victor Dzau, Chairman of the Department of Medicine at the Brigham and Women's Hospital, Harvard Medical School, Boston, Mass.

We intend to uphold the tradition we have created with a series of books in the future. Our aim is to provide a regular update for anyone who wants to maintain a broad-based understudying of cardiology at its very limits.

PREFACE FROM THE SENIOR DEPUTY VICE-CHANCELLOR OF THE UNIVERSITY OF CAPE TOWN

Cardiology is considered by its practitioners to be a discipline, and disciplines are what the word suggests: orderly, systematic ways of thinking and knowing and of adding to knowledge. It is only by being systematic and orderly that cardiologists and other heart scientists have been able to push their knowledge and understandings so far.

Yet the post-modern world has discovered that limits are set by purely disciplinary exploration, while certain problems cannot be fully addressed from within a discipline.

Post-modernism is often considered as synonymous with the assault on the scientific method launched by post-modern French philosophers, for whom there is no truth or even valid conclusion that is not socially or historically or "structurally" determined. Much more significant, however, is the rapid change which has come about in the actual practice of the search for useful knowledge in the post-modern era:

- New disciplines have evolved and are still evolving from combinations or fragmentations of old ones;
- There is a new and enhanced emphasis on multi-, trans- and inter-disciplinarity, and a re-assessment of the unproductive and limiting aspects of disiplinarity (exclusivity, jargon, sterility); and
- New kinds of scientific practice are now very prominent, moving from what Michael Gibbons has called "Mode I" scholarship or research (life-long disciplinary commitment) to "Mode II" (shorter-term teamwork, multi-disciplinarity, project management and deliverables).

Some philosophers have seen the sciences as related to each other in a vertical hierarchy, starting with Mathematics at the bottom and ending with Ethics at the top. Others have more convincingly explored the notion of "consilience" between all scientific disciplinary systems and world-views. Both of these conceptual approaches imply that much can be learnt in one discipline by applying to it the mindset and interrogation modes of the other, since ultimately, all of our knowledge about natural things is connected even if seen through eyes and minds trained in the guilds of the disciplines.

The "Limits of Cardiology" will only be tested if this post-modern Zeitgeist is fully absorbed and applied.

Professor Wieland Gevers, MBChB, MA, DPhil (Oxon), DSc h.c. (Cape Town), DSc h.c. (UPE)
Senior Deputy Vice-Chancellor
University of Cape Town
Cape Town, South Africa

THE HATTER AWARD FOR THE ADVANCEMENT OF CARDIOVASCULAR SCIENCES

The first Hatter Award for the Advancement of Cardiovascular Science was presented to Dr Dzau by the President of the Medical Research Council of South Africa, Professor Malegapuru William Makgoba.

The citation was as follows:

Mr President, may I present to you Dr Victor Dzau, the recipient of the first Hatter Award for the Advancement of Cardiovascular Science, given by the Hatter Institutes of the University of Cape Town and of University College, London.

Dr Dzau has outstanding credentials, both as a physician and a scientist. He is currently Chairman of the Department of Medicine at the Brigham and Women's Hospital at Harvard Medical School, Boston. Previously, he was Chairman of the Department of Medicine at Stanford University, California. He has thus headed two major departments at what are arguably two of the best medical schools in the United States. This is a unique achievement.

His scientific record is equally, or even more, impressive. He is Director of Research at the Brigham and Women's Hospital, Boston. He shares his skills as a leading member of important American expert bodies in the area of vascular biology, including the Advisory Committee to the Director of the National Institutes of Health in the USA. His many publications in the best journals bear testimony to the excellence of his research. He has just become the first Editor of the new journal of the American Physiological Society, *Physiological Genomics.*

Regarding the nature of the Hatter Award, it is designed to remind Dr Dzau of the rich cultural heritage of South Africa and, in particular, its Bushman or San people. They were the original artists of the Cape and their rock art still adorns our interior. Thus, the award is centered on San art.

Mr President, may I ask you to present these awards to Dr Dzau.

CHAPTER 1

Cardiovascular Genetic Manipulation – What are the Opportunities and Limits?

Abeel A. Mangi, MD and Victor J. Dzau, MD

INTRODUCTION

Cardiovascular disease remains the leading cause of death in the western world, with over half a million deaths a year in the United States attributable to coronary artery disease alone. These statistics remain challenging to the clinical community despite the significant progress in therapeutic development. The high incidence of cardiovascular disease is compounded by the aging of our population, with greater numbers of patients presenting for re-do procedures, be they percutaneous transluminal coronary angioplasty (PTCA), coronary artery bypass grafting (CABG), carotid endarterectomies, or infra-inguinal revascularizations. Numerous clinical studies have demonstrated the survival benefits of these invasive procedures when compared to medical modalities alone. However, rising numbers of patients eventually fail surgical or medical treatment and are increasingly left without any treatment options, making the need for aggressive alternative modes of treatment all the more important.

With the recognition of the systemic disease, atherosclerosis, as being a major causative factor in cardiovascular disease and the identification of LDL receptor gene mutation as the genetic basis of familial hypercholesterolemia (FH), it seemed fitting then, that one of the earliest initiatives in cardiovascular gene therapy attempted to treat the monogenic disorder, homozygotic FH. However, the majority of cardiovascular diseases are acquired in the setting of polygeneic predisposition. Thus, gene therapy of common cardiovascular disorders will necessitate a "multi-gene" approach which is far more difficult, and complicated. Additional concerns include the undesirability of systemic exposure to viral vectors.

Effective gene therapy must overcome several significant hurdles. The first, is the identification of the gene whose alteration is linked to disease pathophysiology; or, whose manipulation (by over-expression, or deletion) will result in correction of the pathophysiologic derangement. The complexity of cardiovascular disease has made crossing this first hurdle difficult. However, recent data have shown that genetic manipulation of key gene(s) involved with cardiovascular pathophysiology can sufficiently modify the pathophysiologic process that may result in a therapeutic outcome. For example, the identification of genes encoding for proteins such as vascular endothelial growth factor (VEGF), nitric oxide synthase (NOS), and hemoxygenase-1 (HO-1) have enabled researchers to explore *in vivo* gene therapy. The second hurdle involves targeted *in vivo* delivery of the gene to the cells and tissues of choice. Thus the target cell type in which the transgene mediates or exerts its therapeutic action must be identified. For example, beta-adrenergic over-expression in cardiac myocytes for heart failure therapy, and hirudin over-expression in endothelial cells for thrombolytic therapy. Cell based therapy with genetic engineering is yet another approach. In this case, the cell type is preferably autologous, i.e. it should be obtained from the patient who will be receiving gene therapy. In addition, it would be desirable to introduce the therapeutic gene *ex vivo* that is, in culture prior to *in vivo* application. This gets at the issue of targeted delivery *in vivo* or *ex vivo*. This may encompass a variety of techniques, be they mechanical, such as pressure-induced transfection; chemical, such as liposomal packaging of the plasmid; or biological, that is delivery with the aid of genetically modified retroviruses, adenoviruses or adeno-associated viruses. The critical needs are that the gene be efficiently and effectively delivered to the cell of choice, that the transduction allows stable integration of the engineered gene into the chromosome, that the gene expression be stable over the long term, that the mode of delivery be safe to the patient, and that the means of delivery be preferably tissue specific.

WHAT ARE THE OPPORTUNITIES?

Significant steps have been made in addressing these challenges over the past decade, marking a paradigmatic shift in the application of gene therapy, from the potential treatment of inherited monogenic disease, to the management of acquired disease. We will endeavor to review some of the major accomplishments in this regard (Table 1-1).

In addition, we believe that a second paradigmatic shift is in the making. This involves vascular and myocardial reconstruction, employing genetic manipulations of stem cells and progenitor cells in order to obtain sufficient sources of differentiated and genetically engineered cells of specific types for transplantation therapy. This exciting field termed "regenerative medicine", although very much in its infancy, provides us with a glimpse of what the future of cardiovascular genetic manipulation may hold.

TABLE 1-1:   THE POTENTIALS OF GENETIC MANIPULATION FOR THERAPEUTICS

- As a means of treating inherited systemic disease
- As a means of novel drug delivery to treat organ dysfunction due to common acquired, polygenic diseases
- As a means for organ reconstruction
- As a means for organogenesis
- For in utero/fetal gene therapy
- Use of embryonic stem cells
- For human cloning

A. GENE THERAPY FOR TREATMENT OF GENETIC DISORDERS

In its purest form, gene therapy is the *in vivo* introduction of the normal transgene to replace the defective gene that is responsible for the disorder. The best example of this approach in the cardiovascular area is the treatment of homozygous familial hypercholesterolemia (FH). FH is characterized by a defect in the gene coding for the low density lipoprotein (LDL) receptor that renders the receptor non-functional or dysfunctional. In homozygous FH, both alleles are affected and the natural history of this condition is the early onset of coronary artery disease, with death at an early age as a result. These patients tend to be recalcitrant to traditional lipid lowering medical regimens, such as bile acid resins and hydroxymethylglutaryl (HMG)-CoA reductase inhibitors.[1] These patients also respond poorly to surgical interventions such as portacaval shunting and ileal bypass.[2,3] After demonstrating the feasibility of gene therapy in Wanatabe rabbits[4], Wilson's group conducted a phase I human clinical trial involving *ex vivo* transduction of autologous hepatocytes (obtained by partial hepatectomy) with cDNA encoding the LDL receptor, using a modified retrovirus as the vector for gene transfer. These hepatocytes were then transplanted into the liver by cannulating the portal circulation and infusing the cell preparation through an indwelling catheter. The results demonstrated >90% cell viability after harvesting, approximately 20% transduction rate, significant and prolonged reduction of LDL in 60% of patients, with a 53% increase of *in vivo* LDL catabolism. There was however, some variation in the extent of the metabolic response to the treatment.[5] Unfortunately, the effect was not long lived. Although many technical and medical challenges will have to be overcome before this approach may be helpful in the long term treatment of these patients, this study constitutes a "proof of concept" of gene therapy for cardiovascular genetic disease. Current experimental studies are also examining the use of *in vivo* gene transfer using other vectors such as adenovirus, as an alternate approach.

B. GENE THERAPY AS "DRUG" DELIVERY

Genetic manipulation as a treatment modality may employ the concept of "gene as drug". That is, the gene product is viewed as a therapeutic agent that can produce a therapeutic response in the target tissue. We will highlight several applications of this particular paradigm as it applies to the cardiovascular system.

1. Angiogenesis Gene Therapy

Peripheral vascular insufficiency. There has been much interest over the last 4 years in the use of *in vivo* gene therapy for peripheral vascular disease, spurred on by the discovery of vascular endothelial growth factor (VEGF). With the aging of the population, large numbers of patients are coming to clinical attention with lower extremity ischemia resistant to maximal medical therapy, having failed surgical bypass. These patients, with few or no viable surgical options face possible limb loss, often after a prolonged and inexorable downhill clinical course. VEGF is a mitogen produced by endothelial cells, and targets high affinity receptors on these cells. It is this specificity of VEGF for endothelial cells that makes it such an attractive target for therapeutic angiogenesis, as endothelial cells are the critical cellular elements in the formation of new blood vessels.[6,7,8] The angiogenic effects of intra-arterial administration of acidic fibroblast growth factor (a-FGF)[9] and intramuscular administration of naked VEGF plasmid has been demonstrated successfully in rabbits[10] with the following purported advantage over viral delivery. Since the transfection efficiency is low, it proves to be less toxic systemically[11], while achieving an appropriate local response. Uncontrolled clinical studies have reported improvement in ankle-brachial indices, angiographic and magnetic resonance (MRI) demonstration of new blood vessel formation, as well as the apparent healing of ischemic ulcers and the claim of successful limb salvage in patients who are treated with four intramuscular injections of naked plasmid VEGF cDNA under the control of the cytomegalovirus promoter into the calf[12] as well as after intra-arterial administration into the femoral artery.[13] There is also data to suggest that VEGF injection may actually augment the performance of these collateral vessels by inducing an endothelium dependent relaxation of new blood vessels.[14]

Myocardial ischemia. Similar strategies have been applied to treating myocardial ischemia. One example involves gene transfer of VEGF incorporated in fusigenic hemagglutinating virus of Japan (HVJ)-liposome complexes using intramyocardial injection of ischemic pig hearts, in association with laser trans-myocardial revascularization (TMR) using a high energy carbon dioxide laser pulse. Not only was the level of transgene expression increased in a statistically significant fashion by the addition of TMR, but contractile abnormalities induced by ischemia were completely reversed by the administration of VEGF-TMR as opposed to VEGF alone or TMR alone.[15]

In humans, the direct intra-myocardial injection of naked plasmid VEGF, has been performed in an uncontrolled study in patients with multi-vessel inoperable disease who have failed initial surgical therapy, presenting with functional New York Heart Association (NYHA) Class III or IV angina on a regimen of maximal medical therapy. This study reported a significant reduction in angina as manifested by the a decrease in nitroglycerin use, an improvement in left ventricular ejection fraction in a few patients, with demonstration of improved perfusion as manifested by stress-SPECT imaging and increased collaterals shown by coronary angiography.[16,17] Similar preliminary results have been reported with intramyocardial administration of acidic fibroblast growth factor[18,19] and intracoronary administration of FGF-5 .[20]

In an attempt to optimize gene transfer, similar experiments have been attempted using adenoviral vectors. A replication deficient, recombinant adenovirus theoretically allows a higher transfection efficiency in non-dividing cells than naked plasmid DNA alone, remains highly localized, and expresses VEGF in that area for 1-2 weeks. In a Phase I uncontrolled study, adenoviral administration of rhVEGF as sole therapy was compared to adenoviral administration as an adjunct to coronary artery bypass grafting (CABG). When compared to their own pre-operative condition, patients receiving rhVEGF as sole therapy, reported an improvement in exercise tolerance. There were similar improvements in Rentrop scores on coronary arteriography in both groups, and improvements in sestamibi scans in both groups suggesting that adenoviral delivery of rhVEGF may have a role in myocardial revascularization gene therapy.[21] Clearly, randomized, controlled multi-center studies are needed to evaluate definitively the usefulness of angiogenic gene therapy in peripheral vascular, or coronary artery disease.

2. Antioxidative gene therapy for myocardial protection

With the recent realizations that reactive oxygen species such as superoxide anion (O_2-) and hydrogen peroxide (H_2O_2) contribute not only to ischemic injury, but may play a larger role in reperfusion injury, attention has turned towards developing therapies that may attenuate the free radical injury to the myocardium.[22] The target gene that has attracted the most interest is extracellular superoxide dismutase (ecSOD). EcSOD is a free radical scavenger that catalyzes the dismutation of the superoxide anion to hydrogen peroxide and molecular oxygen. Adenoviral delivery of ecSOD transgene directly into rabbit myocardium reportedly limits the extent of myocardial stunning in a coronary artery occlusion model[23] and preserves post-ischemic cardiac function in transgenic mice engineered to over express ecSOD.[24]

3. Post balloon injury/graft neo-intimal hyperplasia

Neo-intimal hyperplasia continues to be the leading cause of failure of percutaneous transluminal coronary angioplasty (PTCA), as well as of coronary artery bypass grafting (CABG). 30% of patients undergoing PTCA will re-occlude after six months, and 50% of CABG patients will re-occlude after 10 years. The numbers for peripheral arterial bypass grafting are even more dismal, with 20% occluding in the first year. There are two phases during which a bypass graft is threatened. The first is in the immediate intra- or post-operative period, and is attributed either to technical problems in the construction of the bypass, or due to thrombosis. The second phase is generally seen at about 9 months, and the cause is due to accelerated atherosclerosis of the neo-intimal layer.

The development of a neo-intima is critical to the proper functioning of a bypass graft, because it limits the vessel's distensibility and therefore protects its from the increased intraluminal pressure and shear stress when the graft is interposed into the arterial position. It is thought to occur in response to two major stimuli. The first, is manipulation and *ex vivo* ischemia at the time of surgery. The second, is remodeling, or "arterialization" of the vein graft which occurs in response to the increased intraluminal pressure and shear stress that is exerted on the venous wall by the high pressure arterial environment.

Uncontrolled hyperplasia of the neo-intima, however, is detrimental to the long term viability of the graft. This is attributable to smooth muscle cell (SMC) hyperplasia which is a response to vascular injury which unleashes a cascade of cytokines and growth factors, inducing the uncoupling of a regulatory complex that involves cyclin A, Cdk2 and E2F. The transcription factor, E2F, then binds to a highly conserved 8-bp *cis* consensus sequence, and in doing so, transactivates a variety of genes involved in cell cycle regulation, including those encoding c-Myc and proliferating cell nuclear antigen (PCNA). We have examined the effect of the inhibition of E2F action, while other groups have targeted other cell cycle genes in an attempt to address the issue of neo-intimal hyperplasia.

Several groups have attempted to limit neo-intimal hyperplasia using direct adenoviral transduction of the vessel wall with genes designed to block cell cycle progression. For example, p53[25], RB2/p130[26], ribozymes against c-myb mRNA[27], Fas ligand delivery[28], antisense cyclin G1 gene delivery[29], over-expression of human p21[30], ras transdominant negative mutants, which interfere with ras function[31] and adenoviruses encoding a nonphosphorylatable, constitutively active form of Rb was constructed.[32] The primary limitation of these approaches is that adenoviral transduction of the vessel wall itself induces a dense inflammatory response that may further contribute to neointimal hyperplasia.[33]

The G1/S check-point in cell cycle where E2F acts was therefore targeted as an attractive site for blocking cell cycle progression. We hypothesized that by transfecting cells with an excess of exogenous decoy oligonucleotide containing the same 8-bp *cis* consensus sequence, the decoy ODNs would bind E2F, thus preventing the latter from activating E2F responsive cell cycle genes (Figure 1-1). Using this technique, we demonstrated that smooth muscle proliferation can be inhibited[34], and that rabbit internal jugular vein grafts interposed into the carotid artery, did not develop neo-intimal hyperplasia and did not develop atherosclerosis even in the presence of an atherogenic diet.[35] To evaluate the safety and feasibility of E2F decoy in human venous bypass grafts, we performed the Phase II randomized, controlled PREVENT Trial of infrainguinal bypass in patients at high risk for graft failure.

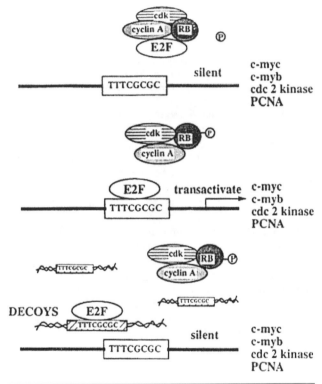

Figure 1-1. Schematic demonstrating the E2F decoy strategy. (Reprinted from PNAS USA. 1995. 92: 5855-59. Permission requested.)

Forty-one age and sex matched patients were prospectively randomized to one of three groups; those treated with E2F decoy, untreated, and those treated with scrambled ODN.[36] After the saphenous vein was harvested, it was treated by a blinded single operator on a sterile back table and immediately returned to the surgeon for implantation into the patient. There were no peri-operative deaths, and an even distribution of postoperative complications across the three groups (p=0.40). There was a 74% reduction in cell proliferation in the treated group, and a statistically significant decrease in time to primary failure (graft occlusion, need for revision, or >75% graft occlusion) in the treated group at 53 weeks (Figure 1-2).

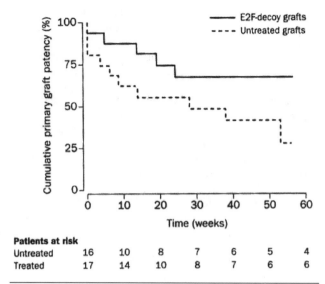

Figure 1-2. Kaplan Meier curve demonstrating cumulative graft patency in E2F treated and control groups in the PREVENT Trial. (Reprinted from Lancet 1999, 354: 1493-98. Permission requested.)

This study has demonstrated that autologous venous bypass grafts can be easily and effectively genetically engineered *ex vivo* to decrease the incidence of primary graft failure in a patient population that is at high risk for early graft occlusion. The procedure is technically feasible, does not add to intra-operative time, and does not appear to pose a safety risk to patients. The *ex vivo* approach appears to shield patients from systemic exposure to the genetic material, and we encountered no adverse side effects. This suggests that this technique may prove to be a useful approach to preventing failures of coronary and peripheral arterial surgical bypasses. It also has implications for the management of angioplasty and stent re-stenosis, as well as for other cardiovascular proliferative diseases. Further large-scale clinical trials would be needed to further validate the efficacy of this technique.

C. GENE THERAPY AS A MEANS OF ORGAN RECONSTRUCTION

The field of gene therapy is expanding to include the paradigm of regeneration, or reconstruction; that is, the transplantation of regeneration competent cells into injured or damaged organs in order to replace lost cells, thereby improving tissue function. Recently, with the recognition of autologous, often circulating, adult stem or progenitor cells in the bone marrow or elsewhere, attention has turned to the possibility of harvesting these cells and possibly genetically manipulating them *ex vivo*, and auto-transplanting them. This exciting field is finding its application primarily in three areas as it pertains to the cardiovascular system.

The first has to do with the endothelial progenitor cell

(EPC), the second has to do with myoblast cells, and the third with embryonic stem cells. We will discuss these approaches in the context of vascular and myocardial reconstruction.

1. Vascular reconstruction

The EPC is derived from the hemangioblast in the bone marrow. These cells can be isolated from human peripheral blood, and can be grown out of the mononuclear fraction in culture using selective medium. The cells are CD34 positive, and this surface marker tends to be down regulated as the cells mature into endothelial cells.[37] With specific growth conditions on cultured matrigel, these cells will differentiate into mature endothelial cells, and assume capillary-like configurations. In addition these cells express VEGF receptors, flk-1 and flt-1[38], and express factor VIII. The loss of factor VIII expression is thought to correlate with senescence.[39] In addition, the cells demonstrate the ability to take up LDL particles. The unique characteristics of these cells make them particularly attractive as a means of therapeutic endothelialization of injured blood vessels, or prosthetic vascular grafts. They may also be used for delivering genes of therapeutic interest through genetic engineering. Our laboratory has demonstrated that lac-Z transduced autologous EPCs can re-endothelialize the denuded arterial bed with 85% coverage at day 7 and 70-80% at day 14, as opposed to 10% at day 7 and 15-20% at day 14 in the group not treated with EPCs (unpublished data). Early endothelial coverage is an obviously desirable treatment for injured blood vessels, especially with the burgeoning use of percutaneous interventional therapy for coronary and peripheral arteries, and now even for the cerebral circulations. Further development of this therapeutic approach revolves around *ex vivo* manipulation of the EPC – achieving endothelialization of the injured vessel wall, with its obvious benefits, as well as transduction with the gene of choice to limit neointimal hyperplasia.

There has also been recent interest in harvesting embryonic stem (ES) cells and inducing those to differentiate into endothelial cells. This ingenious approach involves growing ES cells in a selective culture medium, followed by either direct infection with immortalizing retrovirus PmT; or by initial immunomagnetic bead selection for CD31 followed by PmT infection, and then growing the cells in the presence of G418. These cells acquired all the traits of endothelial cells, and formed capillary tubes when grown on matrigel.[40] This is yet another attractive option for generating endothelial cells.

2. Myocardial reconstruction

The main efforts in myocardial reconstruction have revolved around attempts to perform a cellular cardiomyoplasty. A true cardiomyoplasty is a surgical procedure primarily of historical interest, in which the failing ventricle is wrapped with an externally paced latissimus dorsi muscle, in an attempt to serve as a bridge to transplantation. It has now largely been usurped by mechanical ventricular assist devices. However, the cardiomyoplasty strategy has found new proponents at a cellular level. The description of "satellite cells", that is cells that are somewhat differentiated myogenic precursors, that can actually be harvested from skeletal muscle has served as the major impetus for this field of work.[41] Several groups have demonstrated success in harvesting and growing skeletal myoblasts in culture, and then transplanting them into injured regions of the heart[42], with an apparent improvement in myocardial function as measured by the relationship between stroke work and end diastolic segment length (preload recruitable stroke work – PRSW),[43] improvement in contractile function,[44] as well as improvement in diastolic relaxation.[45] The transplanted cells retain certain phenotypic characteristics, and appear to fuse with existing cardiac fibers.[46,47] Although this is encouraging data, there are several potential concerns with this strategy. The first pertains to cellular retention after transplantation. The consensus appears to be that cellular grafting is extremely inefficient. The cells frequently fail to survive after direct grafting in a cryoinjury model,[48] and only 700 out of 1×10^6 cells are estimated to graft into the heart after injection into a coronary artery 1 week later.[49] A second concern is that transplanted cells tend to assume a slow-twitch type phenotype instead of a cardiac phenotype.[50] The third, and perhaps most pressing concern, however, is the inability of skeletal muscle cells to electrically couple with pre-existing cardiomyocytes. Cardiac myocytes contact one another and communicate via specialized gap junctions composed of hexamers of connexin-43.[51] In fact, these gap junctions are found in virtually every type of mammalian cell except adult skeletal muscle fibers.[52] The inability of transplanted myoblasts to achieve this electrical coupling raises concerns that they may act as arrythmogenic foci when transplanted into the heart, and may, over the long term, impede rather than augment myocardial performance.

A suitable alternative, in our opinion, is to isolate authentic cardiomyocyte precursor cells from the bone marrow. Ferrari et al observed that skeletal muscle is capable of regenerating, and that the source of the cells appears to be the bone marrow. In one set of experiments, bone marrow from a transgenic Lac Z mouse (C57/lacZ) was injected into the injured tibialis anterior (TA) muscle of an immunodeficient scid/bg mouse; in a second set of experiments, bone marrow transplantation was performed from the C57/lacZ mouse into an irradiated scid/bg mouse.[53] In both conditions, small mononuclear cells were seen infiltrating the injured muscle area. Of interest, the newly formed myofibers had the same nuclear staining as did the infiltrating mononuclear cells. These data suggest that circulation derived myogenic progenitors may originate form the bone marrow, and can marginate under injury conditions, to contribute to a pool of resident, more differentiated muscle forming precursors named "satellite cells". Additional data indicates that cardiac myocyte precursor cells exist in the bone marrow. When bone marrow is treated with 5-azacytidine, an agent known to induce differentiation of mesenchymal cells, spontaneously and synchronously beating cells develop, that appear to bear the phenotypic characteristics of differentiated cardiac myocytes.[54] When transplanted into the heart, these cells can actually augment ventricular function.[55] This approach, coupled with the observation that cardiomyocytes when genetically selected from differentiating embryonic stem cells, can form stable intracardiac grafts[56], suggest that it should be possible to achieve cardiac reconstruction or regeneration by isolating precursor cardiac myocytes that would be capable of physiologic integration with the heart, *in vivo*, for the treatment of myocardial infarction, heart failure and cardiomyopathies.

D. GENE THERAPY AS A MEANS OF ORGANOGENESIS

Perhaps the ultimate goal for cardiovascular genetic manipulation involves the construction (as opposed to the reconstruction of diseased organs) of novel, customized, fully functional and completely compatible biologic organs that would simply replace diseased organs in humans and animals. As far-fetched as this approach may appear, some basic concepts in this field are already being addressed. We will review some of these issues in this section.

1. Generating humanoid organs in an animal

Severe shortages in the availability of suitable human donors severely limits the utility of cardiac transplantation for patients with end-stage cardiomyopathies. It is estimated that less than 3 500 cardiac transplantations are performed annually, with over tens of thousands patients dying awaiting cardiac transplantation.[57] This acute shortage of organs has stimulated novel strategies for xenotransplantation.

Xenotransplantation, of course, is limited by physiologic, immunologic, ethical and infectious challenges. Pigs are emerging as the likely source of human "replacement organs"[58] because of their size compatibility with humans, their ease of domestication, and the ability to raise them in large numbers. Swine have long been utilized as a source for insulin and heart valves, and their long history of integration in the human diet limits to some extent, the likelihood of endogenous virus transmission. The major barrier to cross-species transplantation remains hyper-acute rejection, which appears to be triggered by the two major factors. The first is the presence of the alpha-^{1,3} galactose disaccharide (Gal) carbohydrate moiety on the vascular endothelium of lower animals. This moiety is expressed in all mammals except humans and primates, as a result of which, humans have developed pre-formed, circulating antibodies to it. The binding of these antibodies to Gal triggers the complement cascade, which ultimately results in vascular thrombosis and death of the graft.[59] The second has its underpinnings in the physiologic discrepancy between the complement system of humans and lower mammals. Complement regulated proteins are species restricted. The result of this is that porcine complement regulatory proteins are incapable of down regulating human complement – resulting in uncontrollable human complement activation in the presence of a porcine organ.[60]

There are two parallel strategies in the efforts to overcome these biologic limitations to xenotransplantation. The first is by attempting to modify the donor animal; and the second, by modifying the recipient animal. Donor strategies have focused on the two most logical places to start, by attempting to decrease endothelial Gal expression, and by over expressing human complement regulatory proteins in swine. One group has managed to generate Gal knockout and decay accelerating factor (DAF) overexpressing transgenic mice. When Langendorff preparations of hearts from the Gal KO/DAF transgenic animals were perfused with human serum *ex vivo*, there was a statistically significant increase in survival time, as well as in work output when compared to wild type animals over the 40 minute time course of the experiment.[61] In addition, a line of transgenic swine that expresses human CD59 and DAF has been generated. When lymphocytes from these animals were incubated with human or baboon serum, they demonstrated three to five fold resistance to lysis as compared to lymphocytes from wild type littermates. In addition, when transgenic hearts were transplanted into baboons, these transgenic xenografts survived for 6 to 69 hours, as opposed to only 1 to 1.5 hours in wild type animals.[62]

Strategies on the recipient animal side have focused on adsorption of anti-Gal antibodies, and infusions of monoclonal antibodies known to inhibit the complement response. One novel approach being developed however, involves generation of a mixed hematopoietic chimeric recipient, which would recognize both self and donor, as self. The strategy involves treating the donor animal with a "stem cell mobilizing regimen" which involves daily treatments with recombinant porcine stem cell factor (pSCF), IL-3 and human GM-CSF. The recipient animal then undergoes lethal irradiation and T cell depletion, followed by transfusion of the stem cell preparation, which will, in theory reconstitute the bone marrow of the recipient animal. Transplantation is then performed 5-12 months after chimerism is induced. The results demonstrated dramatic improvement in longevity (from 21-44 days in untreated animals, versus 153-362 days in treated animals) of grafts without immunosuppression.[63]

2. Bioengineering for new organ generation

Although organogenesis remains a distant and highly speculative goal, small advances are being made in this field as it pertains to the cardiovascular system. The first is in the heart itself, and the second with the arterial tree.

Cardiac valve disease continues to exert a significant influence on worldwide morbidity and mortality, and valve replacement modalities continue to have significant problems, such as degeneration, thrombo-embolic complications, and the need for prophylactic antibiotics. The ultimate goal of tissue engineering is to engineer a valve out of autologous tissue on a biodegradable scaffold, and form new functional tissue with inherent non-thrombogenicity.[64] In one particular experiment, the scaffold used is a bacterially derived biopolyester, called PHA. Arterial segments are harvested from a sheep carotid artery, and then micro-dissected, and the intima, media and adventitial cell and stroma seeded onto the inside and outside of the polymeric heart valve. The engineered valve is then incubated in a pulsatile flow system (bioreactor) in vitro. This bioreactor allows alteration of flow and pressure across the valve. Valves treated in such a way are then analyzed for cell number, collagen formation, and histology. The cell number after seeding continued to proliferate, with numbers achieving statistical significance when compared to control groups, with migration into pores and formation of tissue bridges between the inner and outer surfaces of the valve. In addition, the cells tend to orient in the direction of flow. There were limitations in extracellular matrix (ECM) deposition, but other groups have demonstrated significant ECM formation with different conditions in the bioreactor.[65,66,67] In the future, genetic engineering should provide further opportunity to develop bioartificial hearts that are both biocompatible and functional.

There have also been significant advances in the construction of arterial conduits. Clinical intervention in order to prevent end-organ damage due to atherosclerotic disease has revolved around bypass of the stenotic vessel with vascular conduits. Although Dacron grafts suffice in larger vessels because of the high flow in these arteries, peripheral and coronary bypass grafting has required the use of autologous tissue, usually the greater saphenous vein. Unfortunately, the longevity of venous grafts is limited, and greater numbers of patients need repeat procedures. The exhaustion of native conduit has necessitated the development of artificial grafts, such as expanded polytetrafluoroethylene (ePTFE) and Dacron. Small diameter (<6mm) prosthetic grafts perform poorly clinically, particularly in the coronary and below-knee femoro-popliteal positions. However, studies have shown that endothelial cell lined prostheses have greater patency than unlined grafts.[68] In addition, these cells have been shown to be amenable to viral transduction, with 40-60% transduction efficiency, and greater than 85% coverage of the prosthesis with endothelial cells[69] suggesting that graft performance may be enhanced by lining the lumen with a non-thrombogenic, biologically active layer. The ease of transduction of these cells makes them attractive targets for genetic manipulation.

Indeed, grafts have been lined with endothelial cells retrovirally transduced to produce hirudin[70] that not only reduced decreased platelet deposition, but also decreased neo-intimal formation at the vascular anastomoses. Hirudin, of course, has been recognized as a factor capable of limiting neo-intimal hyperplasia.[71] Other groups have achieved similar results by transducing the endothelial cells lining the conduit with the tissue plasminogen activator (tPA) gene.[72] This strategy appears to be all the more attractive with the recent discovery of circulating endothelial progenitor cells (EPC)[73] because it eliminates the need for surgical harvesting of autologous veins as a source for endothelial cells. Since these cells are selected for by maintenance in tissue culture for at least one week, they are ideally suited to *ex vivo* genetic manipulation, and have been retrovirally transduced with preprourokinase prior to implantation into a polytetrafluroethylene (PTFE) graft.[74] This group has demonstrated >87% retention of cells in the graft with expression of transgene, similar to our observations in our laboratory (unpublished data).

E. *IN UTERO* OR *EX VIVO* EMBRYONIC OR FETAL MANIPULATION

There has been a persistent interest in *in utero* gene therapy (IUGT). The reporter gene lac Z has been shown to be expressed in the liver and in circulating hematopoietic stem and progenitor cells after a single intra-hepatic in utero retroviral injection.[75] This suggests the possibility of repairing systemic or organ specific genetic lesions *in utero*.

Applications to the cardiovascular system are already finding astonishing preclinical applications. Gene therapy has been used to create an *in utero* patent ductus arteriosus (PDA), which is very desirable in certain congenital cardiac defects. If successful, this technique would buy the clinical team several hours, if not days, of time before having to proceed with surgical intervention. Currently, the only mainstay of achieving a PDA is a prostaglandin infusion. This gene transfer strategy targeted the fibronectin-dependent smooth muscle migration needed for intimal cushion formation. This was achieved by using a HVJ-liposome technique containing antisense mRNA to the fibronectin binding protein mRNA. In doing so, fibronectin translation was inhibited, with arrest of intimal cushion formation, and maintenance of an PDA in sheep.[76] Similar achievements have been made with gene delivery to respiratory epithelium of animals, an obvious choice in diseases such as cystic fibrosis.[77,78]

The burgeoning interest in the molecular biology of cardiac development, along with the implication of certain genes in certain disease phenotypes makes the approach of IUGT very attractive. A few examples include the implication of Nkx 2.5 in atrial septal defects (ASD), TBX5 in both ASD and ventricular septal defect (VSD), JAGGED-1 in pulmonary stenosis and Tetralogy of Fallot, TFAP2B in patent ductus arteriosus (PDA), MEF2C in hypoplastic left heart, Pax3 in persistent truncus arteriosus and Gridlock/HRT2 in aortic coarctation.[79] This wealth of discoveries makes it theoretically possible to repair lethal cardiac defects *in utero*, before their manifestations are ever obvious. In addition, dramatic advances in surgical technique, such as ultrasound guided delivery[80] and embryofetoscopy[81] promise to make this procedure safer and more feasible in the future.

Several issues need to be resolved before this therapy can be applied to human beings. The first is whether or not IUGT is actually capable of curing a disease. Can enough genes be transferred into the appropriate target cells? Will the cells express the gene for an appropriate length of time? Will gene expression be appropriately regulated? Could some mechanism, for example, retroviral silencing eliminate the gene product even after it has been expressed? Transfer of the vector into the maternal bloodstream would be highly undesirable and steps would have to be taken to minimize the possibility of this occurring. In addition, the complications of uterine manipulation in the gravid state cannot be understated – risks of premature labor, infection and bleeding, all of which carry the weight of possible loss of the pregnancy. For the fetus, there would be concerns of the long term, and yet unknown, risks of insertional mutagenesis. Could this interfere with developmental processes or contribute to tumor formation? Finally a question that arises is whether or not viral delivery could result in alteration of the germ line? Ethical issues also need attention before this promising therapy can be brought to the bedside.[82]

F. HUMAN CLONING

It is difficult to mention IUGT without making at least a passing reference to the possibility of human cloning, with all of its ethical weight. Might it be possible to perform somatic cell – nuclear transfer with the goal of generating "personalized" stem cell lines? That is, after transfer of a nucleus from an adult differentiated cell to an enucleated, unfertilized egg to generate a blastocyst, and subsequently, dissociate the inner cell mass of the blastocyst resulting from this procedure in order to generate lines of "custommade" embryonic stem cell lines[83] (Figure 1-3). Might it be possible one day, to be able to engineer a non-sentient human "incubator", if you will, of organs that are custom designed for each of us? Would this be achievable? With the rate of current advances in molecular biology and medicine, it probably would be. Would this be desirable? That is an issue whose scope is too large to be addressed in this chapter alone. But we mention it for the sake of illustrating the fact that genetic manipulation for the cardiovascular system, or for that matter for any system, is still very much in its infancy – the potentials of what we might be capable of achieving years from now truly are limitless.

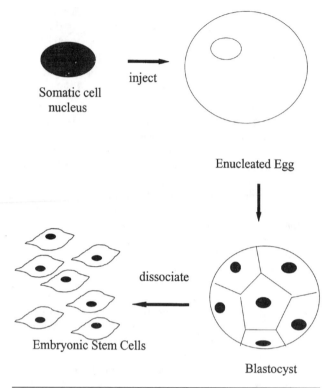

Figure 1-3. *Schematic demonstrating possible strategy by which "custom-made" stem cell lines can be generated using somatic cell nuclear transfer.*

WHAT ARE THE LIMITATIONS?

Technical. There are many challenges in this area involving the identification of therapeutic gene targets, the safe and efficient delivery of the transgene, the stable integration of the transgene into the host chromosome, and the expression of the transgene in cell specific and temporally regulated manners. To date, the technical problems have not been completely overcome. With regards to cell based therapy, the challenges include the difficulty of isolating the target cell, maintaining viability of the cell, as well as its capacity to regenerate. In this context, it will be desirable to avoid immunosuppression, therefore making autologous sources of target cells and tissues the most favorable. Successful tissue engineering or cell transplantation may involve the development of biomaterials to serve as scaffolds, or reservoirs of autologous genetically manipulated cells that are capable of integrating well within the engrafted tissue.

Medical. The medical challenges of genetic manipulation require serious soul searching on the part of physicians. Who should be treated? How much better is genetic manipulation than "traditional therapies" which are constantly improving? What are the risks of gene therapy versus its benefits, and how does the physician use this information to make clinically relevant decisions? Finally, who will pay for this therapy? Will patients want genetic information disclosed to insurance companies? What are the insurance ramifications for the offspring and relatives of these patients?

Ethical and societal. While most (but not all) would agree that gene therapy for life threatening conditions is probably reasonable, can gene therapy for non-lethal conditions be rationalized? Moreover, can gene therapy as a means of prevention, or gene therapy to enhance health, be justified? Will society permit genetic manipulation of the germ line? Will human in utero gene therapy ever enter clinical use? Will we ever use human embryonic stem cells or fetal cells for therapeutic use? Will human beings accept xenotransplantation as a common procedure? Finally, will we ever allow the cloning of personal "custom-made" human stem cells (as in after somatic cell nuclear transfer)?

CONCLUSIONS

Innovative advances in basic science have allowed the rapid translation of genetic information to manipulation for clinical therapy. The initial results that we outlined above, have been impressive. As our understanding of stem cell biology and organ regeneration has matured, it has allowed us to explore new and exciting applications for genetic manipulation. Clinical results once thought unachievable, such as myocardial reconstruction, vascular reconstruction, and in utero gene transfer are actually, for the first time, within the realm of possibilities.

ACKNOWLEDGEMENTS

This work was supported by Grants HL 35610, HL 58516, HL 59316 and HL 54527 from the National Heart, Lung and Blood Institute. VJD is the recipient of a National Heart, Lung and Blood Institute Merit Award. AAM is the recipient of the Linton Research Fellowship from the Department of Surgery, Massachusetts General Hospital, Boston, MA and is supported by The National Research Service Award 1F32 NHLBI 10503-01 from the National Institute of Health.

REFERENCES

1. Uauy R., Vega, GL, Grundy SM and Bilheimer DM. Lovastatin therapy in receptor-negative familial hypercholesterolemia: Lack of effect on low density lipoprotein concentrations or turnover. J Pediatr. 113, 387-392 (1988).

2. Starzl TE et al. Portacaval shunt in patients with familial hypercholesterolemia. Ann Surg. 198; 273-83 (1988).

3. Deckelbaum RJ, Lees, RS, Small DM, Hedberg SE an Grundy SM. Failure of complete bile diversion and oral bile acid therapy in the treatment of homozygous familial hypercholesterolemia. New Engl J Med. 296; 465-470 (1977).

4. Ishibashi S et al. Hypercholesterolemia in low density lipoprotein receptor knock out mice and its reversal by adenovirus mediated gene therapy. J Clin Invest. 92; 883-893 (1993).

5. Grossman, M, Rader DJ, Muller DWM, Kolansky DM, Kozarsky K, Clark BJ, Stein EA, Lupien PJ, Brewer HB, Raper SE, Wilson JM. A pilot study of *ex vivo* gene therapy for homozygous familial hypercholesterolemia. Nat Med. 1(11): 1148-1154 (1995).

6. Leung DW, Cachianes G, Kuang WJ, Goeddel DV, Ferrrara N. Vascular endothelial growth factor is a secreted angiogenic mitogen. Science. 246; 1306-9 (1989).

7. Keck PJ, Hauser SD, Krivi G, Sanzo K, Warren T, Feder J, Connolly DT. Vascular permeability factor, an endothelial cell mitogen related to PDGF. Science. 246; 1309-12. (1989).

8. Risau W. Mechanisms of angiogenesis. Nature. 386; 671-4. (1997).

9. Tabata, H, Silver M and Isner JM. Arterial gene transfer of acidic fibroblast growth factor for therapeutic angiogenesis *in vivo*: critical role of secretion signal in use of naked DNA. Cardiovasc Res. 35; 470-9 (1997).

10. Tsumuri Y, Kearney M, Chen D, Silver M, Takeshita S, Yang J, Symes JF, Isner JM. Treatment of acute limb ischemic by intramuscular injection of vascular endothelial growth factor gene. Circulation. 96[suppl II]: II-382—II-388 (1997).

11. Ledley FD. Nonviral gene therapy: the promise of genes as pharmacologic products. Human gene ther. 6; 1129-44 (1995).

12. Baumgartner I, Peiczek A, Manor O, Blair R, Kearney M, Walsh K and Isner JM. Constitutive expression of phVEGF165 after intramuscular gene transfer promotes collateral vessel development on patients with critical limb ischemia. Circulation. 97; 1114-1123 (1998).

13. Isner JM, Pieczak A, Schainfeld R et al. Clinical evidence of angiogenesis following intra-arterial gene transfer of VEGF. Lancet. 348; 370-74 (1996).

14. Takeshita S, Isshiki T, Ochiai M, Eto K, Mori H, Tanaka E, Umetania K, Sato T. Endothelium-dependent relaxation of collateral microvessels after intramuscular gene transfer of vascular endothelial growth factor in a rat model of hindlimb ischemia. Circulation. 98; 1261-3 (1998).

15. Sayeed-Shah U, MJ Mann, J Martin, S Grachev, S Reimold, R Laurence, V Dzau, LH Cohn. Complete reversal of ischemic wall motion abnormalities by combined use of gene therapy with transmyocardial laser revascularization. J Thorac Cardiovasc Surg. 116; 763-9 (1998).

16. Losordo DW, PR Vale, JF Symes, CH Dunnington, DD Esakof, M Maysky, AB Ashare, K Lathi, JM Isner. Gene therapy for myocardial angiogenesis: initial clinical results with direct myocardial injection of phVEGF as sole therapy for myocardial ischemia. Circulation. 98: 2800-04 (1998).

17. Henry TD, Rocha-Singh K, Isner JM, Kereiakes DJ, Giordano FJ, Simons, M, Losordo DW, Hendel RC, Bonow RO, Rothman JM, Borbas ER, McCluskey ER. Results of intracoronary recombinant human vascular endothelial growth factor (rhVEGF) administration trial. Circulation. 31: 65A (1998).

18. Selke FW, Jianyi L, Stamler A, Lopez JJ, Thomas KS, Simons M. Angiogenesis induced by acidic fibroblast growth factor as an alternative method of revascularization for chronic myocardial ischemia. Surgery. 120; 180-88 (1996).

19. Harada K, Grossman W, Friedman M, Edelman ER, Prasad PW, Keighley CS, Manning WJ, Selke FW, Simons M. Basic fibroblast growth factor improves myocardial function in chronically ischemic porcine hearts. J Clin Invest. 94; 623-30 (1994).

20. Giordano FJ, Ping P, McKirnan D, Nozaki S, Demaria AN, Dillmann WH, Mathieu-Costello O, Hammond HK. Intracoronary gene transfer of fibroblast growth factor 5 increases blood flow and contractile function in an ischemic region of the heart. Nat Med. 2; 534-9 (1996).

21. Rosengart TK, Lee LY, Patel SR, Sanbron TA, Parikh M, Bergman GW, Hachamovitch R, Szulc M, Kligfield PD, Okin PM, Hahn RT, Devereaux RB, Post MR, Hackett NR, Foster T, Grasso TM, Lesser LM, Isom W, Crystal RG. Angiogenesis gene therapy: phase I assessment of direct intramyocardial administration of an adenovirus vector expressing VEGF121 cDNA to individuals with clinically significant severe coronary artery disease. Circulation. 100; 468-74 (1999).

22. Bolli R. Oxygen derived free radicals and myocardial reperfusion injury: an overview. Cardiovasc Drugs Ther. 5(suppl 2); 249-68 (1991).

23. Li Q, Bolli R, Qiu Y, Tang X-L, Murphree SS, French BA. Gene therapy with extracellular superoxide dismutase attenuates myocardial stunning in conscious rabbits. Circulation. 8; 1438-48 (1998).

24. Chen EP, Bittner HB, Davis RD, Folz R, Tright PV. Extracellular superoxide dismutase transgene overexpression preserves postischemic myocardial function in isolated murine hearts. Circulation 94[suppl II]: II-241–II-417 (1996).

25. Ascher E; Scheinman M; Hingorani A; Seth P, Marella VK; Jacob T. Ann Vasc Surg 14(4):385-92 (2000).

26. Claudio PP; Fratta L; Farina F; Howard CM; Stassi G, Numata S; Pacilio C; Davis A; Lavitrano M; Volpe M; Wilson JM, Trimarco B; Giordano A; Condorelli G. Adenoviral RB2/p130 gene transfer inhibits smooth muscle cell proliferation and prevents restenosis after angioplasty. Circ Res 85(11):1032-9 (1999).

27. Macejak DG; Lin H; Webb S; Chase J; Jensen K; Jarvis TC; Leiden JM; Couture L Adenovirus-mediated expression of a ribozyme to c-myb mRNA inhibits smooth muscle cell proliferation and neointima formation *in vivo*. J Virol;73(9):7745-51 (1999).

28. Luo Z; Sata M; Nguyen T; Kaplan JM; Akita GY Walsh K. Adenovirus-mediated delivery of fas ligand inhibits intimal hyperplasia after balloon injury in immunologically primed animals. Circulation 99(14):1776-9 (1999).

29. Nian Ling Zhu, Lingtao Wu, Peng Xuan Liu, Erlinda M. Gordon, W. French Anderson, Vaughn A. Starnes, and Frederick L. Hall. Downregulation of Cyclin G1 Expression by Retrovirus-Mediated Antisense Gene Transfer Inhibits Vascular Smooth Muscle Cell Proliferation and Neointima Formation Circulation 1997 Jul 15; 96(2):628-35.

30. Chang MW, Barr E, Lu MM, Barton K, Leiden JM. Adenovirus-mediated over-expression of the cyclin/cyclin-dependent kinase inhibitor, p21 inhibits vascular smooth muscle cell proliferation and neointima formation in the rat carotid artery model of balloon angioplasty. J Clin Invest 1995 Nov; 96(5):2260-8.

31. Indolfi C, Avvedimento EV, Rapacciuolo A, Di Lorenzo E, Esposito G, Stabile E, Feliciello A, Mele E, Giuliano P, Condorelli G, et al. Inhibition of cellular ras prevents smooth muscle cell proliferation after vascular injury *in vivo*. Nat Med 1995 Jun; 1(6):541-5.

32. Chang MW, Barr E, Seltzer J, Jiang YQ, Nabel GJ, Nabel EG, Parmacek MS, Leiden JM. Cytostatic gene therapy for vascular proliferative disorders with a constitutively active form of the retinoblastoma gene product. Science 1995 Jan 27; 267(5197):518-22.

33. Newman KD, Dunn PF, Owens JW, Schulick AH, Virmani R, Sukhova G, Libby P, Dichek DA. Adenovirus-mediated gene transfer into normal rabbit arteries results in prolonged vascular cell activation, inflammation and neointimal hyperplasia. J Clin Invest. 96; 2955-65 (1995).

34. Morishita R., GH Gibbons, M Horiuchi, KE Ellison, M Nakajima, L Zhang, Y Kaneda, T Ogihara, VJ Dzau. A gene therapy strategy using a transcription factor decoy of the E2F binding site inhibits smooth muscle proliferation in vivo. Proc Natl Acad Sci USA. 92: 5855-5859 (1995).

35. Mann, MJ, GH Gibbons, RS Kernoff, FP Diet, PS Tsao, JP Cooke, Y Kaneda, VJ Dzau. Genetic engineering of vein grafts resistant to atherosclerosis. Proc Natl Acad Sci USA. 92: 4502-4506 (1995).

36. Mann, MJ., AD Whittemore, MC Donaldson, M Belkin, MS Conte, JF Polak, EJ Orav, A Ehsan, G Dell'Acqua, VJ Dzau. *Ex-vivo* gene therapy of human vascular bypass grafts with E2F decoy: the PREVENT single-centre, randomized, controlled trial. Lancet. 354 (9189): 1493-98 (1999).

37. Fina L, Molgaard HV, Robertson D et al. Expression of the CD34 gene in vascular endothelial cells. Blood 75; 2417-26 (1990).

38. Hlatky L, Hahnfeldt P, Tsionou C, Coleman CN. Vascular endothelial growth factor: environmental controls and effects in angiogenesis. Br J Cancer. 74; S151-6 (1996).

39. Johnson TE, Umbenhaue DR, Hill R et al. Karyotypic and phenotypic changes during in vitro aging of human endothelial cells. J Cell Physiol. 150; 17-27 (1992).

40. Balconi G, Spagnuolo R, Dejana E. Development of endothelial cell lines from embryonic stem cells: a tool for studying genetically manipulated endothelial cells in vitro. Arterioscler Thromb Vasc Biol 20; 1443-51 (2000).

41. Rando TA and HM Blau. Primary mouse myoblast purification, characterization, and transplantation for cell-mediated gene therapy. J Cell Biol. 125; 1275-87 (1994).

42. Chiu RC-J, Zibaitis A, Kao RL. Cellular cardiomyoplasty: myocardial regeneration with satellite cell implantation. Ann Thorac Surg. 60; 12-18 (1995).

43. Taylor DA, Atkins BZ, Hungspreugs P, Jones TR, Reedy MC, Hutcheson KA, Glower DD, Kraus WE. Regenerating functional myocardium: improved performance after skeletal myoblast transplantation. Nat Med. 4; 929-933 (1998).

44. Murry CE, Wiseman RW, Schwartz SM, Haruschka SD. Skeletal myoblast transplantation for repair of myocardial necrosis. J Clin Invest. 98; 2512-2523 (1996).

45. Atkins BZ, Hueman MT, Meuchel J, Hutcheson KA, Glower DD, Taylor DA. Cellular cardiomyoplasty improves diastolic properties of injured heart. J Surg Res. 85; 234-242 (1999).

46. Yao S-N, Kurachi K. Implanted myoblasts not only fuse with myofibers but also survive as muscle precursor cells. J Cell Sci. 105; 957-963 (1995).

47. Atkins BZ, Lewis CW, Kraus WE, Hutcheson KA, Glower DD, Taylor DA. Intracardiac transplantation of skeletal myoblasts yields two populations of striated cells *in situ*. Ann Thorac Surg 67; 124-9 (1999).

48. Taylor DA, Atkins BZ, Hungspreugs P, Jones TR, Reedy MC, Hutcheson KA, Glower DD, Kraus WE. Regenerating functional myocardium: improved performance after skeletal myoblast transplantation. Nat Med. 4; 929-933 (1998).

49. Robinson SW, Cho PC, Levitsky HI, Olson JL, Hruban RH et al. Arterial delivery of genetically labeled skeletal myoblasts to the murine heart: long term survival and phenotypic modification of implanted myoblasts. Cell Transplant. 5; 77-91 (1996).

50. Murry CE, Wiseman RW, Schwartz SM, Haruschka SD. Skeletal myoblast transplantation for repair of myocardial necrosis. J Clin Invest. 98; 2512-2523 (1996).

51. Kalderon N, Epstein ML, Gilula NB.Cell to cell communication and myogenesis. J Cell Biol.75; 788-806 (1977).

52. Beyer EC, Kister J, Paul DL, Goodenough DA et al. Antisera directed against connexin 43 peptide react with 43kD protein localized to gap junctions in myocardium and other tissues J Cell Biol. 108; 595-605 (1989).

53. Ferrari G, Cusella-De Angelis G, Coletta M, Paolucci E, Stornaiuolo A, Cossu G, Mavilio F. Muscle regeneration by bone marrow derived myogenic progenitors. Science. 279; 1528-30 (1998).

54. Makino S, Fukuda K, Miyoshi S, Konishi F, Kodama H, Pan J, Takahashi T, Hori S, Abe H, Hata J, Umezawa A, Ogawa S. Cardiomyocytes can be generated from marrow stromal cells *in vitro*. J Clin Invest. 103; 697-705 (1999).

55. Tomita S, Li R-K, Weisel RD, Mickle DAG, Kim E-J, Sakai T, Jia Z-Q. Autologous transplantation of bone marrow cells improves damaged heart function. Circulation. 100[suppl II]: II-247 – II-256 (1999)..

56. Klug MG, Soonpas MH, Koh GY, Fields LJ. Genetically selected cardiomyocytes from differentiating embryonic stem cells form stable intracardiac grafts. J Clin Invest. 98; 216-24 (1996).

57. Hosenpud JD, Bennett LE, Keck BM, Fiol B, Boucek MM, Novick RJ. The registry of the international society for heart and lung transplantation: fifteenth official report – 1998. J Heart Lung Transplant 17; 656-68 (1998).

58. Adams DH, Chen RH, Kadner A. Cardiac xenotransplantation: clinical experience and future direction. Ann Thor Surg. 70: 320-6 (2000).

59. Galili U, Clark MR, Shohet SB, Buehler J, Macher BA. Evolutionary relationship between the natural anti-Gal antibody and the Gal alpha 1,3 epitope in primates. PNAS USA. 84; 1369-73 (1987).

60. Platt JL, Dalmasso AP, Vercelloti GM, Lindman BJ, Turman MA, Bach FH. Endothelial cell proteoglycans in xenotransplantation. Transplant Proc. 22; 1066 (1990).

61. Van Denderen BJW, Salvaris E, Romanella M, Aminian A, Katerelos M, Tange MJ, Pearse MJ, D'Apice AJF. Combination of decay-accelerating factor expression and a 1,3-galactosyltransferase knockout affords added protection from human complement mediated injury. Transplantation. 64; 882-88. (1997).

62. Byrne GW, McCurry KR, Martin MJ, McLellan SM, JL Platt and JS Logan. Transgenic pigs expressing human CD59 and decay accelerating factor produce an intrinsic barrier to complement mediated damage. Transplantation. 63; 149-55 (1997).

63. Schwarze ML, Menard MT, Fuchimoto Y, Huang CA, Houser S, Mawulawde K, Alliosn KS, Sachs DH, Madsen JC. Mixed hematopoietic chimerism induces long term tolerance to cardiac allografts in miniature swine. Ann Thor Surg. 70l 131-9 (2000).

64. Siduan R, Hoerstrup SP, Sperling JS, Daebritz SH, Martin DP, Schoen FJ, Vacanti JP, Mayer JE. Tissue engineering of heart valves: in vitro experience. Ann Thorac Surg 70; 140-4 (2000).

65. Niklason LE, Langer RS. Advances in tissue engineering of blood vessels and other tissues. Transplant Immunol. 5; 303-6 (1997).

66. Niklason LE, Gao J, Abbott WM et al. Functional arteries grown in vitro. Science. 284; 289-93 (1999)..

67. Ziegler T, Nerem RM. Tissue engineering a blood vessel: regulation of vascular biology by mechanical stresses. J Cell Biochem. 56; 204-9 (1995).

68. Zilla P; Preiss P; Groscurth P; Rosemeier F; Deutsch M; Odell J; Heidinger C; Fasol R; von Oppell U. 1994. Clinical in vitro endothelialization of femoro-popliteal bypass grafts: an actuarial follow-up over three years. J Vasc Surg. 19; 540-8..

69. Wilson JM, Biryini LK, Salomon RN, Libby P, Callow AS, Mulligan RC. Implantation of vascular grafts lined with genetically modified endothelial cells. Science. 244; 1344-46. 1989..

70. Lundell A, Kelly AB, Anderson J, Marijianowski M, Rade JJ, Hanson SR, Harker LA. Reduction in vascular lesion formation by hirudin secreted from retrovirus-transduced confluent endothelial cells on vascular grafts in baboons. Circulation. 100; 2018-24 (1999).

71. Rade JJ, Schulick AH, Virmani R, Dichek DA. Local adenoviral-mediated expression of recombinant hirudin reduces neointima formation after arterial injury. Nat Med 2(3):293-8 (1996).

72. Huber TS, Welling TH, Sarkar R, Messina LM, Stanley JC. Effects of retroviral-mediated tissue plasminogen activator gene transfer and expression on adherence and proliferation of canine endothelial cells seeded onto expanded polytetrafluoroethylene. J Vasc Surg. 22(6):795-803 (1995).

73. Asahara T; Murohara T; Sullivan A; Silver M; van der Zee R; Li T; Witzenbichler B; Schatteman G; Isner JM Isolation of putative progenitor endothelial cells for angiogenesis. Science 275:964-7 (1997).

74. Boyer M, Townsend LE, Vogel LM, Falk J, Reitz-Vick D, Trevor KT, Villalba M, Bendick PJ, Glover JL. Isolation of endothelial cells and their progenitor cells from human peripheral blood. J Vasc Surg 31; 181-9 (2000).

75. Clapp DW, Freie B, Lee W-H, Zhang Y-Y. Molecular evidence that in situ transduced fetal liver hematopoietic stem/progenitor cells give rise to medullary hematopoiesis in adult rats. Blood, 86; 2113-2122 (1995).

76. Mason CA, Bigras JL, O'Blenes SB, Zhou B, McIntyre B, Nakamura N, Kaneda Y, Rabinovitch M. Gene transfer in utero biologically engineers a patent ductus arteriosus in lambs by arresting fibronectin dependent neo-intimal formation. Nat Med 5; 176-92 (1999)..

77. Sekhon HS and Larson JE. In utero gene transfer into the pulmonary epithelium. Nat Med. 1; 1201-3 (1995)) Vincent MC, Trapnell BC, Baughman RP, Wert SE, Whitsett JA, Iwamoto HS. Adenovirus mediated gene transfer to the respiratory tract of fetal sheep in utero. Hum Gene Ther. 6(8); 1019-28 (1995).

78. Pitt BR, Schwarz MA, Pilewski JM, Nakayama D, Mueller GM, Robbins PD, Watkins SA, Albertine KH, Bland RD. Retrovirus mediated gene transfer in lungs of living fetal sheep. Gene Ther. 2(5); 344-50 (1995).

79. Srivastava D and Olson EN. A genetic blueprint for cardiac development. Nature 407; 221-225. (2000).

80. Wang G, Williamson PR, Mueller G, Thomas P, Davidson BL, McCray PB. Ultrasound guided gene transfer to hepatocytes in utero. Fetal Diagn Ther 13(4); 197-205 (1999).

81. Surbek DV, Tercanli S and Holzgreve W. Transabdominal first trimester embryofetoscopy as a potential approach to early in utero stem cell transplantation and gene therapy. Ultrasound Obstet Gynecol. 15(4); 302-7 (2000).

82. Zanjani ED and Anderson WF. Prospects for in utero gene therapy. Science. 285; 2084-2087 (1999).

83. Wilmut I, Schnieke AE, McWhir J, Kind AJ, Campbell KH. Viable offspring derived from fetal and adult mammalian cells. Nature. 385(6619): 810-3 (1997)

Crossovers between Functional and Proliferative Signaling in the Pathogenesis of Heart Failure: Approaching the Limits?

Arnold M. Katz

New concepts regarding the pathophysiology and treatment of heart failure are appearing at an accelerating rate. Driven by a remarkable collaboration between the basic and clinical sciences, the pace of discovery has increased to the extent that concepts almost universally accepted only a decade ago are now viewed as obsolete, and in some cases, wrong. This article, which uses an historical approach to describe the trajectory of discovery in this field, asks whether the current pace of discovery might be approaching a limit.

SCIENTIFIC PROGRESS AND PARADIGM SHIFTS

Thomas Kuhn, in his "The Structure of Scientific Revolutions",[1] describes scientific progress in terms of a series of paradigm shifts. These begin when the finding of "anomalies" that violate the expectations of an existing "normal science" stimulates a search for data and concepts to explain the anomalies. When the new data and concepts are sufficiently revolutionary to invalidate the foundations of the former normal science, a paradigm shift takes place.

A classical paradigm shift occurred in the 17th Century, when Harvey's discovery of the circulation, along with autopsy studies of patients who died of heart failure caused by rheumatic valvular disease, revealed anomalies that overthrew the normal science based on ancient Greek cosmology. Our current understanding of heart failure is in the midst of another paradigm shift that is as remarkable as that which occurred almost 400 years ago.

FROM EXCESS PHLEGM TO IMPAIRED CARDIAC PUMPING

The works attributed to Hippocrates, most of which were written from the 5th – 3rd Century BC, describe patients with shortness of breath, edema, and anasarca, many of whom suffered from heart failure.[2] Hippocrates, who provides explicit instructions as to how to drain pleural effusions, attributed this fluid to an excess of "phlegm" (the cold humor) moving from the brain to the chest. This explanation, along with Galen's view that the heart is the source of heat that it distributes through the body, was part of a paradigm that dominated medical thinking in the West for almost 2 000 years (Figure 2-1). It was not until 1628, when Harvey described the circulation, that it became possible to understand the hemodynamics of heart failure (for descriptions written before the 20th Century, see references 3–5).

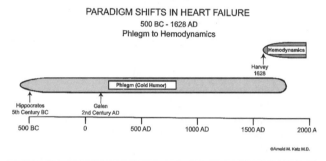

Figure 2-1. *According to Hippocrates, pleural effusions are caused when an excess of the cold humor (phlegm) moves from the brain to the chest. This paradigm, which was supported by Galen, lasted almost 2 000 years, until Harvey's description of the circulation in 1628 stimulated a paradigm shift that overthrew this explanation of heart failure.*

Harvey's discovery of the Circulation made it possible for Mayow, in 1674, to recognize how mitral stenosis causes right ventricular dilatation (Figure 2-2). Vieussens, in a text published posthumously in 1715, proposed that the pleural effusions seen in this syndrome are caused when serum separates from the blood that backs up behind the narrowed mitral valve. These views, by invalidating the concepts based on Hippocrates and Galen, stimulated a classical paradigm shift.

THE HYPERTROPHIC RESPONSE: EARLY OBSERVATIONS

In 1707, shortly after Mayow's observation that obstruction to blood leaving the heart causes ventricular dilation, Lancisi distinguished between increased cavity size (dilatation) and increased wall thickness (hypertrophy) in enlarged hearts. Morgagni, in 1761, recognized the causal link between chronic overload and hypertrophy. These observations set the stage for a remarkable, and now generally overlooked, century of discovery that focused on the different patterns of growth in failing hearts (Figure 2-2). This

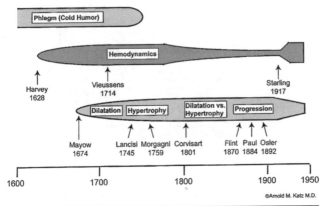

Figure 2-2. Throughout the 18th and 19th Centuries, emphasis on the mechanisms responsible for heart failure focused on changes in the size and shape of diseased hearts. The progressive nature of dilatation (remodeling) was well understood by the middle of the 19th Century, which ended with a clear understanding that hypertrophy too was progressive. This emphasis on changes in the size and shape of the failing heart ended after publication of Starling's Law of the Heart returned attention to the hemodynamics of this syndrome.

began in 1801 when Corvisart distinguished between clinical manifestations associated with eccentric hypertrophy (dilatation) and concentric hypertrophy, and continued throughout the 19th Century with the recognition that cardiac enlargement is progressive, and eventually kills the patient. Flint, in the 1850s, suggested that hypertrophy protects the patient from the adverse effects of dilatation, but by the 1880s, Paul and Osler had noted that the hypertrophy itself is also associated with progression. This focus on the hypertrophic response of the failing heart ended around 1920, when publication of Starling's Law of the Heart returned attention to the abnormal hemodynamics in heart disease.

SALT AND WATER RETENTION

The clinical picture in heart failure had, since the time of Hippocrates, been dominated by the signs and symptoms of fluid overload. Although a role for the kidney in casing fluid retention had been proposed in the 16th Century, this mechanism did not assume practical importance until 1920, when Saxl and Heilig discovered the diuretic properties of an organic mercurial that was being used to treat syphilitic heart disease.[6] Although this demonstrated that drugs affecting renal function could effectively treat heart failure (Figure 2-3), mercurial diuretics are of limited value as they have to be given by injection, and more importantly, if used more than twice weekly, they lose their effectiveness. For the next 40 years, therefore, heart failure research emphasized the kidneys in the effort to develop more

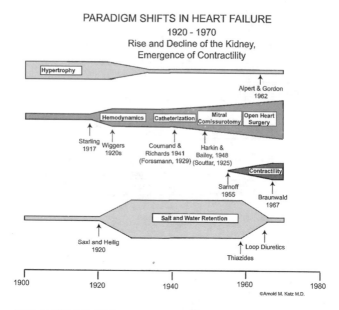

Figure 2-3. *Discovery of the diuretic properties of organic mercurials in 1920 stimulated research in renal physiology that led to the development of thiazide and loop diuretics. At the same time, basic research in cardiac hemodynamics, followed by the introduction of cardiac catheterization, provided the basis for modern cardiac surgery. The increasing pace of discovery continued with the description of myocardial contractility in 1955, recognition that myocardial contractility is depressed in the failing heart in 1967, and the identification of the first molecular abnormality in the failing heart in 1962.*

powerful diuretics that could be given orally. This ended successfully in the 1950s and 1960s with the discovery first of the thiazides, and then of the loop diuretics. The availability of these drugs, which made it possible to cause a diuresis so effective as to exchange congestion for a low output state, returned the focus in heart failure research to the heart.

Discovery of the renal abnormalities responsible for salt and water retention, and the subsequent recognition of the importance of peripheral vasoconstriction in patients with heart failure, highlighted the role of the neurohumoral response in this syndrome.[7] As noted below, unexpected effects of drugs that block this response are providing a major impetus for the paradigm shift that is currently dominating heart failure today.

RETURN TO HEMODYNAMICS

During the era when renal physiology dominated research in heart failure, knowledge of the hemodynamic abnormalities in heart disease continued to advance (Figure 2-3). Between World War I and World War II, research in this field was dominated by Wiggers, who characterized the hemodynamics of valvular, congenital, and ischemic heart disease. These studies, which could only be pursued in animal models, were incorporated into clinical medicine following the introduction of cardiac catheterization in the late 1940s. At the same time, advances in the treatment of cardiac injury during World War II provided surgeons the experience that led to the successful operative treatment of rheumatic mitral stenosis. By the 1960s, open heart surgery and the development of prosthetic valves made it possible to palliate most forms of structural heart disease.[8] At the same time, the causes of heart failure in the industrialized world were changing; rheumatic fever, which had been a scourge through the early years of the 20th Century, virtually disappeared, and most children with congenital heart disease could be cured, or at least palliated, by surgery performed during infancy. At the same time, new causes of heart failure emerged in developed countries. Ischemic heart disease and idiopathic dilated cardiomyopathy are now the major causes of systolic dysfunction, while diastolic dysfunction, which has reached epidemic status in the elderly, is due most commonly to increased afterload on the left ventricle caused by hypertensive heart disease and the reduced aortic compliance that accompanies normal aging.

Vasodilators and inotropes. Renewed emphasis on the hemodynamic causes of heart failure, along with evidence that myocardial contractility is depressed in this syndrome (Figure 2-4) had a major impact on therapy, and led to the clinical testing of two new classes of drugs. These were vasodilators, which by reducing afterload improve energetics and increase cardiac output, and newly developed

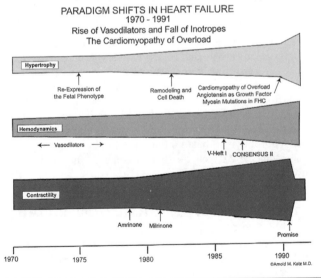

Figure 2-4. *During the 1970s and 1980s, the short-term benefits of new inotropic agents stimulated efforts to increase contractility in the failing heart. The importance of hemodynamics was highlighted by short-term improvement following administration of several classes of vasodilators, and a survival benefit for a vasodilators reported in V–Heft I, and CONSENSUS I. The end of this era was heralded by evidence that inotropic therapy worsened prognosis. The maladaptive features of hypertrophy attracted little attention until 1990, when evidence began to emerge that heart failure is exacerbated by the growth response in overloaded hearts, that angiotensin II evokes a proliferative response, and that myosin mutations cause hypertrophic cardiomyopathy.*

inotropic agents, such as amrinone and milrinone, which were initially believed to hold the key to reversing the depressed contractility. Short term clinical trials showed that both vasodilators and inotropic drugs improve hemodynamics and symptoms in heart failure, and two survival trials reported in the late 1980s, V–Heft I[9] and CONSENSUS I,[10] demonstrated that the combination of isosorbide dinitrate and hydrazine (V–Heft I) and an ACE inhibitor (CONSENSUS I) improved survival. As a result, in 1990 it was generally believed that the judicious use of diuretics, vasodilators and inotropes could solve most of the problems in these patients.

Angiotensin converting enzyme inhibitors. The finding that ACE inhibitors significantly prolong survival in heart failure[9–12] was initially interpreted within the established paradigm that heart failure is a hemodynamic disorder that can be helped by afterload reduction, while the initial short–term benefits of inotropes supported the view that the best way to treat this syndrome is to increase contractility in the failing heart. However, the latter view received a major setback when the promise trial, using milrinone, had to be stopped prematurely because this inotrope significantly reduced survival.[13] This adverse effect, which was confirmed in subsequent trials,[14] provided solid evidence that there is much more to heart failure that decreased contractility, and highlighted to the need to slow progression, as well as to relieve symptoms.

Hypertrophic response. The hypertrophic response, which had dominated thinking about heart failure in the 19th Century, attracted little notice throughout the 20th Century. It was not until 1990 that evidence began to emerge that the prognosis in heart failure is worsened when overload causes hypertrophy,[15] that angiotensin II can stimulate a proliferative response,[16] and that myosin mutations cause hypertrophic cardiomyopathy.[17] Together, these findings heralded the paradigm shift that has now come to dominate thinking about heart failure; that the major problem in this syndrome is a maladaptive growth response that accelerates myocardial cell death in damaged and overloaded hearts.

THE CARDIOMYOPATHY OF OVERLOAD

Throughout the 1990s, clinical trials with vasodilators yielded anomalous results in terms of the "normal science" that viewed heart failure largely as a hemodynamic disorder (Figure 2-5). These trials demonstrated that, in spite of providing short-term clinical improvement, most vasodilators worsen prognosis in heart failure.[18-19] The latter include α–adrenergic blockers, short–acting L–type calcium channel blockers, minoxidil, prostacyclin, ibopamine, moxonidine, flosequinan, and phosphodiesterase inhibitors. Among the vasodilators, only the combination of isosorbide dinitrate and hydralazine, ACE inhibitors, and angiotensin II receptor blockers, have a survival benefit. An even more striking

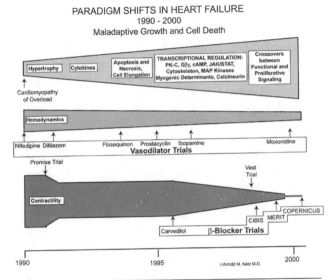

Figure 2-5. Evidence that proliferative signaling caused by mediators of the neurohumoral response is a major cause of the poor prognosis in heart failure came from clinical trials which showed that most vasodilators worsen prognosis, and that β blockers, in spite of their negative inotropic effects, improve survival.

anomaly that challenged the traditional view that heart failure is simply a hemodynamic disorder caused by weakened heart muscle is the recent demonstration that β blockers, in spite of a negative inotropic action that initially worsens heart failure, improve long-term prognosis.[20-23]

Maladaptive growth and accelerated cardiac cell death. One explanation for the anomalous findings of the clinical trials reviewed above is that the neurohumoral response, which increases circulating levels of such mediators as norepinephrine and angiotensin II, has a deleterious long-term effect on the failing heart. Many of these harmful effects occur because when vasodilators stimulate the neurohumoral response by lowering blood pressure. The significance of this response lies in the fact that most neurohumoral mediators not only stimulate fluid retention, vasoconstriction and myocardial contractility, but also activate a deleterious long–term response in which stimuli that cause cardiac myocytes to enlarge (hypertrophy) also damage the failing heart. The latter occurs because the proliferative stimuli that initially normalize wall stress by causing hypertrophy also accelerate cell death and cause progressive dilatation.[19,24-25] The latter is especially harmful in the adult heart because the myocytes are terminally differentiated cells that have little capacity to divide, so that cells which die cannot be replaced. For these reasons, overload and neurohumoral mediators such as norepinephrine and angiotensin II establish a vicious cycle of cell death, increased overload, maladaptive proliferative signaling, and further cell death. Other causes of this vicious cycle include cell deformation, which stimulates cell adhesion molecules and cytoskeletal proteins that activate proliferative signal transduction cascades, and intracellular messengers, such as calcium and cyclic AMP. These and other mechanisms operate in heart failure to activate proliferative signaling by such transcriptional regulators as protein kinase–C, the heterotrimeric G proteins, the cytokine-activated JAK/STAT pathway, and mitogenic and stress-activated MAP kinase pathways. These concepts represent a new paradigm which states that the major problem in heart failure is not the hemodynamic abnormalities, but instead is the poor prognosis that results from growth stimuli which accelerate deterioration and cell death in the failing heart.

Proliferative vs functional responses. Key to understanding the mechanism by which the neurohumoral response accelerates progression in heart failure is that many mediators of this response activate proliferative as well as functional responses (Table 2–1). The latter, which include chronotropic, inotropic and lusitropic stimulation of the heart, are part of the response that allows organisms to survive attack by "fight and flight" (Figure 2-6). Proliferative responses, on the other hand, represent a more primitive means of defense seen in prokaryotes, which literally grow their way out of trouble. This occurs in bacteria, where rapid proliferation generates individuals able to survive a change in the external environment, such as the appearance of an antibiotic. In eukaryotes, where proliferative responses evolve much more slowly than functional responses, the former increase the number of cells in proliferating tissue, such as the bone marrow, where this response replaces erythrocytes lost after hemorrhage and provides leukocytes needed to fight infection. In the heart, whose terminally cardiac myocytes have little or no capacity to divide, proliferative signaling is responsible for a hypertrophic response. However, features of this response, such as apoptosis and the cell elongation that causes remodeling, accelerate progression in heart failure. This can explain both the ability of angiotensin II and norepinephrine to shorten survival in this syndrome, and the beneficial effects of neurohumoral blockade on prognosis.

TABLE 2–1. PRACTICAL IMPORTANCE OF CROSSOVERS BETWEEN FUNCTIONAL AND PROLIFERATIVE SIGNALLING

	SHORT-TERM EFFECT	LONG-TERM EFFECT
VASODILATORS		
Direct acting*	**Afterload reduction**[F]	*Transcriptional activation*[P]
ACE inhibitors	**Afterload reduction**[F]	Transcriptional inhibition[P]
AT$_1$ receptor blockers	**Afterload reduction**[F]	Transcriptional inhibition[P]
INOTROPES		
β agonists♣	↑**Cardiac output**[F]	*Transcriptional activation*[P]
PDE inhibitors♣♣	↑**Cardiac output**[F]	*Transcriptional activation*[P]
β–BLOCKERS	↓*Cardiac output*[F]	**Transcriptional inhibition**[P]
SPIRONOLACTONE	**Diuresis**[F]	**?Transcriptional inhibition**[P]

Bold = beneficial
Italic = Deleterious
[F] Functional signalling
[P] Proliferative signalling
* Minoxidil, short–acting Ca channel blockers, prazocin, prostacyclin, ibopamine, PDE inhibitors, moxonidine
♣ Xamoterol, dobutamine
♣♣ Milrinone, vesnarinone, pimobendan, etc.

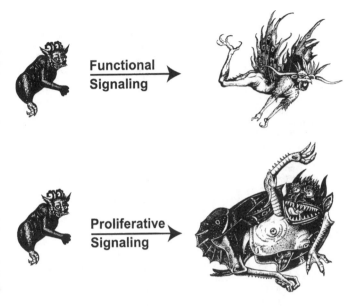

Figure 2-6. Functional signaling, which modifies the behavior of pre-existing structures by post-translational modifications, enables an organism to survive using such responses as fight or flight. In the case of proliferative signaling, transcriptional changes make it possible for an organism to grow its way out of trouble. From Katz, Physiology of the Heart (3rd Ed), Philadelphia, Lippincott/Williams & Wilkins, 2001.

IS THERE A LIMIT TO HEART FAILURE THERAPY?

A scientist living at the time of the paradigm shift that followed Harvey's discovery of the circulation would have had no basis for predicting today's paradigm shift. For this reason, it is presumptuous to try to predict future advances in our understanding of heart failure. The complexity of the current paradigm of molecular biology makes it unlikely that understanding of maladaptive proliferative signal transduction will soon be complete, although the pace of discovery is now so rapid that even this limit may be reached more quickly than now seems possible. After all, the understanding of cardiac function that began in the 20th Century with studies of organ physiology, expanded in the 1960s to include cell biochemistry, and over the past decade has incorporated molecular biology.[26] What then could be the next step in this process? If scientific progress continues to develop at its current pace, by the end of the 21st Century we may well pass the limits set by molecular biology to enter a new era, one where principles based on quantum mechanics will be used in the search for new understanding and new means to treat heart failure.

REFERENCES

1. Kuhn TS. The Structure of Scientific Revolutions. 2nd Ed. Chicago, The University of Chicago Press, 1970.

2. Katz AM, Katz PB. Diseases of the heart in the works of Hippocrates. Brit Heart J 1962;24:257–264.

3. Jarcho S. The Concept of Heart Failure. From Avicenna to Albertini. Cambridge MA, Harvard Univ Press, 1980.

4. Katz AM. Evolving Concepts of Heart Failure: Cooling Furnace, Malfunctioning Pump, Enlarging Muscle. Part I. Heart failure as a disorder of the cardiac pump. J Cardiac Failure. 1997;3:319–334.

5. Katz AM. Evolving Concepts of Heart Failure: Cooling Furnace, Malfunctioning Pump, Enlarging Muscle. Part II. Hypertrophy and dilatation of the failing heart. J Cardiac Failure. 1998;4:67–81.

6. Saxl P, Heilig R. üer die diuretiche Wirkung von Novasurol und anderen Quecksilberinjektionen. Wein klin Wochenschr 1920;33:943.

7. Francis GS, Goldsmith SR, Levine TB, Olivari MT, Cohn JN (1984). The neurohumoral axis in congestive heart failure. Ann Int Med 101:370-377.

8. Acierno LJ. The History of Cardiology. London, Parthenon, 1994.

9. Cohn JN, Archibald DG, Ziesche S, Franciosa JA,Harston WE, Tristani FE, Dunkman WB, Jacobs W, Francis GS, Cobb FR, Shah PM, Saunders R, Fletcher RD, Loeb HS, Hughes VC, Baker B (1986). Effect of vasodilator therapy on mortality in chronic congestive heart failure. Results of a Veterans Administration cooperative study(V–HeFT). New Eng J Med 314:1547–52.

10. CONSENSUS Trial Study Group. Effects of enalapril on mortality in severe congestive heart failure: Results of the Cooperative North Scandinavian Enalapril Survival Study (CONSENSUS). New Eng J Med 1987;316:1429–35.

11. The SOLVD Investigators. Effect of enalapril on mortality and the development of heart failure in asymtomatic patients with reduced left ventricular ejection fraction. New Eng J Med 1992;327:685–691.

12. Pfeffer MA, Braunwald E, Moy LA, Basta L, Brown EJ Jr, Cuddy TE, Davis BR, Geltman EM, Goldman S, Flaker CG, Klein M, Lamas GA, PAcker M, Rouleau J, Rouleau JL, Rutherford J, Wertheimer JH, Hawkins CM on behalf of the SAVE Investigators. Effect of captopril on mortality and morbidity in patients with left ventricular dysfunction after myocardial infarction. Results of the survival and ventricular enlargement trial. New Eng J Med 1992;327:669–677.

13. Packer M, Carver, JR, Rodeheffer RJ, Ivanhoe, RJ, DiBianco, R, Zeldis, SM, Hendrix, GH, Bommer, WJ, Elkayam, U, Kukin, ML, Mallis, GI, Sollano, JA, Shannon, J, Tandon, PK, and DeMets, DL. Effect of oral milrinone on mortality in severe heart failure. New Eng J Med. 1991;325:1468–1475.

14. Cohn JN, Goldstein SO, Greenberg BH, Lorell BH, Bourge RC, Jaski BE, Gottlieb SO, McGrew F, Demets DL, White BG. A dose-dependent increase in mortality among patients with severe heart failure. N Engl J Med. 1998; 339:1810–1816.

15. Katz AM. Cardiomyopathy of overload. A major determinant of prognosis in congestive heart failure. New Eng J Med 1990;322:100–110.

16. Katz AM. Angiotensin II: Hemodynamic regulator or growth factor? J Mol Cell Cardiol 1990;22:739747.

17. Geisterfer–Lowrance AAT, Kass S, Tanigawa G, Vosberg H–P, McKenna W, Seidman CE, Seidman JG. A molecular basis for familial hypertrophic cardiomyopathy: A β cardiac myosin heavy chain gene missense mutation. Cell 1990;62:999–1006.

18. Packer M, Cohn JN (1999). Consensus recommendations for the management of heart failure Am. J Cardiol 83(Suppl 2a);1A–38A.

19. Katz AM. Heart Failure: Pathophysiology, Molecular Biology, and Clinical Management. Philadelphia, Lippincott/Williams & Wilkins, 2000.

20. Packer M, Bristow MR, Cohn JN, Colucci WS, Fowler MB, Gilbert EM, Shusterman NH for the US Carvedilol Heart Failure Study Group. New Eng J Med 1996;334:1349–1355.

21. LeChat P, Packer M, Chalon S, Cucherat M, Arab T, Boissel J–P. Clinical effects of β–adrenergic blockade in chronic heart failure. Circulation 1998;98:1184–1191.

22. CIBIS–II Investigators and Committees The cardiac insufficiency bisoprolol study II (CIBIS–II): A randomised trial. Lancet 1999;353:9–13.

23. Merit–HF Study Group. Effect of metoprolol CR/XL in chronic heart failure: Metoprolol CR/XL randomized intervention trial in congestive heart failure (MERIT–HF) Lancet 1999;353:2001–2007.

24. Eichhorn EJ, Bristow MR. Medial therapy can improve the biological properties of the chronically failing heart. Circulation 1996;94:2285–2296.

25. Mann DL Mechanisms and models in heart failure: A combinatorial approach. Circulation 1999;100:999–1008.

26. Katz AM. Molecular biology in cardiology, a paradigmatic shift. J Mol Cell Cardiol 1988;20:355–366.

CHAPTER 3

Defining the Limits of Acute Coronary Syndromes

Harvey D. White

INTRODUCTION

Acute coronary syndromes are now defined according to the presence or absence of ST-segment elevation on the presenting electrocardiogram (ECG) rather than the presence or absence of Q waves. This chapter will focus on non-ST-elevation acute coronary syndromes, and discuss new advances in our understanding of the pathophysiology, the development of new prognostic markers, the importance of risk stratification, new antiplatelet and antithrombotic treatments, and how best to integrate percutaneous coronary intervention (PCI) into the management of these patients.

Most patients admitted to coronary care units have non-ST-elevation acute coronary syndromes. Between 5% and 17% suffer myocardial infarction (MI) within a month after admission, and 3-15% die within a year. The rate of revascularization procedures performed in patients with non-ST-elevation acute coronary syndromes varies from 5% to 85% worldwide, perhaps reflecting uncertainty as to the value of performing such procedures in particular subgroups of patients.[1]

Much has been learned about plaques and how to distinguish those vulnerable to rupture from those that are stable. Vulnerable plaques have a rich lipid core, a thin fibrous cap and increased numbers of macrophages, T-lymphocytes and activated intimal smooth muscle cells.[2]

NEW CARDIAC MARKERS

Troponin complex. The troponin complex that regulates the calcium-dependent interactions between myosin and actin in the myocyte is made up of three sub-units: C, T and I. Troponin T is involved in contraction, and troponin I is involved in inhibiting contraction. Between 6% and 8% of troponin T and 2-3% of troponin I are found free in the cytosolic pool. The cardiac troponins are sensitive and reliable markers of myocyte necrosis, and have recently been defined as the "gold standard" for the diagnosis of MI.[3] While only one troponin T assay has been available until recently, there are about 20 different troponin I assays with a wide variety of cut-off values, and discrepancies have been found between the results obtained using different assays.[4] Troponin I is also affected by heterophilic antibodies.[5] Troponin assays show lower concentrations in heparinized plasma than in serum,[6] and each assay should be evaluated separately.

Troponin levels are elevated in about 30% of patients presenting with non-ST-elevation acute coronary syndromes, and provide useful prognostic information, with a clear gradient of risk as levels increase.[7] However, a normal troponin test does not guarantee a benign course. For instance, in the Platelet Receptor Inhibition in Ischemic Syndrome Management (PRISM) Study, 3.5% of the patients with a troponin T level below the diagnostic threshold (<0.1 μg/L) died or suffered MI within 30 days. The release pattern of the troponins over time is similar to that of creatine kinase (CK)-MB, meaning that patients presenting within 6 hours of symptom onset may have a normal troponin T test and still be at high risk. For this reason it is important that troponin tests are done at admission and repeated 6-8 hours later.

Troponins are particularly important because they identify patients at short- and long-term risk, they correlate with the pathophysiology of acute coronary syndromes (i.e. the presence of thrombus in the coronary artery), and they identify patients who potentially have the most to gain from various treatment strategies. Troponin testing is thus a valuable addition to the history, examination and ECG. The prognostic value of the troponins is out of proportion to the extent of myocyte necrosis and impairment of left ventricular function, perhaps reflecting preceding episodes of micromyocyte necrosis following embolization of platelets from ulcerated or fissured plaques. In other words, elevated troponin levels in the setting of ischemia reflect the thrombogenic activity of a ruptured or fissured plaque.

In the PRISM Study, the 30-day risk of death/MI was 13.7% in patients with elevated troponin T levels (>0.1 μg/L) and 13.0% in those with elevated troponin I levels (>1.0 μg/L). Figure 3-1 shows the risk of death/MI at various time points in trials of the glycoprotein IIb/IIIa receptor antagonists, abciximab, tirofiban and lamifiban, and the low-molecular-weight heparins, dalteparin and enoxaparin. In all seven trials[8-14] there was a clear association between elevated troponin levels and risk.

The Platelet IIb/IIIa Antagonists for the Reduction of Acute Coronary Syndrome Events in a Global Organization Network (PARAGON)-B Study was the first trial to prospectively measure troponin levels at enrolment in a substudy of 1 100 patients, and reported that patients with an elevated troponin T level ($\geq$0.1 μg/L) had a worse outcome at 30 days, with an odds ratio for the composite endpoint of

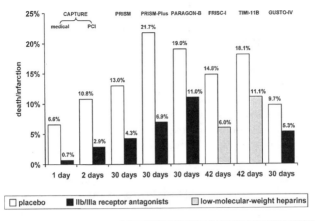

Figure 3-1. *Association between elevated troponin levels and the rates of death/MI at various time points in the CAPTURE Trial[8] of abciximab, the PRISM[9] and PRISM-Plus Studies[10] of tirofiban, the PARAGON-B Trial[11] of lamifiban, the FRISC-I Study[12] of dalteparin, the TIMI-11b Trial[13] of enoxaparin, and the GUSTO-IV Trial[14] of abciximab.*

death/MI/recurrent ischemia of 1.5 (95% confidence interval 1.1-2.1).[11] The importance of elevated troponin levels as a risk factor was confirmed in the Global Use of Strategies to Open Occluded Coronary Arteries in Acute Coronary Syndromes (GUSTO)-IV Non-ST-Elevation Trial, which reported 30-day death/MI rates of 9.7% in patients with elevated troponin T levels versus 5.3% in those with normal troponin levels.[15]

Ottani et al have recently performed a meta-analysis of trials totalling over 5,000 patients, and calculated odds ratios of 4.19 (95% confidence interval 2.01-4.20) for the short-term risk of an event (i.e. in-hospital or within 30 days)[16] and 2.05 (95% confidence interval 1.98-4.11) for longer-term risk (up to 150 days). There was no difference in the prognostic values of troponin T versus troponin I.

The prognostic value of third-generation assays for troponin T (cut-off point 0.03 µg/L) and troponin I (cut-off point 1.0 µg/L) was confirmed in the Fragmin During Instability in Coronary Artery Disease (FRISC-II) Study.[17] Several angiographic studies have reported that evidence of thrombus, complex lesions and impairment of Thrombolysis in Myocardial Infarction (TIMI) flow were more common in patients with elevated troponin levels than in those with normal levels.[18,19]

While the troponins are useful markers of necrosis, the fact that they remain elevated for up to 14 days means that they cannot be used to diagnose re-MI within this timeframe, and so CK-MB and its isoforms will continue to be important markers because of their specificity for (re)-MI.

Cardiac inflammatory markers. A number of other cardiac inflammatory markers may well prove important in the future. The most likely candidate is high-sensitivity C-reactive protein, which may be useful in long-term risk stratification. This and another marker, serum amyloid-A, are produced in the liver, and both have similar release patterns. Other markers currently under investigation include interleukin-6, intercellular adhesion molecule (ICAM)-1, and infectious seropositivity for chlamydia.[20] Fatty acid binding proteins may also play a role in the future. Markers of hemostatic risk such as von Willebrand factor, D-dimers, fibrinogen, anti-Xa and anti-IIa titres could potentially be used to identify patients at high risk. Markers of platelet function are also being developed, such as P-selectin levels and glycoprotein IIb/IIIa receptor occupancy.

RISK STRATIFICATION

Risk stratification not only provides important prognostic information for the patient and relatives, but also determines the treatment strategy. Patients at low risk can be discharged early, while those at high risk should have early angiography and revascularization if appropriate. Patients at intermediate risk may be best managed with a "watch and see" strategy. Risk stratification should be performed on a continuous basis throughout the period of observation rather than being done only when the patient is first seen. A variety of risk factors have been identified, and various models for risk stratification have been developed that incorporate clinical factors, the patient's history and the results of noninvasive and invasive investigations (Table 3-1).[21-23] It is important to note that certain clinical features are not included in risk stratification models, and the clinical assessment should always be regarded as paramount, e.g. a patient who is grey, sweating and anguished is at higher risk than one who is relaxed and appears well.

TABLE 3-1: RISK STRATIFICATION IN NON-ST-ELEVATION ACUTE CORONARY SYNDROMES

	GUSTO-IIB[21]	PURSUIT[22]	TIMI-11B[23]
Age	✓	✓	✓
Cardiac markers	✓	✓	✓
ST-segment deviation	✓	✓	✓
Congestive heart failure	✓	✓	
Prior coronary artery disease or myocardial infarction	✓	✓	✓
Risk factors	✓	✓	✓
Prior beta-blocker therapy		✓	
Prior aspirin therapy		✓	✓
Prior coronary artery bypass grafting	✓	✓	✓
Renal insufficiency	✓		
Severe chronic obstructive respiratory disease	✓		

Different markers are used to assess acute risk and long-term risk, and the European Society of Cardiology guidelines[24] divide patients into these two categories (Table 3-2).

TABLE 3-2: EUROPEAN SOCIETY OF CARDIOLOGY RECOMMENDATIONS FOR THE TREATMENT OF PATIENTS WITH NON-ST-ELEVATION ACUTE CORONARY SYNDROMES[24]

Markers of underlying disease (i.e. long-term risk)
→ *Clinical markers*
  • Age
  • History of prior myocardial infarction
  • History of severe angina
  • Diabetes
→ *Angiographic markers*
  • Left ventricular dysfunction
  • Extent of coronary artery disease
→ *Biological markers*
  • Level of C-reactive protein
Markers of thrombotic risk (i.e. acute risk)
  • Recurrent chest pain
  • ST-segment depression
  • Dynamic ST-segment changes
  • Elevated troponin levels
  • Thrombus detected at angiography

The timing of risk stratification is important, and it is recommended that patients are assessed initially and then reviewed at 6-8 hours for recurrence of ischemia, response to treatment, and results of cardiac marker investigations, particularly troponins. Further assessments should be done at 24 hours and again prior to discharge (Table 3-3).

Table 3-4 summarizes the guidelines for risk stratification published recently by the American College of Cardiology (ACC) and American Heart Association (AHA).[25] Special emphasis is given to the tempo and momentum of ischemia, the patient's age (the most powerful determinant of risk), troponin levels and ECG features, based on a number of studies such as TIMI-IIIb,[26] which showed that ST-segment depression of 0.5 mm was a significant risk factor for the composite endpoint of death/MI at 1 year. A

TABLE 3-3: RISK STRATIFICATION IN NON-ST-ELEVATION ACUTE CORONARY SYNDROMES

→ *At presentation*
  • Clinical examination
  • Electrocardiogram
  • Cardiac markers
→ *At 6-8 hours*
  • Recurrence of ischaemia
  • Cardiac markers
→ *At 24 hours*
  • Recurrence of ischaemia
  • Cardiac markers
  • Response to therapy
→ *Predischarge*
  • Left ventricular function
  • Catheterisation
  • Inducible ischemia

TABLE 3-4:   AMERICAN COLLEGE OF CARDIOLOGY/AMERICAN HEART ASSOCIATION GUIDELINES FOR RISK STRATIFICATION IN PATIENTS PRESENTING WITH NON-ST-ELEVATION ACUTE CORONARY SYNDROMES[25]

FEATURE	HIGH-RISK	INTERMEDIATE-RISK	LOW-RISK
History	Accelerating tempo over 48 hours	Previous history, prior aspirin use	
Characteristics of pain	Prolonged and ongoing (>20 minutes of rest pain)	Prolonged (>20 minutes) rest angina now resolved, rest angina (<20 minutes or relieved by nitroglycerin)	New-onset (within 2 weeks), Canadian Cardiovascular Society Class III or IV angina
Clinical features	Pulmonary edema, new/worse murmur of mitral regurgitation, third heart sound, new/worse rales, low blood pressure, bradycardia, tachycardia, age >75 years	Age >70 years	
ECG features	Rest angina with transient ST-segment changes (>0.05 mV), new bundle branch block, sustained ventricular tachycardia	T-wave inversion (>0.2 mV), pathological Q waves	Normal or unchanged ECG during episode of angina
Cardiac markers	Markedly elevated troponin T or I (>0.1 µg/L)	Slightly elevated troponin T (>0.01 but <0.1 µg/L)	Normal

follow-up study from Auckland[27] showed that patients presenting with 0.5mm of ST-segment depression had significantly higher mortality rates than those with normal ECGs or T-wave inversion (10% versus 4% at 1 year and 18% versus 6% at 4 years) (Figure 3-2).

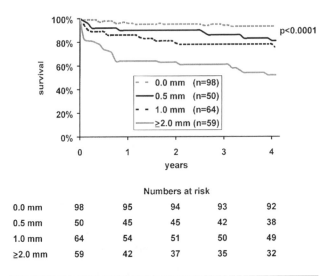

Figure 3-2. *Survival over 4-year follow-up in patients presenting with non-ST-elevation acute coronary syndromes with either a normal ECG or T-wave inversion and various degrees of ST-segment depression. The p value is a log rank comparison over the follow-up period. [Reproduced with permission from: Hyde TA, et al. Four-year survival of patients with acute coronary syndromes without ST-segment elevation and prognostic significance of 0.5-mm ST-segment depression. Am J Cardiol 1999; 84: 379-85.]*

The Platelet Glycoprotein IIb/IIIa in Unstable Angina: Receptor Suppression Using Integrilin Therapy (PURSUIT) Investigators[22] developed a multivariate model from 33 candidate variables, although most of the prognostic infor-

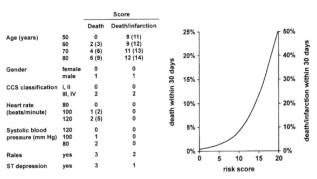

Figure 3-3. *Risk stratification model for the endpoints of death and death/ MI within 30 days in the PURSUIT Trial. Points were given for each predictive factor. With respect to age and heart rate, separate points were given for the enrolment diagnoses of unstable angina and MI (indicated in brackets). CCS=Canadian Cardiovascular Society. [Reproduced with permission from: Boersma E, et al. Predictors of outcome in patients with acute coronary syndromes without persistent ST-segment elevation: results from an international trial of 9461 patients. Circulation 2000; 101: 2557-67.]*

mation was contained in seven variables, namely age, gender, Canadian Cardiovascular Society angina classification, heart rate, blood pressure, the presence of rales, and the presence of ST-segment depression. Different models were developed for the endpoints of death and death/MI (Figure 3-3), and for the admission diagnoses of MI and non-ST-elevation acute coronary syndrome without MI (Figure 3-4).

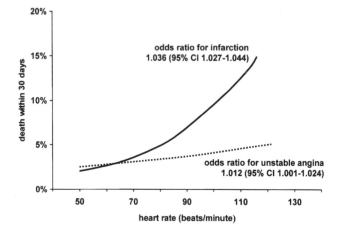

Figure 3-4. Univariate relation between continuous baseline characteristics and 30-day mortality in the PURSUIT Trial. The solid line indicates patients with MI and the dotted line indicates patients with unstable angina. [Reproduced with permission from: Boersma E, et al. Predictors of outcome in patients with acute coronary syndromes without persistent ST-segment elevation: results from an international trial of 9 461 patients. Circulation 2000; 101: 2557-67.]

The TIMI Investigators evaluated 12 baseline characteristics (Table 3-5), and devised a risk model according to the number of risk factors (Figure 3-5).[23] The advantage of this model is its simplicity, but it differs from those developed by the PURSUIT[22] and GUSTO-IIb[21] Investigators (Table 3-1). It should be noted that none of these studies measured troponin levels in a large proportion of their patients.

TABLE 3-5:   BASELINE CHARACTERISTICS INCLUDED IN THE TIMI RISK SCORE FOR UNSTABLE ANGINA/NON-ST-ELEVATION ACUTE CORONARY SYNDROMES[28]

→ Age ≥65 years
→ ≥3 risk factors for coronary artery disease
→ Prior stenosis of ≥50%
→ Prior myocardial infarction
→ Prior coronary artery bypass grafting
→ Prior percutaneous revascularisation
→ ST-segment deviation
→ ≥2 anginal events in the previous 24 hours
→ Aspirin therapy within the previous 7 days
→ Intravenous unfractionated heparin within the previous 24 hours
→ Elevated cardiac markers
→ Prior congestive heart failure

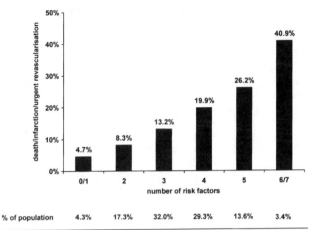

Figure 3-5. TIMI risk stratification model for the composite endpoint of death/MI/urgent revascularization in patients with unstable angina/non-ST-elevation acute coronary syndromes. [Reproduced with permission from: Antman EM, et al. The TIMI risk score for unstable angina/non-ST elevation MI: a method for prognostication and therapeutic decision making. JAMA 2000; 284: 835-42.]

MANAGEMENT OF ACS

The management of patients with acute coronary syndromes should be focussed on etiology,[28] and the primary aims of treatment in non-ST-elevation acute coronary syndromes are to reduce initial symptoms and to prevent MI. Patients with an increased oxygen demand or decreased oxygen supply (e.g. those with anemia or thyrotoxicosis) need to be managed differently than those with a severe coronary artery stenosis causing mechanical obstruction. Patients with vasospasm require other therapies such as nitrates and calcium-channel blockers, and patients with evidence of inflammation may be best treated with statins.[29] The choice of management also depends on whether an invasive or a conservative strategy is planned.

Aspirin. Aspirin reduces the risk of death/MI by about 50% in patients with non-ST-elevation acute coronary syndromes.[1] However, up to 20% of patients may be resistant to aspirin, and some cannot tolerate it. Clopidogrel could be used as an alternative in these patients, although there are no data to support its use in this situation.

Unfractionated heparin. Unfractionated heparin is effective in reducing symptoms of angina, but the evidence for its use is not compelling. A meta-analysis of all unfractionated heparin trials did not quite reach statistical significance for the endpoint of death/MI at 30 days.[30]

GLYCOPROTEIN IIB/IIIA RECEPTOR ANTAGONISTS

IIb/IIIa receptor antagonists block the final common pathway to platelet aggregation. They have the potential to reduce platelet aggregation at the site of plaque rupture, erosion or fissuring, and to reduce the amount of platelet thrombus and embolization causing myocyte necrosis. Abciximab was shown in the c7E3 Fab Antiplatelet Therapy in Unstable Refractory Angina (CAPTURE) Study to reduce the amount of thrombus present at coronary arteriography,[31] and the PRISM-Plus Study reported that tirofiban reduced peak troponin levels.[32]

In 16 trials of IIb/IIIa receptor antagonists totalling over 32 000 patients with acute coronary syndromes, the mortality rate was reduced by 30% at 48/96 hours (p<0.03), but the mortality reductions at 30 days and 6 months were not significant. The composite endpoint of death/MI was significantly reduced by 24% at both 30 days and 6 months.[33]

Seven trials, including the recent High-Dose Eptifibatide in Elective Coronary Stenting (ESPRIT) Trial, have shown that IIb/IIIa receptor antagonists reduce the composite endpoint of death/MI by approximately 35% at 30 days in patients undergoing angioplasty.[34,35] When instituted prior to the procedure, they have the potential to reduce platelet aggregation and the amount of platelet thrombus caused by the disruption of the endothelium with the angioplasty balloon.

These clinical effects could well be class effects, but may vary in different populations treated with different dosing regimens. For example, the Integrilin (Eptifibatide) to Minimize Platelet Aggregation and Coronary Thrombosis (IMPACT)-II Study,[36] which administered eptifibatide as a 135 μg/kg bolus followed by a 0.5 μg/kg/minute infusion, reported a 15% reduction in death/MI at 30 days, whereas the ESPRIT Trial,[35] which administered eptifibatide as two 180 μg/kg boluses followed by a 2 μg/kg/minute infusion, reported a 38% reduction in death/MI at 30 days.

"Upstream" treatment with IIb/IIIa receptor antagonists:
IIb/IIIa receptor antagonists may be beneficial in three situations: with angioplasty, prior to angioplasty or surgery ("upstream" treatment) and with medical therapy alone. Upstream treatment was assessed in the CAPTURE, PRISM-Plus and PURSUIT Trials, and the combined results in over 12 000 patients demonstrated a significant reduction in death/MI (from 4.3% to 2.9%) in the period prior to intervention (Figure 3-6). Most of this reduction pertained to MI (excluding enzyme release with PCI) rather than death. From the time of the intervention up until 48 hours afterwards the effect was greater, but after that time there was no effect.

Although many interventionists claim that they perform PCI acutely after a patient is admitted, this has not been demonstrated in clinical trials. In the PURSUIT Trial, for instance, only 28% of patients randomized in North America underwent PCI within the first 96 hours. Given the logistical difficulties of performing procedures at night and in the weekend, upstream use of a IIb/IIIa receptor antagonist is a sensible measure, preventing 14 preprocedural events per 1,000 patients treated. Upstream IIb/IIIa receptor

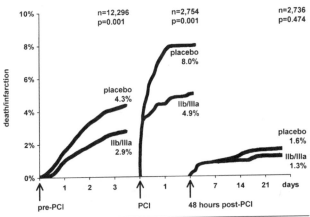

Figure 3-6. Rates of death/MI before, during and after PCI in the CAP-TURE,[8] PRISM-Plus[10] and PURSUIT[37] Trials comparing IIb/IIIa receptor antagonists with placebo in patients with non-ST-elevation acute coronary syndromes. [Reproduced with permission from: Boersma E, et al. Platelet glycoprotein IIb/IIIa receptor inhibition in non-ST-elevation acute coronary syndromes: early benefit during medical treatment only, with additional protection during PCI. Circulation 1999; 100: 2045-8.]

antagonist therapy may also benefit patients undergoing coronary bypass surgery. In the PRISM-Plus Study, the 30-day incidence of death/MI was reduced from 16.8% to 12.2% in patients undergoing coronary bypass surgery who received tirofiban.[10]

For patients treated with medical therapy alone, the 30-day rates of death/MI were reduced by 7% with eptifibatide in the PURSUIT Trial (p=NS),[37] 25% with tirofiban in the PRISM-Plus Study (p=NS),[10] and 42% with tirofiban in the PRISM Study (p<0.05).[9]

Which patients should receive IIb/IIIa receptor antagonists? There are a number of patient groups at whom IIb/IIIa receptor antagonist therapy should be targeted (Table 3-6), including patients at high risk and, in particular, those with ST-segment depression or elevated troponin levels.[9,11,31] In the PRISM Study,[9] tirofiban reduced the risk of death/MI in patients with elevated troponins to a level similar to that of patients without elevated troponins. In the PARAGON-B Study, lamifiban had no beneficial effect overall. However, in patients with troponin levels of >0.1 µg/L there was a reduction in the 30-day composite endpoint of death/MI/recurrent ischemia from 19.4% to 11.0% (p=0.01).[11] Diabetic patients are also at high risk, and in the PRISM-Plus Study their incidence of death/MI at 30 days was reduced from 19.2% to 11.2% with tirofiban.[10]

Patients who are already on aspirin therapy at admission are a particularly high-risk group[23,38] because the aspirin has usually been prescribed for secondary prevention purposes (due to a previous coronary event or important coronary artery disease) or for primary prevention purposes (e.g. they are considered high-risk because of a strong family history of coronary disease). If such patients present with an acute coronary syndrome, it signifies that they

TABLE 3-6:   INDICATIONS FOR INTRAVENOUS GLYCOPROTEIN IIB/
IIIA RECEPTOR ANTAGONISTS

→ Elevated troponin levels

→ ≥0.5 mm of ST-segment depression

→ Elevated cardiac enzymes

→ Patients undergoing percutaneous coronary intervention

→ Patients with high-risk features:

  • Age >65 years

  • Ejection fraction of <50%

  • Haemodynamic instability

  • Angiographic evidence of thrombus

  • Percutaneous coronary intervention within the previous 6 months

  • Previous coronary artery bypass surgery

  • Previous myocardial infarction

  • Pulmonary oedema

→ Diabetes

→ Patients already on aspirin at admission

→ Recurrent ischaemia

→ Inpatients awaiting surgery for left main coronary artery disease

have broken through the antiplatelet and anti-inflammatory effects of the aspirin, and could mean either that they are unresponsive to aspirin, or that they have a large thrombus load associated with plaque rupture or fissuring. IIb/IIIa receptor antagonists have been shown to benefit patients already on aspirin,[10,38] e.g. in the PURSUIT Trial eptifibatide reduced the risk of death/MI at 30 days from 17.3% to 14.9% in patients already on aspirin.[38]

Patients with intracoronary thrombus detected at angiography are also at high risk. In the PRISM-Plus Study[39] the presence of thrombus was found to increase the 30-day risks of death from 2% to 5%, MI from 4% to 9%, and recurrent ischemia from 5% to 9%. Given that IIb/IIIa receptor antagonists have been shown to reduce the amount of angiographic thrombus,[31] their use may also be indicated in patients with angiographic thrombus unsuitable for PCI who are waiting for surgery within the next few days.

GUSTO-IV and CAPTURE Trials. The results of the GUSTO-IV Trial have recently been reported.[14] In this trial, 7 800 patients who presented within 24 hours of the onset of ≥5 minutes of chest pain at rest and had either ≥0.5 mm of ST-segment depression or elevated troponin I or T levels were randomized to receive either a placebo infusion, abciximab for 24 hours, or abciximab for 48 hours. The aim of the trial was to test an intensive medical regimen, and only 1.6% of patients underwent PCI in the first 48 hours. Abciximab was found to have no effect on the primary 30-day composite endpoint of death/MI (the latter defined as a CK-MB level of three times normal), with rates of 8.0% in the placebo group, 8.2% in the 24-hour abciximab group, and 9.1% in the 48-hour abciximab group. In the subset of patients with elevated troponin levels, the event rates were 10.0%, 10.0% and 11.6%, respectively. Abciximab also had no effect in patients with ST-segment depression (with event rates of 8.4%, 8.5% and 9.9%, respectively), nor in patients with both elevated troponins and ST-segment depression. These results are markedly inconsistent with previous trials, and at least three explanations have been put forward.

Firstly, the trial had poor statistical power due to the low frequency of the primary composite endpoint. However, even when the results were analysed using a more traditional definition of MI (viz. a CK-MB level of twice normal), raising the event rate in the placebo group to about 13%, there was still no evidence that abciximab was beneficial. Secondly, the trial population was markedly different from those in previous trials in that a large proportion of the patients were women (37.6% overall and 49.1% of the patients randomized in Eastern Europe). In addition, this was the first trial to use troponin levels as an entry criterion. Previous trials have used evidence of ischemia as an entry criterion,[10,11,37,40] however, 20% of the patients in GUSTO-IV did not have ST-segment depression. While an elevated troponin level signifies that myocyte necrosis has occurred, it does not indicate the timing (which could have occurred up to 14 days previously) nor the etiology of myocyte necrosis, which could be due to causes other than ischemia, such as coronary spasm, pulmonary embolism, right ventricular MI, myocarditis or heart failure.

GUSTO-IV confirmed that troponins are an important factor in risk stratification. Death/MI (the latter defined as a CK-MB level of three times normal) occurred within 30 days in 9.7% of patients with elevated troponin T levels ($>0.1\mu g/L$) versus 5.3% of those with normal troponin T levels. Even using the more traditional definition of MI (a CK-MB of twice normal), the event rate was still lower than was seen in patients with elevated troponin levels in other trials of IIb/IIIa receptor antagonists.[9,11] The risk profile of this patient population was therefore unexpectedly low.

A third possible explanation for the lack of benefit seen with abciximab in GUSTO-IV could be the effects of the drug itself or the duration of treatment. Although the infusion was only given for 48 hours, abciximab can affect platelets for up to 2 weeks. Besides competitively blocking IIb/IIIa receptors, abciximab also blocks vitronectin receptors. It has also been shown to be procoagulant in low doses.[41] A recent study has suggested that it may increase leukocyte rolling in an *ex vivo* model, which may outweigh the reduction in leukocyte aggregation.[42] Although no studies have precisely determined the optimal level of platelet inhibition, the level of inhibition achieved by the abciximab bolus attenuates during the course of the infusion, and it may be that a prolonged low level of platelet inhibition causes procoagulant effects.[43] In a study of abciximab in patients undergoing PCI, the incidence of clinical events correlated with the level of platelet inhibition at 8 hours. Only 7% of patients with platelet inhibition of >80% suffered an MI or required coronary bypass surgery compared with 46% of those with lesser levels of platelet inhibition.[44]

The CAPTURE Study also tested abciximab in patients treated medically for 24 hours prior to PCI, and showed that it decreased the frequency of MI compared with placebo. However, unlike the patients in GUSTO-IV, all of these patients were resistant to aspirin and heparin, and continued to have pain.[8] They were also shown on angiography to have anatomy suitable for PCI, and many had evidence of thrombus. Furthermore, any prothrombotic effects of abciximab may be unimportant after PCI, when the coronary artery stenosis has been reduced.

If all of the randomized IIb/IIIa receptor antagonist studies are combined in which patients received medical treatment primarily and revascularization procedures only at the physician's discretion, there is a significant 8% reduction in death/MI at 30 days (from 11.8% to 10.6%, p<0.02) (Figure 3-7). These are powerful data obtained from over 30 000 patients, with an overall reduction of 12 events per 1 000 patients treated. The two most compelling trials within this data set are PRISM-Plus, which reported a 30% reduction in death/MI, and PURSUIT, which reported an 11% reduction. In the subgroup of patients with elevated troponins, there was a 22% reduction in death/MI at 30 days (Figure 3-8).[9,11,14]

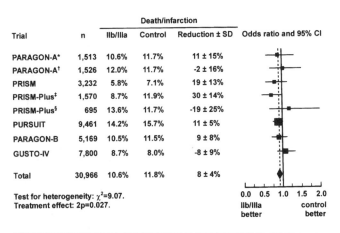

| Trial | n | Death/infarction | | Reduction ± SD | Odds ratio and 95% CI |
		IIb/IIIa	Control		
PARAGON-A*	1,513	10.6%	11.7%	11 ± 15%	
PARAGON-A†	1,526	12.0%	11.7%	-2 ± 16%	
PRISM	3,232	5.8%	7.1%	19 ± 13%	
PRISM-Plus‡	1,570	8.7%	11.9%	30 ± 14%	
PRISM-Plus§	695	13.6%	11.7%	-19 ± 25%	
PURSUIT	9,461	14.2%	15.7%	11 ± 5%	
PARAGON-B	5,169	10.5%	11.5%	9 ± 8%	
GUSTO-IV	7,800	8.7%	8.0%	-8 ± 9%	
Total	30,966	10.6%	11.8%	8 ± 4%	

Test for heterogeneity: χ^2=9.07.
Treatment effect: 2p=0.027.

0.0 0.5 1.0 1.5 2.0
IIb/IIIa   control
better   better

Figure 3-7. Rates of death/MI at 30 days in trials[9-11,14,37,40] comparing IIb/IIIa receptor antagonists with control treatment in patients with non-ST-elevation acute coronary syndromes who were also receiving aspirin therapy and in whom immediate PCI was not planned. CI=confidence interval, SD=standard deviation. *Low-dose lamifiban. †High-dose lamifiban. ††Tirofiban plus heparin versus heparin alone. §Tirofiban alone versus heparin alone. [Modified with permission from: White HD. Targeting therapy in unstable angina. J Invas Cardiol 1998; 10 Supplement D: 12D-21D.]

Do Tirofiban and Abciximab Have Similar Efficacy? The (TARGET) Trial[69] compared tirofiban with abciximab in patients undergoing PCI either for an acute coronary syndrome or for stable angina. Tirofiban was administered according to the regimen previously tested in the Randomized Efficacy Study of Tirofiban for Outcomes and Restenosis (RESTORE) Trial[70] and abciximab was administered according to the regimen previously tested in the Evalua-

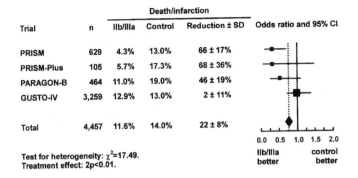

Trial	n	IIb/IIIa	Control	Reduction ± SD	Odds ratio and 95% CI
			Death/infarction		
PRISM	629	4.3%	13.0%	66 ± 17%	
PRISM-Plus	105	5.7%	17.3%	68 ± 36%	
PARAGON-B	464	11.0%	19.0%	46 ± 19%	
GUSTO-IV	3,259	12.9%	13.0%	2 ± 11%	
Total	4,457	11.6%	14.0%	22 ± 8%	

Test for heterogeneity: χ^2=17.49.
Treatment effect: 2p<0.01.

Figure 3-8. Rates of death/MI at 30 days in patients with elevated troponin levels in the PRISM,[7] PRISM-Plus,[10] PARAGON-B[11] and GUSTO-IV[14] Trials. In GUSTO-IV, MI was defined as a CK-MB level of three times normal. Here, MI is defined as a CK-MB level of twice normal. CI=confidence interval, SD=standard deviation.

tion of Platelet IIb/IIIa Inhibition in Stenting (EPISTENT) Trial.[71] All patients in TARGET also received aspirin, clopidogrel and heparin (70 IU/kg intravenous bolus), with a target activated clotting time of 250 seconds. The primary endpoint of death/MI/urgent revascularization occurred in 6.0% of the tirofiban group versus 4.8% of the abciximab group within 72 hours, and in 7.5% of the tirofiban group versus 6.0% of the abciximab group within 30 days (p=0.037). In patients undergoing PCI for acute coronary syndromes, the rates of the primary endpoint at 30 days were 8.3% with tirofiban versus 6.2% with abciximab, whereas in those undergoing elective PCI the rates were 4.7% versus 6.3% respectively (p=0.038), indicating that there was an association between treatment randomization and clinical indications for PCI. The superiority of abciximab became evident right from the first CK-MB assay performed 8 hours after the procedure. There was no difference in major bleeding between the two groups, but there was an increase in minor bleeding with abciximab. Possible explanations for these findings may include the dosing regimens used in the trial and the duration of platelet inhibition achieved.

The TARGET results show that abciximab is superior to tirofiban when administered to patients arriving in the catheterization laboratory who have not received upstream treatment with a IIb/IIIa antagonist.

Guidelines. A number of studies have evaluated the cost-effectiveness of IIb/IIIa receptor antagonists.[45,46] The recent guidelines issued by the European Society of Cardiology[24] and by the ACC and AHA[25] give a Class A recommendation (i.e. based on at least one randomized controlled trial) for the use of IIb/IIIa receptor antagonists and PCI in unstable angina or non-ST-elevation MI. Both guidelines also give a Class A recommendation for the use of IIb/IIIa receptor antagonists in acute coronary syndromes, based on the data from PRISM,[9] PRISM-Plus,[10] PURSUIT[37] and CAPTURE.[8]

LOW-MOLECULAR-WEIGHT HEPARINS

As yet, there is no compelling evidence that the low-molecular-weight heparins as a group are superior to unfractionated heparin in the management of acute coronary syndromes. A meta-analysis of five trials of dalteparin, enoxaparin and fraxiparin calculated that there was no significant overall reduction in death/MI during short-term follow-up,[30] although it should be noted that the combined event rates in these trials (2.2% in patients given low-molecular-weight heparin and 2.3% in those given unfractionated heparin) were much lower than in the IIb/IIIa receptor antagonist trials (Figure 3-9). However, individual low-molecular-weight heparins have shown some promise. The two enoxaparin trials (the Efficacy and Safety of Subcutaneous Enoxaparin in Non-Q-Wave Coronary Events (ESSENCE) Trial[47] and the TIMI 11B[48] Trial) and a prospective meta-analysis of these two studies[49] showed that enoxaparin reduced the incidence of death/MI by 18% at 42 days (p=0.02) compared with unfractionated heparin. The low-molecular-weight heparin, dalteparin, was shown in the FRISC-I Study to reduce death/MI[12] compared with placebo.

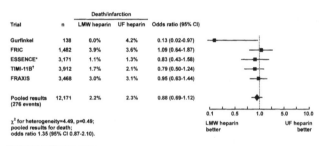

Trial	n	Death/infarction		Odds ratio (95% CI)
		LMW heparin	UF heparin	
Gurfinkel	138	0.0%	4.2%	0.13 (0.02-0.97)
FRIC	1,482	3.9%	3.6%	1.09 (0.64-1.87)
ESSENCE*	3,171	1.1%	1.3%	0.83 (0.43-1.58)
TIMI-11B†	3,912	1.7%	2.1%	0.79 (0.50-1.24)
FRAXIS	3,468	3.0%	3.1%	0.95 (0.63-1.44)
Pooled results (276 events)	12,171	2.2%	2.3%	0.88 (0.69-1.12)

χ^2 for heterogeneity=4.49, p=0.49; pooled results for death; odds ratio 1.35 (95% CI 0.87-2.10).

*Figure 3-9. Rates of death/MI at the completion of treatment in randomized trials comparing short-term low-molecular-weight (LMW) heparin with unfractionated (UF) heparin in patients with non-ST-elevation acute coronary syndromes.[47,48,66-68] CI=confidence interval. *The median duration of therapy was 2.6 days in both groups. †Unequal duration of treatment. [Reproduced with permission from: Eikelboom JW, et al. Unfractionated heparin and low-molecular-weight heparin in acute coronary syndrome without ST elevation: a meta-analysis. Lancet 2000; 355: 1936-42.]*

Low-molecular-weight heparins do have some practical advantages over unfractionated heparin (Table 3-7), such as convenience in that there is no need to monitor the activated partial thromboplastin time and no need for intravenous lines. Cost-effectiveness data show that in some health systems, the use of low-molecular-weight heparins saves money.[50] The greatest benefits of low-molecular-weight heparins appear to be in patients with elevated troponins, patients with ST-segment depression, patients over the age of 65 years, patients on aspirin, and patients with previous or current MI.[12,47,48]

Combination of IIb/IIIa receptor antagonists and low-molecular-weight heparins. In the Antithrombotic Combination Using Tirofiban and Enoxaparin (ACUTE-1) Study,[51]

TABLE 3-7: ADVANTAGES OF LOW-MOLECULAR-WEIGHT
HEPARIN COMPARED WITH UNFRACTIONATED
HEPARIN

→ Convenience: no intravenous lines and no need to monitor activated partial thrombin times

→ Cost-effective

→ Higher anti-Xa to anti-IIa ratio with enhanced ability to inhibit thrombin generation

→ Lack of platelet activation and inhibition of von Willebrand factor release

→ Less thrombocytopenia

→ Reliable anticoagulant effect due to high bioavailability and minimal protein binding

→ Resistance to inactivation by platelet factor 4

55 patients were randomized to receive either tirofiban plus enoxaparin or tirofiban plus unfractionated heparin. At 48 hours, 84% of the patients treated with enoxaparin had *ex vivo* platelet inhibition of >70% compared with only 65% of those treated with unfractionated heparin, although this trend did not reach statistical significance (p=0.16). There was also less variability in the degree of platelet inhibition in the patients treated with enoxaparin. In addition, although not closely related to clinical bleeding, bleeding times were less prolonged with enoxaparin (20.7 minutes versus 30 minutes with unfractionated heparin, p=0.35).

In the recent ACUTE-2 Study,[52] 525 patients were randomized to receive either tirofiban plus enoxaparin or tirofiban plus unfractionated heparin. There was no difference in major or minor bleeding, nor in the need for transfusion, between the two groups. The incidence of thrombocytopenia was low and similar in both groups, and there was no difference in death, MI or stroke.

INTEGRATION OF REVASCULARIZATION STRATEGIES

In the Organization to Assess Strategies for Ischemic Syndromes (OASIS) Registry, which compared revascularization rates in six countries, the countries with higher revascularization rates (Brazil and the United States) had higher bleeding and stroke rates — but not lower rates of cardiovascular death or MI — than the countries with lower revascularization rates (Australia, Canada, Hungary and Poland).

Six trials have compared an invasive treatment strategy with a conservative treatment strategy in which patients underwent revascularization procedures only if they developed recurrent or inducible ischemia (Figure 3-10). Four of these trials were conducted exclusively in patients with non-ST-elevation acute coronary syndromes,[53-56] one was conducted in patients with post-MI ischemia,[57] and one was conducted in patients with either ST-segment elevation or ST-segment depression.[58] One of these trials concluded

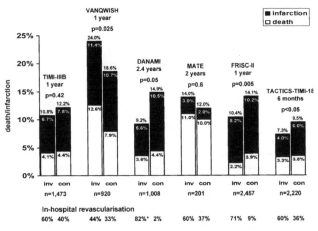

Figure 3-10. Rates of death/MI at various timepoints in six trials comparing invasive (inv) with conservative medical management (con) in patients with acute coronary syndromes. Three of these trials were conducted in patients with non-ST-elevation acute coronary syndromes,[53-55] one was conducted in patients with post-MI angina,[57] and one was conducted in patients with either ST-segment elevation or ST-segment depression who were ineligible for thrombolytic therapy.[58] *At 2 months. [Reproduced with permission from: White HD. The rationale for early conservative medical management of acute coronary syndromes. IMJ. In press 2001.]

that a conservative strategy was better[54] and three trials favored an invasive strategy.[53,55] Both approaches are therefore supported by clinical trial evidence.

The Veterans' Study[59] reported that patients with impaired left ventricular function (i.e. an ejection fraction of <40%) had better outcomes when treated by surgical revascularization. Revascularization has also been shown to relieve angina and to prolong life in patients with left main coronary artery disease and in patients with both triple-vessel disease and impaired left ventricular function.[60]

In the six trials comparing invasive with conservative treatment, the percentage of patients who were randomized to receive conservative treatment but then underwent revascularization procedures varied from 2%[57] to 40%[58] (Figure 3-10). It should be noted that in some of the trials there was actually little difference in revascularization rates between the invasive and conservative treatment groups, e.g. in the Veterans' Affairs Non-Q-Wave Infarction Strategies in Hospital (VANQWISH) Trial, revascularization was performed in 33% of the conservative treatment group and 44% of the invasive treatment group. In contrast, only 9% of the conservative treatment group in the FRISC-II Study underwent revascularization, as opposed to 71% of the invasive treatment group.

The Danish Trial in Acute Myocardial Infarction (DANAMI)[57] compared invasive with conservative treatment in 1 008 patients under the age of 70 who developed post-MI ischemia after receiving thrombolytic therapy (viz. Braunwald Class C angina,[61] including silent ischemia in 56.5% and exercise-induced ischemia in 28%). The incidence of MI was reduced by almost 40% (from 14.9% to 9.2%, p=0.05) in the invasive treatment group.

In the VANQWISH Trial there was a high operative mortality rate (11.6%) among patients who underwent early surgical revascularization. This may have been due to the urgency of the operation, as acuity is known to be one of the most powerful predictors of a bad outcome after coronary bypass surgery.[62] The operative mortality rate among patients whose surgery was not performed acutely was 3.4%.

The FRISC-II Study reported that intervention was beneficial after an initial period of dalteparin therapy (4 days in patients undergoing PCI and 7 days in those undergoing coronary bypass surgery). At 1 year, mortality was reduced from 3.9% to 2.2% (p<0.02), MI was reduced from 11.6% to 8.6% (p=0.02) and readmissions were reduced from 57% to 37% (p<0.001).[63] The patients who benefited from revascularization were those with ST-segment depression and those with elevated troponin T levels (>0.03 μg/L). However, there was no significant benefit in patients who had ST-segment depression with normal troponin T levels (n=301). Similarly, there was no significant benefit in patients who had elevated troponin T levels without ST-segment depression (n=800). There was, however, a significant reduction in death/MI at 12 months in patients in the invasive treatment group who had both ST-segment depression and elevated troponin T levels (n=756).[19]

TACTICS-TIMI-18. The Treat Angina With Aggrastat and Determine Cost of Therapy with an Invasive or Conservative Strategy (TACTICS-TIMI-18) Trial, is a large and influential trial, which supports the use of early tirofiban and PCI in the treatment of acute coronary syndromes.[56] The trial enrolled 2 220 patients presenting with unstable or minimal-effort angina and ECG changes, elevated troponins or a history of prior MI, PCI or coronary bypass surgery (i.e. largely intermediate/high-risk patients according to ACC/AHA guidelines).[25] The patients were randomized to receive either invasive or conservative treatment, and all received heparin, aspirin and tirofiban for 48-108 hours. Patients in the invasive treatment group underwent catheterization between 0 and 48 hours and revascularization if the anatomy was suitable.

Patients in the conservative treatment group did not undergo revascularization procedures unless they had refractory angina (>10 minutes of rest pain with ECG changes), hemodynamic instability, a positive exercise test or stress echocardiogram, new MI or hospitalization with unstable angina, class III or IV angina. The study prospectively evaluated the TIMI risk score[26] and the use of troponin levels in determining the optimal treatment strategy. The primary endpoint was a composite of death/MI (defined as a CK-MB level of at least three times normal with PCI)/rehospitalization for acute coronary syndromes within 6 months of follow-up.

During the initial hospital admission, 97% of the invasive group and 51% of the conservative group underwent cardiac catheterization. In the invasive group, 41% of patients underwent PCI, 19% had surgery and 40% had no intervention. In the conservative group, 36% of patients underwent revascularization procedures during the initial hospital admission. At 6 months there was a reduction in the primary composite endpoint from 19.4% in the conservative group to 15.9% in the invasive group (odds ratio 0.78, p=0.025). There was no difference in death rates. The incidence of rehospitalization was reduced in the invasive group from 13.7% to 11.0% (p=0.054). Invasive treatment was beneficial in patients with elevated troponin levels, reducing the primary composite endpoint from 24.2% to 14.3%, but not in patients with a low TIMI risk score (0-2). The mean duration of the tirofiban infusion prior to catheterization in the invasive group was 24 hours. The 30-day mortality rate in patients who underwent surgical revascularization was 3.5%.

TACTICS-TIMI-18 shows that intermediate- and high-risk patients benefit from aspirin, a IIb/IIIa receptor antagonist (e.g. tirofiban) and unfractionated heparin, and should undergo early angiography with revascularization if possible. A cost-effectiveness analysis of this approach is awaited. If facilities are poor, patients with ST-segment changes and elevated troponins should be transferred under cover of heparin, aspirin and a IIb/IIIa receptor antagonist to an appropriate center.

There are two possible alternatives to the treatment strategy tested in TACTICS-TIMI-18. The first is to administer low-molecular-weight heparin prior to intervention, as used in the FRISC-II trial.[55] It should be noted, however, that the patients in FRISC-II received low-molecular-weight heparin for 4 to 7 days, and there was an increase in the infarction rate in patients who underwent procedures. The incidence of periprocedural infarction was reduced by tirofiban in TACTICS-TIMI-18, but not by low-molecular-weight heparin in the FRISC-II Trial.

The second alternative is to withhold upstream treatment with IIb/IIIa antagonists and instead administer abciximab in the catheterization laboratory. However, it is known that upstream treatment with a IIb/IIIa antagonist reduces the risk of preprocedural infarction, and so withholding it would expose patients to a greater risk of preprocedural infarction, which would increase with the length of the delay prior to intervention.

There is now strong evidence that better outcomes are achieved with higher usage rates of proven therapies.[64] Future advances, including new combinations of current therapies, will almost certainly improve patient outcomes (Figure 3-11).

Secondary prevention. Following presentation with a non-ST-elevation acute coronary syndrome, it is important that secondary preventive measures are instituted. These

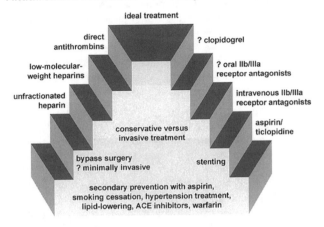

Antithrombin Treatment   **Antiplatelet Treatment**

Figure 3-11. Strategies to improve the treatment of patients with non-ST-elevation acute coronary syndromes, including new combinations of current therapies. [Modified with permission from: White HD. Optimal treatment of patients with acute coronary syndromes and non-ST-elevation MI. Am Heart J 1999; 138: S105-S114.]

should include lifestyle changes such as smoking cessation, achievement of ideal weight, a regular exercise programme, an appropriate low-cardiovascular-risk diet, and achievement of optimal diabetic and blood pressure control where necessary. Pharmacological measures are also indicated, such as aspirin, beta-blockers, lipid-modifying agents, and angiotensin-converting-enzyme (ACE) inhibitors in patients with decreased ejection fractions or another risk factor.[65] Appropriate education and enrollment in rehabilitation programs should also be undertaken. Diabetics need excellent blood pressure and glycemic control.

SUMMARY

1. Risk stratification is of major importance in non-ST-elevation acute coronary syndromes. Not only does it provide important prognostic information for the patient and relatives; it also determines the treatment strategy. Patients at low risk can be discharged early, while those at high risk should have early angiography and revascularization if appropriate. Patients at intermediate risk may be best managed either with a "watch and see" strategy or by PCI, the latter favoured by a recent study. Patients at high risk should undergo intervention. Risk stratification should be performed on a continuous basis throughout the period of observation rather than being done only when the patient is first seen. The clinical assessment should always be regarded as paramount. Two other important signs are elevated troponin levels and ST-segment depression.

2. Troponin levels are elevated in about 30% of patients presenting with non-ST-elevation acute coronary syn-

dromes, and provide useful prognostic information, with a clear gradient of risk as levels increase.[7] The prognostic value of the troponins is out of proportion to the extent of myocyte necrosis and impairment of left ventricular function. Elevated troponin levels reflect the thrombogenic activity of a ruptured or fissured plaque. However, a normal troponin test does not guarantee a benign course.

3. Therapy is by aspirin, heparin, IIb/IIIa receptor antagonists and revascularization. In one study favoring relatively early intervention after a few days of low-molecular-weight heparin, the patients who benefited "with increased survival" from revascularization were those with both ST-segment depression and elevated troponin T levels (>0.03 mg/L). However, there was no significant benefit in patients who had just one of these signs. The increased incidence of periprocedural MI was not reduced by low-molecular-weight heparin. In a recent study that reported benefits from intervention between 4 and 48 hours after pretreatment with a IIb/IIIa receptor antagonist, intervention was not associated with an increased risk of periprocedural MI. Again, the patients who benefited were those at higher risk.

Secondary prevention measures must be instituted. These should include lifestyle changes such as smoking cessation, achievement of ideal weight, a regular exercise programme, an appropriate low-cardiovascular-risk diet, and optimal diabetic and blood pressure control where necessary. Pharmacological measures are also indicated, such as aspirin, beta-blockers, lipid-modifying agents, and angiotensin-converting-enzyme (ACE) inhibitors.

ABBREVIATIONS AND ACRONYMS

ACE	angiotensin-converting-enzyme
ACUTE	Antithrombotic Combination Using Tirofiban and Enoxaparin Studies
CAPTURE	c7E3 Fab Antiplatelet Therapy in Unstable Refractory Angina Study
CK-MB	creatine kinase-MB
DANAMI	Danish Trial in Acute Myocardial Infarction
ECG	electrocardiogram
ESPRIT	High-Dose Eptifibatide in Elective Coronary Stenting Trial
ESSENCE	Efficacy and Safety of Subcutaneous Enoxaparin in Non-Q-Wave Coronary Events Trial

FRISC	Fragmin During Instability in Coronary Artery Disease Studies
GUSTO	Global Use of Strategies to Open Occluded Coronary Arteries in Acute Coronary Syndromes Trials
ICAM-1	intercellular adhesion molecule-1
IMPACT	Integrilin (Eptifibatide) to Minimize Platelet Aggregation and Coronary Thrombosis Studies
MI	myocardial infarction
OASIS	Organization to Assess Strategies for Ischemic Syndromes
PARAGON	Platelet IIb/IIIa Antagonists for the Reduction of Acute Coronary Syndrome Events in a Global Organization Network Studies
PCI	percutaneous coronary intervention
PRISM	Platelet Receptor Inhibition in Ischemic Syndrome Management Study
PRISM-Plus	Platelet Receptor Inhibition in Ischemic Syndrome Management in Patients with Unstable Signs and Symptoms Study
PURSUIT	Platelet Glycoprotein IIb/IIIa in Unstable Angina: Receptor Suppression Using Integrilin Therapy Trial
TACTICS-TIMI-18	Treat Angina With Aggrastat and Determine Cost of Therapy with an Invasive or Conservative Strategy (TIMI-18) Trial
TIMI	Thrombolysis in Myocardial Infarction Trials
VANQWISH	Veterans' Affairs Non-Q-Wave Infarction Strategies in Hospital Trial

REFERENCES

1. White HD. Unstable angina: ischemic syndromes. In: Topol EJ, editor. Comprehensive cardiovascular medicine. Philadelphia: Lippincott-Raven Publishers; 1998. p. 395-423.

2. Libby P. Molecular bases of the acute coronary syndromes. Circulation 1995; 91: 2844-50.

3. Jaffe AS, Ravkilde J, Roberts R, et al. It's time for a change to a troponin standard. Circulation 2000; 102: 1216-20.

4. Apple FS. Clinical and analytical standardization issues confronting cardiac troponin I. Clin Chem 1999; 45: 18-20.

5. Fitzmaurice TF, Brown C, Rifai N, et al. False increase of cardiac troponin I with heterophilic antibodies. Clin Chem 1998; 44: 2212-4.

6. Stiegler H, Fischer Y, Vazquez-Jimenez JF, et al. Lower cardiac troponin T and I results in heparin-plasma than in serum. Clin Chem 2000; 46: 1338-44.

7. Heeschen C, Hamm CW, Goldmann B, et al. Troponin concentrations for stratification of patients with acute coronary syndromes in relation to therapeutic efficacy of tirofiban. Lancet 1999; 354: 1757-62.

8. The CAPTURE Investigators. Randomised placebo-controlled trial of abciximab before and during coronary intervention in refractory unstable angina: the CAPTURE Study.Lancet 1997; 349: 1429-35.

9. The Platelet Receptor Inhibition in Ischemic Syndrome Management (PRISM) Study Investigators. A comparison of aspirin plus tirofiban with aspirin plus heparin for unstable angina. N Engl J Med 1998; 338: 1498-505.

10. The Platelet Receptor Inhibition in Ischemic Syndrome Management in Patients Limited by Unstable Signs and Symptoms (PRISM-Plus) Study Investigators. Inhibition of the platelet glycoprotein IIb/IIIa receptor with tirofiban in unstable angina and non-Q-wave myocardial infarction. N Engl J Med 1998; 338: 1488-97.

11. Harrington RA, on behalf of the PARAGON-B Investigators. The PARA-GON-B study. Presented at the Late Breaking Clinical Trials II Session, 49th Annual Scientific Sessions of the American College of Cardiology; Anaheim, California, USA; March 14, 2000.

12. Fragmin During Instability in Coronary Artery Disease (FRISC) Study Group. Low-molecular-weight heparin during instability in coronary artery disease. Lancet 1996; 347: 561-8.

13. Antman EM, McCabe CH, Premmereur J, et al. Enoxaparin for the acute and chronic management of unstable angina/non-Q wave myocardial infarction: results of TIMI 11B [abstract]. Circulation 1998: 98 Suppl I: I-504.

14. Simoons ML. GUSTO IV ACS: outcome of 7,800 patients with acute coronary syndromes randomised to placebo or abciximab for 1 or 2 days. Presented at the Hot Line I Session, XXII Congress of the European Society of Cardiology; Amsterdam, The Netherlands; August 28, 2000.

15. Wallentin LC. GUSTO IV ACS: substudy comparing outcomes for the combination of abciximab with standard unfractionated heparin or low molecular weight heparin. Presented at the Hot Line I Session, XXII Congress of the European Society of Cardiology; Amsterdam, The Netherlands; August 28, 2000.

16. Ottani F, Galvani M, Nicolini F, et al. Elevated cardiac tropon levels predict the risk of adverse outcome in patients with acute coronary syndromes. Am Heart J 2000; 140: 917-27.

17. Lindahl B, Diderholm E, Lagerqvist B, et al. Troponin I and T are comparable for risk stratification in unstable coronary artery disease [abstract]. Eur Heart J 2000: 21 Abstract Supplement: 521.

18. Heeschen C, van den Brand MJ, Hamm CW, et al. Angiographic findings in patients with refractory unstable angina according to troponin T status. Circulation 1999; 104: 1509-14.

19. Lindahl B, Diderholm E, Lagerqvist B, et al. Invasive vs noninvasive strategy in relation to troponin T level and ECG findings a FRISC-2 substudy [abstract]. Eur Heart J 2000: 21 Abstract Supplement : 469.

20. Wong C-K, Amos DJ, White HD. Does infection have a role in the pathogenesis of coronary artery disease? NZ Med J 2000; 113: 190-2.

21. Armstrong PW, Fu Y, Chang W-C, et al. Acute coronary syndromes in the GUSTO-IIb Trial: prognostic insights and impact of recurrent ischemia. Circulation 1998; 98: 1860-8.

22. Boersma E, Pieper KS, Steyerberg EW, et al. Predictors of outcome in patients with acute coronary syndromes without persistent ST-segment elevation: results from an international trial of 9461 patients. Circulation 2000; 101: 2557-67.

23. Antman EM, Cohen M, Bernink PJ, et al. The TIMI risk score for unstable angina/non-ST elevation MI: a method for prognostication and therapeutic decision making. JAMA 2000; 284: 835-42.

24. Bertrand ME, Simoons ML, Fox KAA, et al. Management of acute coronary syndromes: acute coronary syndromes without persistent ST segment elevation: recommendations of the Task Force of the European Society of Cardiology. Eur Heart J 2000; 21: 1406-32.

25. Braunwald E, Antman EM, Beasley JW, et al. ACC/AHA guidelines for the management of patients with unstable angina and non-ST-segment elevation myocardial infarction: a report of the American College of Cardiology/American Heart Association Task Force on Practice Guidelines (Committee on the Management of Patients with Unstable Angina). J Am Coll Cardiol 2000; 36: 970-1062.

26. Cannon CP, McCabe CH, Stone PH, et al. The electrocardiogram predicts one-year outcome of patients with unstable angina and non-Q wave myocardial infarction: results of the TIMI III Registry ECG Ancillary Study. J Am Coll Cardiol 1997; 30: 133-40.

27. Hyde TA, French JK, Wong C-K, et al. Four-year survival of patients with acute coronary syndromes without ST-segment elevation and prog-

nostic significance of 0.5-mm ST-segment depression. Am J Cardiol 1999; 84: 379-85.

28. Braunwald E. Unstable angina: an etiologic approach to management [editorial]. Circulation 1998; 98: 2219-22.

29. Ridker PM, Rifai N, Pfeffer MA, et al. Inflammation, pravastatin, and the risk of coronary events after myocardial infarction in patients with average cholesterol levels. Circulation 1998; 98: 839-44.

30. Eikelboom JW, Anand SS, Malmberg K, et al. Unfractionated heparin and low-molecular-weight heparin in acute coronary syndrome without ST elevation: a meta-analysis. Lancet 2000; 355: 1936-42.

31. Hamm CW, Heeschen C, Goldmann B, et al. Benefit of abciximab in patients with refractory unstable angina in relation to serum troponin T levels. N Engl J Med 1999; 340: 1623-9.

32. Januzzi JL, Hahn SS, Chae CU, et al. Effects of tirofiban plus heparin versus heparin alone on troponin I levels in patients with acute coronary syndromes. Am J Cardiol 2000; 86: 713-7.

33. Kong DF, Califf RM, Miller DP, et al. Clinical outcomes of therapeutic agents that block the platelet glycoprotein IIb/IIIa integrin in ischemic heart disease. Circulation 1998; 98: 2829-35.

34. Topol EJ, Serruys PW. Frontiers in interventional cardiology. Circulation 1998; 98: 1802-20.

35. Kleiman NS, Califf RM. Results from late-breaking clinical trials sessions at ACCIS 2000 and ACC 2000. J Am Coll Cardiol 2000; 36: 310-25.

36. The IMPACT-II Investigators. Randomised placebo-controlled trial of effect of eptifibatide on complications of percutaneous coronary intervention: IMPACT-II. Lancet 1997; 349: 1422-8.

37. The PURSUIT Trial Investigators. Inhibition of platelet glycoprotein IIb/IIIa with eptifibatide in patients with acute coronary syndromes. N Engl J Med 1998; 339: 436-43.

38. Alexander JH, Harrington RA, Tuttle RH, et al. Prior aspirin use predicts worse outcomes in patients with non-ST-elevation acute coronary syndromes. Am J Cardiol 1999; 83: 1147-51.

39. Zhao X-Q, Throux P, Snapinn SM, et al. Intracoronary thrombus and platelet glycoprotein IIb/IIIa receptor blockade with tirofiban in unstable angina or non-Q-wave myocardial infarction: angiographic results from the PRISM-PLUS Trial (Platelet Receptor Inhibition for Ischemic Syndrome Management in Patients Limited by Unstable Signs and Symptoms). Circulation 1999; 100: 1609-15.

40. The PARAGON Investigators. International, randomized, controlled trial of lamifiban (a platelet glycoprotein IIb/IIIa inhibitor), heparin, or both in unstable angina. Circulation 1998; 97: 2386-95.

41. Peter K, Schwarz M, Ylnne J, et al. Induction of fibrinogen binding and platelet aggregation as a potential intrinsic property of various glycoprotein IIb/IIIa ($a_{IIb}b_3$) inhibitors. Blood 1998; 92: 3240-9.

42. Simon DI, Chen Z, Xu H, et al. Platelet glycoprotein ibalpha is a counterreceptor for the leukocyte integrin Mac-1 (CD11b/CD18). J Exp Med 2000; 192: 193-204.

43. Murphy RT, Quinn M, Dooley M, et al. Abciximab fails to fully inhibit internal pool of GP IIb/IIIa receptors in patients undergoing coronary angioplasty [abstract]. Circulation 2000: 102 Suppl II: II-428.

44. Steinhubl SR, Kottke-Marchant K, Moliterno DJ, et al. Attainment and maintenance of platelet inhibition through standard dosing of abciximab in diabetic and nondiabetic patients undergoing percutaneous coronary intervention. Circulation 1999; 100: 1977-82.

45. Heeschen C, Hamm CW, Heidenreich P, et al. Costs and effectivity of treatment with tirofiban in patients with acute coronary syndromes: results from the PRISM trial [abstract]. Eur Heart J 2000: 21 Abstract Supplement: 218.

46. Szucs TD, Meyer BJ, Kiowski W. Economic assessment of tirofiban in the management of acute coronary syndromes in the hospital setting: an analysis based on the PRISM PLUS Trial. Eur Heart J 1999; 20: 1253-60.

47. Cohen M, Demers C, Gurfinkel EP, et al. A comparison of low-molecular-weight heparin with unfractionated heparin for unstable coronary artery disease. N Engl J Med 1997; 337: 447-52.

48. Antman EM, McCabe CH, Gurfinkel EP, et al. Enoxaparin prevents death and cardiac ischemic events in unstable angina/non-Q-wave myocardial infarction: results of the Thrombolysis in Myocardial Infarction (TIMI) 11B Trial. Circulation 1999; 100: 1593-601.

49. Antman EM, Cohen M, Radley D, et al. Assessment of the treatment effect of enoxaparin for unstable angina/non-Q-wave myocardial infarction: TIMI 11B-ESSENCE meta-analysis. Circulation 1999; 100: 1602-8.

50. Mark DB, Cowper PA, Berkowitz SD, et al. Economic assessment of low-molecular-weight heparin (enoxaparin) versus unfractionated heparin in acute coronary syndrome patients: results from the ESSENCE Randomized Trial. Circulation 1998; 97: 1702-7.

51. Cohen M, Throux P, Weber S, et al. Combination therapy with tirofiban and exoxaparin in acute coronary syndromes. Int J Cardiol 1999; 71: 273-81.

52. Cohen M, Theroux P, Frey MJ, et al. Anti-thrombotic combination using tirofiban and enoxaparin: the ACUTE II Study [abstract]. Circulation 2000: 102 Suppl II: II-826.

53. The TIMI IIIB Investigators. Effects of tissue plasminogen activator and a comparison of early invasive and conservative strategies in unstable angina and non-Q-wave myocardial infarction: results of the TIMI IIIB Trial. Circulation 1994; 89: 1545-56.

54. Boden WE, O'Rourke RA, Crawford MH, et al. Outcomes in patients with acute non-Q-wave myocardial infarction randomly assigned to an invasive as compared with a conservative management strategy. N Engl J Med 1998; 338: 1785-92.

55. Fragmin and Fast Revascularisation During Instability in Coronary Artery Disease (FRISC II) Investigators. Invasive compared with non-invasive treatment in unstable coronary-artery disease: FRISC II Prospective Randomised Multicentre Study. Lancet 1999; 354: 708-15.

56. Cannon C, on behalf of the TACTICS-TIMI-18 Investigators. TACTICS-TIMI-18. Presented at the Late Breaking Clinical Trials Plenary Session XII, American Heart Association's Scientific Sessions 2000; New Orleans, Louisiana, USA; November 16, 2000.

57. Madsen JK, Grande P, Saunamki K, et al. Danish multicenter randomized study of invasive versus conservative treatment in patients with inducible ischemia after thrombolysis in acute myocardial infarction (DANAMI). Circulation 1997; 96: 748-55.

58. McCullough PA, O'Neill WW, Graham M, et al. A prospective randomized trial of triage angiography in acute coronary syndromes ineligible for thrombolytic therapy: results of the Medicine Versus Angiography in Thrombolytic Exclusion (MATE) Trial. J Am Coll Cardiol 1998; 32: 596-605.

59. Luchi RJ, Scott SM, Deupree RH, et al. Comparison of medical and surgical treatment for unstable angina pectoris: results of a Veterans Administration cooperative study. N Engl J Med 1987; 316: 977-84.

60. Yusuf S, Zucker D, Peduzzi P, et al. Effect of coronary artery bypass graft surgery on survival: overview of 10-year results from randomised trials by the Coronary Artery Bypass Graft Surgery Trialists Collaboration. Lancet 1994; 344: 563-70.

61. Braunwald E. Unstable angina: a classification. Circulation 1989; 80: 410-4.

62. Jones RH, Hannan EL, Hammermeister KE, et al. Identification of preoperative variables needed for risk adjustment of short-term mortality after coronary artery bypass graft surgery. The Working Group Panel on the Cooperative CABG Database Project. J Am Coll Cardiol 1996; 28: 1478-87.

63. Wallentin L, Lagerqvist B, Husted S, et al. Outcome at 1 year after an invasive compared with a non-invasive strategy in unstable coronary-artery disease: the FRISC II invasive randomised trial. Lancet 2000; 356: 9-16.

64. Thiemann DR, Coresh J, Oetgen WJ, et al. The association between hospital volume and survival after acute myocardial infarction in elderly patients. N Engl J Med 1999; 340: 1640-8.

65. Heart Outcome Prevention Evaluation Study Investigators. Effects of ramipril on cardiovascular and microvascular outcomes in people with diabetes mellitus: results of the HOPE Study and MICRO-HOPE Substudy. Lancet 2000; 355: 253-9.

66. Gurfinkel EP, Manos EJ, Mejail RI, et al. Low molecular weight heparin versus regular heparin or aspirin in the treatment of unstable angina and silent ischemia. J Am Coll Cardiol 1995; 26: 313-8.

67. Klein W, Buchwald A, Hillis SE, et al. Comparison of low-molecular-weight heparin with unfractionated heparin acutely and with placebo for 6 weeks in the management of unstable coronary artery disease: Fragmin in Unstable Coronary Artery Disease Study (FRIC). Circulation 1997; 96: 61-8.

68. The FRAXIS Study Group. Comparison of two treatment durations (6 days and 14 days) of a low molecular weight heparin with a 6-day treatment of unfractionated heparin in the initial management of unstable angina or non-Q wave myocardial infarction: FRAXIS (Fraxiparine in Ischaemic Syndrome). Eur Heart J 1999; 20: 1553-62.

69. Topol EJ, for the TARGET Investigators. TARGET (Do Tirofiban and Reopro Give Similar Efficacy) Trial. Presented at the Late Breaking Clinical Trials Plenary Session XII, American Heart Association Scientific Sessions 2000; New Orleans, Louisiana, USA; November 15, 2000.

70. The RESTORE Investigators. Effects of platelet glycoprotein IIb/IIIa blockade with tirofiban on adverse cardiac events in patients with unstable angina or acute myocardial infarction undergoing coronary angioplasty. Circulation 1997; 96: 1445-53.

71. The EPISTENT Investigators. Randomised placebo-controlled and balloon-angioplasty-controlled trial to assess safety of coronary stenting with use of platelet glycoprotein-IIb/IIIa blockade. Lancet 1998; 352: 87-92.

EDITORS' NOTE

Owing to the importance of the TACTICS-TIMI-18 and TARGET Trials, presented at the American Heart Association meeting in New Orleans in November, 2000, Professor Harvey White kindly agreed to update his article to incorporate the results of these trials at the galley proof stage. Hence references 69 to 71 are quoted out of sequence in the text. We appreciate his major efforts to keep his article as up to date as possible in this fast moving area.

CHAPTER 4

The Global Epidemic of Atherosclerotic Cardiovascular Disease

Salim Yusuf, Stephanie Ôunpuu, Sonia Anand

The last century has witnessed the most dramatic improvements in health in history for most populations. During this period, life expectancy at birth has increased by an average of over 25 years. The health status and dominant disease profile of human societies have historically been linked to the level of their economic development and social organization. With industrialization, the major causes of death and disability, in the more advanced societies, have shifted from a predominance of nutritional deficiencies and infectious diseases, to chronic diseases such as cardiovascular disease, cancer, and diabetes. This shift from a dominance of the acute communicable diseases to the chronic degenerative diseases, has been termed "the epidemiologic transition".

EPIDEMIOLOGICAL TRANSITION

At any given time, different countries of the world or even different regions within a country are at different stages of the epidemiologic transition. This transition occurs between different disease categories (e.g. deaths from childhood diarrhea and malnutrition giving way to adult chronic diseases), and also within specific disease categories (e.g. across different cardiovascular diseases, rheumatic heart disease of the young giving way to chronic artery diseases of middle age or valve calcification, degeneration and heart failure of the elderly). The epidemiologic transition can at times shift back when dramatic changes in social and economic conditions occur resulting in a resurgence of diseases of poverty and infections (e.g. in the last 10 years in Russia, life expectancy has shortened and there has been an increase in infectious diseases). Therefore, the epidemiologic transition is both global and regional, within and across diseases and is potentially reversible. Table 4-1 provides a schema of the epidemiologic transition as it relates to CVD.

During the past 30 years, large declines in cardiovascular disease (CVD) death rates have been experienced in several

TABLE 4–1: MODIFIED MODEL OF THE STAGES OF EPIDEMIOLOGIC TRANSITION AS IT PERTAINS TO CARDIOVASCULAR DISEASES (CVD)

Stages of Development	Deaths from CVD (% of total deaths)	Predominant CVDs	Regional Examples
1. Age of pestilence and famine	5 to 10	Rheumatic heart disease, infectious, and nutritional cardiomyopathies	Sub-Saharan Africa, rural India, South America
2. Age of receding pandemics	10 – 35	As above + hypertensive heart disease and hemorrhagic strokes	China
3. Age of degenerative and man-made diseases	35 – 55	All forms of strokes, ischemic heart disease at young ages, increasing obesity and diabetes	Urban India, former socialist economies, aboriginal communities
4. Age of delayed degenerative diseases	< 50	Stroke and ischemic heart disease at old age	Western Europe, North America, Australia, New Zealand
5. Age of Health Regression and Social Upheaval	35 – 55	Re–emergence of deaths from rheumatic heart disease, and infections and increase in ischemic and hypertensive diseases in the young	Russia

During Stages 1 to 4, life expectancy increases, whereas in Stage 5 life expectancy decreases compared to stages 4 and even 3.

western countries, whereas substantial increases have been experienced in developing countries. These contrasting trends are expected to continue. Over the next three decades, premature morbidity and mortality attributable to CVD will almost double globally from 85 million disability adjusted life years (DALY) in 1990, to 140–160 million DALY in 2020, with about 80% of this burden occurring in developing countries[1,2] (Table 4-2). Other than subSaharan Africa, all geographic regions are already experiencing substantial disease burden from ischemic heart disease (IHD) (Table 4-3) and can anticipate substantial increases in mortality rates over the next decade.

Reasons for increases in CVD. The expected increases in CVD in developing countries are probably a result of at least three contributing factors: First, decreasing mortality from acute infectious diseases and increases in life expectancy will result in a higher proportion of individuals reaching middle and old age. Second, lifestyle and socioeconomic changes associated with urbanisation in developing nations will lead to higher levels of risk factors for CVD. Third, special susceptibility of certain populations (e.g. due to specific genes) may lead to a greater impact on clinical events compared to western populations.

TABLE 4–2:   CONTRIBUTION OF NON-COMMUNICABLE DISEASES
(NCD) AND VARIOUS INDIVIDUAL DISEASES TO THE
GLOBAL MORTALITY AND GLOBAL BURDEN OF
DISEASE IN 1998, SUBDIVIDED BY LOW INCOME
COUNTRIES (LIC) & MIDDLE INCOME COUNTRIES
(MIC)

Disease Category	Contribution to total global mortality (%)	Contribution to total burden of disease (%)	LIC + MIC Contribution to global NCD mortality (%)	LIC + MIC Contribution to NCD burden of disease (%)
Total NCD	**58.8**	**43.0**	77	85
Total CVD	30.9	10.3	78	86.3
Total Cancers	13.4	5.8	72	79
Diabetes*	1.1	0.8	73	73
COPD	4.1	2.0	87.5	91.4

LIC = Low income country
MIC = Middle income country
NCD = Noncommunicable disease
COPD = Chronic Obstructive Pulmonary Disease

Source: Derived from estimates provided in World Health Report 1999

The rates projected in Table 4–3 are based solely upon
demographic changes. If the prevalence of various CVD
risk factors also rise as a consequence of adverse lifestyle
changes accompanying industrialization and urbanization,
the rates of CVD mortality and morbidity could rise even
higher than the projected rates. Further, both the degree
and the duration of exposure to the CVD risk factors would
increase as a result of higher risk factor levels coupled with
a longer life expectancy. Higher prevalence of both risk factors for CVD and disease rates in urban compared to rural
communities in India[3,4] and China[5] provide evidence of
these trends.

TABLE 4–3:   ESTIMATES OF ACUTE MYOCARDIAL INFARCTION
MORTALITY RATES (PER 100,000) BY REGION* AND
GENDER (ALL AGES)[1]

Region	Men		Women		Percentage increase	
	1990	2000	1990	2000	men	women
EME	212	228	206	210	+8	+2
FSE	283	372	309	363	+32	+18
India	141	166	136	154	+18	+16
China	66	80	69	75	+21	+9
OAI	68	82	67	77	+21	+15
SSA	36	36	45	43	0	–4
LAC	81	95	76	87	+17	+14
MEC	124	139	118	124	+12	+5
Total World	118	133	120	127	+13	+6

* EME: European Market Economies
  FSE: Formerly Socialist Economies of Europe
  OAI: Other Asia and Islands
  SSA: Sub–Saharan Africa
  LAC: Latin American Countries
  MEC: Middle Eastern Crescent

Lifestyle changes and nutrition. Lifestyle changes observed in countries undergoing transition include changes
in diet, physical activity and tobacco use. The globalization
of food production and marketing has resulted in greatly

increased availability of cheap vegetable oils and fats, and increased consumption of energy-dense foods which may be poor in dietary fibre and several micronutrients.[6,7] Other characteristics of this *nutrition transition* include a shift from plant to animal protein, and shifts towards refined carbohydrates and sweets, and increased prevalence of obesity. This transition now occurs even in countries and groups with a relatively low level of income, and is further accelerated by urbanisation. In South Africa for example, length of time living in an urban environment has been directly associated with increased dietary fat and decreased carbohydrate consumption, and a shift from plant to animal sources of protein.[6] National nutrition surveys conducted in Brazil during 1974/75 and 1989 have demonstrated both a striking increase in the prevalence of overweight and obesity (from 21% of the population in 1974/75 to 33% in 1989), and that overweight/obesity is positively associated with income and urban residence.[8] Data from the China Health and Nutrition Surveys in eight Chinese provinces indicate that between 1989 and 1991, the prevalence of relatively high fat consumption was increased among adults living in urban areas and among higher income groups. For example in urban areas, 46% of high income participants, 38% of middle income participants and 20% of low income participants consumed >30% energy as fat, compared to 25%, 19%, 14% of high, middle and low income participants in rural areas. Differences were also observed in activity patterns. From 1989 to 1991, the prevalence of sedentary activity patterns increased substantially among urban residents in all income groups, a trend not observed among rural residents. Over the same time period, an increased prevalence of overweight was observed in the high and middle income groups but not in the low income group.[9]

Smoking. Smoking rates vary widely by geographic region and gender, and trends towards increased tobacco consumption in most "transitional" countries contrast with the decreases observed in most industrialised nations. Increased tobacco smoking in the Former Socialist Economies (FSE), Latin America, Middle East Crescent, India and China will lead to large increases in chronic disease mortality attributable to tobacco. For example mortality in India that is attributable to tobacco will rise from 1% in 1990 to 13% in 2020. In the FSE, mortality attributable to tobacco will rise from 14% to 23% in the same time period.[10] It is estimated that by 2025, tobacco attributable deaths in China will be a staggering two million annually.[11]

Thrifty gene hypothesis. The metabolic response to these altered CVD risk profiles may vary in specific populations. One such hypothesis has been referred to as the "thrifty gene hypothesis", which describes a process of selective survival, where a population was occasionally exposed to adverse environmental conditions and associated famine. For example selection of a gene that increases the efficiency of fat storage through an over secretion of insulin in response to a meal, would favor survival in a period of famine. However a high level of energy intake (because of the relatively easy access to "rich" foods) with urbanisation may lead to a less desirable response that includes obesity, hyperinsulinemia, diabetes, and atherosclerosis. Such gene-environment interactions may relate to higher blood pressure levels (e.g. salt retention or sensivity genes), or higher homocysteine levels (due to higher consumption of meats and lower consumption of vegetables interacting with various genes that affect homocysteine synthesis or break down).

Ethnic groups and risk. Studies from Canada, United Kingdom, Singapore, South Africa and Mauritius have consistently demonstrated very high rates of coronary heart disease (CHD) among individuals of South Asian origin (Figure 4-1), intermediate rates among those of European origin with the lowest rates among those of African or Chinese origin. However the extent to which these variations in CHD by ethnicity are due to genetic factors or environmental factors remains unclear. Recent studies have identified candidate genes that may correlate with CVD and with its risk factors such as obesity, plasma lipoproteins, elevated blood pressure, and elevated blood glucose. The relative frequencies of various genes among different ethnic groups is not known. An assessment of the relevance of varying gene frequencies or expression that may ultimately lead to differences in CVD between populations must also incorporate information on a host of environmental factors such as lifestyle or nutritional and possible programming factors.[12]

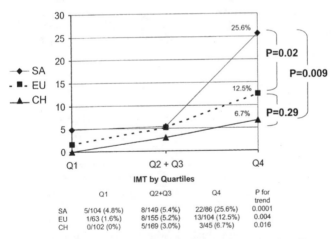

	Q1	Q2+Q3	Q4	P for trend
SA	5/104 (4.8%)	8/149 (5.4%)	22/86 (25.6%)	0.0001
EU	1/63 (1.6%)	8/155 (5.2%)	13/104 (12.5%)	0.004
CH	0/102 (0%)	5/169 (3.0%)	3/45 (6.7%)	0.016

*Note: Overall P value <0.0001, comparing slopes of atherosclerosis vs CVD between SA, CH and EU. For a particular level of atherosclerosis, the rates of clinical events vary between the three ethnic groups. P for trend is within each ethnic group. (Reproduced with permission from the Lancet 2000; 356: 279-84.) SA = South Asians; EU = Europeans; CH = Chinese

Figure 4-1. *Prevalence of cardiovascular disease for given levels of carotid atherosclerosis*

ONGOING STUDIES

SHARE. In order to overcome some of the limitations of the currently available data and to obtain standardised information across ethnic groups both within and across many different countries, we have been involved in facilitating three studies. First, SHARE (Study of Health Assessment and Risk in Ethnic groups) explores the relationship of environmental (nutrition, tobacco use, lifestyle and psychosocial factors) and genetic factors, as well as subclinical atherosclerosis, in about 1,300 individuals from four groups (Canadians of European, South Asian, Chinese and Aboriginal descent).[13] An initial publication indicates that, as expected, South Asians had the highest rates of CVD, Europeans were slightly lower and Chinese had markedly lower rates. However, the degree of atherosclerosis (measured utilizing B-mode carotid ultrasonography) was the highest among Europeans with significantly lower rates in South Asians and Chinese (with only a modest difference among these two latter groups). Although the degree of carotid atherosclerosis correlated with the prevalence of clinical events, for any given level of atherosclerosis, South Asians had significantly higher rates of CV events compared to the other ethnic groups. This suggests that the propensity to plaque rupture or thrombosis, leading to clinical events, may vary by ethnic group (Figure 4-1). The classical risk factors (lipids, glucose abnormalities, blood pressure and tobacco use) did correlate with clinical events, with some emerging risk factors (e.g. elevated levels of plasminogen activator inhibitor-1 and lipoprotein (a)), also adding predictive information. However, after inclusion of all measured risk factors and degree of atherosclerosis, South Asian ethnicity conferred additional risk. This suggests that some additional factor(s) that are yet unidentified are of importance among South Asians. By contrast the lower rates of CVD among Chinese compared to the Europeans was entirely explained by the risk factors and atherosclerosis, indicating that if Chinese adopt Western lifestyles, their rates of CVD will tend to approximate those observed in European populations.

INTER-HEART. In a second study, a group of scientists are collaborating in a large international, multi-centre, hospital-based incident case-control study (INTER-HEART). Approximately 12 000 incident cases of acute myocardial infarction in men and women admitted to the coronary care unit, and a similar number of hospital-based controls matched by age and gender are expected to be enrolled over the next three to four years from about 50 countries. Women are expected to comprise about 20% of all participants. The majority of subjects will be recruited from the Middle East, South Asia, Southeast Asia, China, Eastern Europe, Russia, and Latin America with significant numbers from Africa, North America and Western Europe. These studies are initial steps towards exploring the causes of CVD in different populations across the world. In addition to exploring the importance of known and emerging risk factors for CVD, INTER-HEART will assess if the impact of these risk factors vary by region or ethnicity.

Prospective large cohort studies. The findings of such studies will undoubtedly have to be explored in further detail in prospective large cohort studies that combine a range of methodologies (e.g. proximal societal level determinants, plus individual level information on nutrition, lifestyle factors, biological markers as well as genetic variations) in several of the participating countries (Figure 4-2). Such studies are already being initiated in several developing countries (e.g. the Prospective Urban-Rural Epidemiologic Study in South India involving 5000 urban residents and 5000 rural residents). Similar studies in different parts of the world will provide valuable information upon which a global strategy for CVD prevention can be developed that is both ethnically and regionally sensitive.[14]

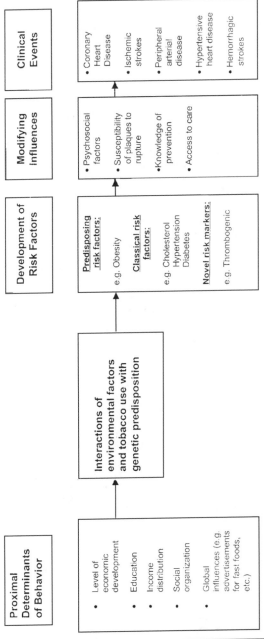

Figure 4-2. Schema for societal level ''Pathway'' for the development of atherothrombotic cardiovascular diseases

ACKNOWLEDGEMENTS

Salim Yusuf holds a Heart and Stroke Foundation of Ontario Chair in Cardiovascular Research and is a Senior Scientist of the Medical Research Council of Canada.

Sonia Anand was supported by a Heart and Stroke Foundation of Ontario Research Fellowship, and is a recipient of a Medical Research Council of Canada Clinician Scientist Award.

Stephanie Ounpuu was appointed by a Heart and Stroke Foundation of Ontario Research Fellowship and is currently a Fellow of the Population Health Research Institute.

REFERENCES

1. Murray CJ, Lopez AD (eds.). The Global Burden of Disease: A Comprehensive Assessment of Mortality and Disability From Disease, Injuries and Risk Factors in 1990 and Projected to 2020. USA, Harvard School of Health, 1996.
2. Murray CJ. Quantifying the burden of disease: The technical basis for disability-adjusted life years. Bull WHO 1994; 72: 429–45.
3. Gupta R, Prakash H, Kaul V. Cholesterol lipoproteins, rural-urban differences and prevalence of dyslipidaemia among males in Rajasthan. JAPI 1997;45:275–279.
4. Gupta R, Gupta VP. Meta-analysis of coronary heart disease prevalence in India. Ind Heart J 1996;48:241–45.
5. People's Republic of China-United States Cardiovascular and Cardiopulmonary Epidemiology Research Group. An epidemiological study of cardiovascular and cardiopulmonary disease risk factors in four populations in the People's Republic of China. Circulation 1992;85:1083–96.
6. Drewnoski A, Popkin BM. The nutrition transition: new trends in the global diet. Nutr Rev 1997;55:31–43.
7. Lang T. The public health impact of globalisation of food trade. In: Shetty PS, McPherson K (eds). Diet, Nutrition and Chronic Disease: Lessons From Contrasting Worlds. Chichester, UK: Wiley; 1997:173–87.
8. Sichieri R, Coitinho DC, Leao MM, Recine E, Everhart JE. High temporal, geographic, and income variation in body mass index among adults in Brazil. Am J Public Health 1994;84:793–98.
9. Popkin BM, Paeratakul S, Ge K, Fengying Z. Body weight patterns among the Chinese: Results from the 1989 and 1991 China Health and Nutrition Survey. Am J Public Health 1995;85:690–94.
10. World Health Organisation. Tobacco or Health: A Global Status Report. Geneva: World Health Organization, 1997.
11. Peto R. Tobacco–related deaths in China. Lancet 1987;2:211.
12. Reddy KS, Yusuf S. Emerging epidemic of CVD in the developing countries. Circulation 1997; 97:596–601.
13. Anand SS, Yusuf S, Vuksan V, Devanesen S, Teo KK, Montague PA, Kelemen L, Yi Q, Lonn E, Gerstein H, Hegele RA, McQueen M, for the SHARE investigators. Differences in risk factors, atherosclerosis, and cardiovascular disease between ethnic groups in Canada: the Study of Health Assessment and Risk in Ethnic groups (SHARE). Lancet 2000; 356: 279–84.
14. Institute of Medicine. Howson CP, Reddy S, Ryan TJ, Bale JR (eds). Control of Cardiovascular Diseases in Developing Countries: Research, Development, and Institutional Strengthening. Washington DC: National Academy Press, 1998.

CHAPTER 5

Mortality in Heart Failure; Selected Aspects of Pathophysiology and the Implications of Recent Clinical Trials

Philip A Poole-Wilson

DEFINITIONS

Many definitions of heart failure have been put forward.[1-3] Most have emphasised a physiological feature of the syndrome. The best known definition is "a pathophysiological state in which an abnormality of cardiac function is responsible for the failure of the heart to pump blood at a rate commensurate with the requirements of the metabolising tissues".[4] This definition has the advantage that it identifies an abnormality of cardiac function as a requirement for the diagnosis but suffers from the disadvantages that it is only true on exercise, not at rest, and cannot be applied in epidemiological studies or even at the bedside. The major requirement of the metabolising tissues is presumably oxygen. A more practical definition is "a clinical syndrome caused by an abnormality of the heart and recognised by a characteristic pattern of haemodynamic, renal, neural and hormonal responses".[5,6] This definition again requires an abnormality of the heart to be present but also recognises the complex body response to a limitation of the heart to act as a pump. Th European Society of Cardiology defined heart failure as requiring "symptoms of heart failure, objective evidence of cardiac dysfunction and a response to treatment directed towards heart failure".[7] This definition is practical and has been used in many epidemiological studies.

Heart failure can usefully be categorised as acute (pulmonary oedema), circulatory collapse (cardiogenic shock) or chronic heart failure. Many adjectives are added to chronic heart failure such as congestive, undulating, overt, treated, compensated and decompensated. This is often the jargon of the practical physician. This chapter is concerned with chronic heart failure.

Several phrases are redundant or unhelpful.[8] These are often used as shorthand by doctors to convey clinical phenotypes; as such they have value but do not contribute to an understanding of the entity of heart failure. Such phrases include right and left sided heart failure (the commonest cause of right sided heart failure is left ventricular failure !!!), forward and backward heart failure, and high and low output failure.

Some phrases in common usage present clinical challenges. The best known of these is diastolic or systolic heart failure. In general the distinction between these two entities is the size of the end-diastolic volume of the heart at rest, such that diastolic heart failure is the presence of the clinical syndrome of heart failure in association with a normal or near normal ejection fraction. Diastolic heart failure is common in the elderly, hypertensive patients and associated with a fibrotic heart; it is notoriously difficult to treat and few clinical trials have been undertaken in patients with diastolic heart failure.

EPIDEMIOLOGY

Heart failure is common, becoming more common, is detectable in the community, has effective treatments and is costly to health systems in the Western world.[9-12] For these reasons heart failure once the Cinderella of cardiology in comparison to the sirens of intervention, hypertension and lipidology, has become a topic of major interest. Numerous studies have reported a prevalence of up to 3% of the entire population and an annual incidence of up to 1.5% (Fig. 5-1).[9,10]

An important observation is that the mean age of heart failure in the community is 76 years.[13,14] This is at least ten to fifteen years greater than populations studied in most clinical trials.[15-23] The reason for the increasing incidence of heart failure are two fold. First the management of coronary heart disease has reduced mortality generating a population of patients with known damage to the myocardium who

- **Prevalence** 0.5 - 2 %; 10% in those over 75 years

- **Incidence** 0.2 - 0.5 % per annum and increasing

- **Men:women is 60:40**. Ratio reverses in the very old

- 5% of hospital admissions and bed occupancy

- 40% readmission rate in one year

- 40% of hospital admissions dead in one year

- Approximately 2% of total health budget

Cowie et al Eur heart J 1997;18:208-225

Figure 5-1. Epidemiology of heart failure

will later go on to develop heart failure. Coronary artery disease is by far the commonest cause of heart failure (more than 80%).[13] The second reason is that populations are changing their demographic structure with a greater proportion of elderly persons. This is a consequence of the healthier environment in which they live. Since heart failure and coronary heart disease are chronic diseases more common in the elderly, the prevalence will necessarily increase.

Contemporary information on the outcome of heart failure in the population is difficult to obtain. A recent study from the suburbs of London (Fig. 5-2) shows that a high proportion of incidence cases of heart failure die within three months of diagnosis.[14] Subsequently the rate of death is approximately 10% per annum. An important point is that the relationship between survival and time from diagnosis is not linear. The inclusion of patients in trials who had heart failure diagnosed at different times from the onset, leads to a heterogeneous population with results which may be difficult to interpret.

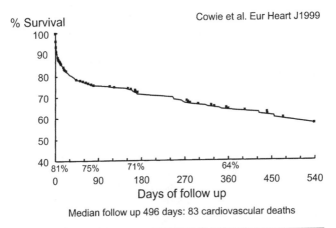

Median follow up 496 days: 83 cardiovascular deaths

Figure 5-2. Survival curve 220 incident cases of heart failure

Numerous factors and clinical findings relate to prognosis. Indeed any symptom, sign or measurement which relates to the severity of heart failure will in general predict prognosis. Patients with heart failure develop worsening heart failure and usually die of the consequences of heart failure, commonly classified as sudden death or progressive heart failure. Heart size, exercise capacity and measurements of hormonal activation (the simplest is a low serum sodium) are strong predictors of a poor prognosis. In severe chronic heart failure the expected survival is 6 months whereas with mild heart failure the mean survival is up to 6 years; in a population the mean survival is about 4 years.

PURPOSE OF TREATMENT AND DEMONSTRATION OF EFFICACY

As in other branches of medicine there are only two purposes in treating heart failure. One is to extend the duration

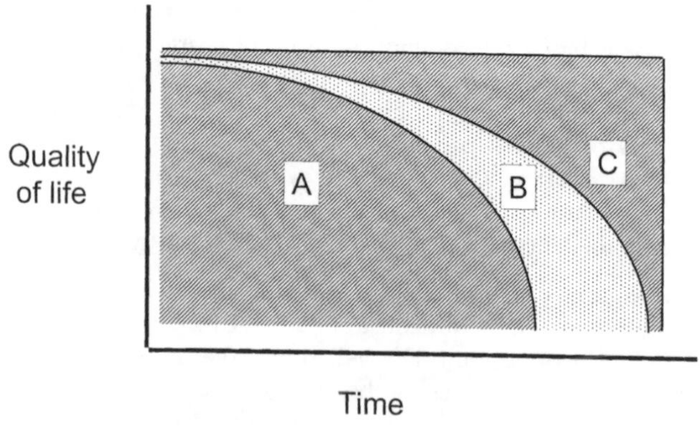

Figure 5-3. Quality of life. Duration versus symptoms

of life and the second to improve the quality of life. Most modern treatments have achieved both to some degree (Fig. 5-3).

There is currently a debate concerning the issue as to whether patients should be more involved in the decisions over health strategies which may improve quality at the cost of longevity. That may be particularly relevant in an elderly population where co-morbid conditions can interact with heart failure to diminish the quality of life to an unacceptable degree. Some drugs, flosequinan for example, had a beneficial effect on symptoms but were withdrawn from the market because of an increase in mortality.

Many clinical trials have been undertaken in heart failure. Conventionally at the present time the outcome of these trials is assessed by the measurement of primary or secondary endpoints. That is a concept which can be challenged. From a humanitarian point of view, the purpose of a trial should be to improve the goals of treatment namely longevity and quality of life. Often the primary endpoint of a clinical trial is chosen so as to optimise the possibility that the trial is positive rather than answering a clinical relevant question. An example is the use of a primary endpoint such as mortality and admission to hospital with heart failure. In theory at least in such a trial, the drug could do harm in terms of another endpoint such as overall mortality and hospitalisation whilst achieving a positive result in this limited endpoint. It is necessary for there to be a hierarchy of endpoints (Fig. 5-4) by which trials should be assessed. The choice of primary endpoint should not be left to the whim of a Steering Committee or to the wishes of industry, drug agencies or governments.

Many governments are at present focused on the delivery of healthcare. That is totally appropriate. A current mantra is that treatment should be assessed by what is called evidence-based medicine. That is a mixture of evidence obtained from clinical trials together with some degree of clinical experience. Such a viewpoint is to be expected from governments or those concerned with overall healthcare delivery. From the doctors point of view a more sensible

Mortality
Mortality & hospitalisation
Mortality & hospitalisation & others

> eg Myocardial infarction, Stroke
> Peripheral vascular disease
> Need for a specified therapy

Freedom from a stated list of unwanted outcomes.

> Event free survival

Cause specific mortality

> eg Sudden death, Arrhythmic death
> Myocardial infarction
> Progression of heart failure

Quality of life

Figure 5-4. Hierarchy of end-points in clinical trials

concept is patient based medicine (Fig. 5-5) because the doctor is concerned with the individual patient and the characteristics of that patient which may determine outcome. From the patient's standpoint what is required is patient based evidence; that is the knowledge of whether any treatment will impact favourably on that individual patient. Such information is rarely available in medicine and clinical judgement is the compromise.

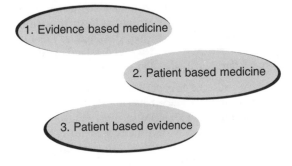

Figure 5-5. Current mantra on application of medical knowledge

CONCEPTS AND TREATMENT IN HEART FAILURE

The last two decades have seen substantial advances in the treatment of heart failure. Concepts have changed. A number of those concepts are illustrated in Fig. 5-6. In the middle of the last century heart failure was considered as a disease focused on the effect of the malfunction of the heart on the kidney causing sodium and water retention. Later the progression of heart failure was attributed to an increase in after-load increasing the stress on an already compromised myocardium. More recently the concept of remodelling has emerged whereby the heart changes its

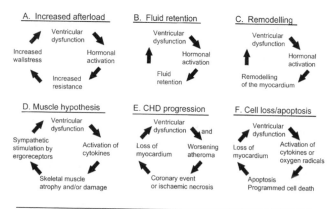

Figure 5-6. Spirals of heart failure

architecture and function in response to damage and central haemodynamics but independent of hypertension or valve abnormalities. Other ideas have included the hypothesis that the symptoms of heart failure originate from changes in skeletal muscle[24-27] causing neural traffic to the brain. Much of the progression of heart failure may be due to further coronary events and not to the pathological processes of heart failure itself. Finally the most popular current concept is that the progression of heart failure is linked to the continuing loss of myocytes possibly by the process of apoptosis. This has led to the possibility of inhibiting progression with new drugs.

A key problem is a determination of the underlying cause of heart failure. Traditionally heart failure due to failure of the myocardium is attributed to coronary heart disease or to cardiomyopathies, which are sub-classified as dilated, hypertrophic or restrictive. A better understanding might be based on a different classification (Fig. 5-7).

The commonest cause of heart failure is loss of myocytes and often heart failure is exacerbated by incoordinate contraction of the ventricles. Extracellular abnormalities including alterations of architecture and the occurrence of fibrosis within the myocardium can be critical. Abnormalities in the function of the cells themselves relate to alterations of calcium control or of the contractile protein (Fig. 5-8). This remains a controversial area and it is often difficult to distinguish between changes in the myocardium, which are a consequence of heart failure and those which are the cause of heart failure.

The single most widely studied abnormality in the function of the myocyte in heart failure is a failure to take up calcium from the cytosol by the calcium ATPase sited on the sarcoplasmic reticulum.

In heart failure a complex body response is initiated. This includes the activation of neural, hormonal, inflammatory and immunological pathways. Numerous growth pathways are activated (Fig. 5-9). Identification of any single pathway, which can be manipulated with benefit for patients with heart failure, has proved elusive. Another way of considering the problem relates to the key proteins which make up

1. **Loss of muscle**

2. **Incoordinate contraction and abnormal timing of contraction**

3. **Extracellular** Fibrosis, altered extracellular architecture, shape and size of ventricle
   Slippage of cells, fibre orientation

4. **Cellular** 1. Change of cell structure
   Hypertrophy, ? hyperplasia, ? addition of sarcomeres

   2. Change of cell function - systolic and/or diastolic

Calcium release/ and or uptake	Response of contractile proteins to calcium
Receptor down regulation	Altered contractile proteins (isoforms)
Reduced c-AMP	Altered phosphorylation of contractile proteins
Sarcoplasmic reticulum dysfunction	? energy deficient state
Reduced number of ion channels or pumps	

Many of these factors combine to cause systolic or diastolic failure. Diastolic heart failure is common in the presence of hypertrophy, fibrosis or ischaemia

Figure 5-7. *Underlying causes of chronic heart failure due to the myocardium*

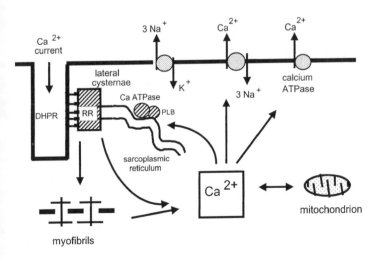

Figure 5-8. *Calcium exchange*

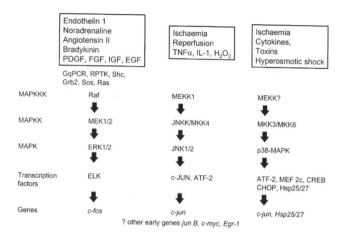

Figure 5-9. Growth pathways under stress

cardiac muscle (Fig. 5-10). Abnormalities of those proteins associated with contraction, in general, have led to hypertrophic cardiomyopathy. Several genetic abnormalities of proteins and the cytoskeleton and nucleus have been linked to dilated cardiomyopathy. Whether these are single gene abnormalities or whether they are gene abnormalities which are necessary for an interaction with other genes or other activating factors remains uncertain.

Contraction	actin, myosin, troponin, tropomyosin
Sarcomere	titin, α-actinin, myonesin, C-protein
Cytoskeleton	tubulin, desmin, actin
Membrane	vinculin, talin, dystrophin, spectrin
Intercalated disc	Desmosomes: *desmoplakin, desmin* Fascia adherens: *N-cadherin, vinculin* Gap junctions: *connexin*
Nucleus membrane	emerin, lamin

Figure 5-10. Key proteins in heart muscle

ORIGIN OF SYMPTOMS IN HEART FAILURE

A major problem in heart failure has been the origin of symptoms. Recent work has demonstrated that in patients in whom fluid volumes have been controlled symptoms are not related to central haemodynamics.[24-26] More likely they are related to the many changes which occur in skeletal muscle (Fig. 5-11). An important consequence is that until that skeletal muscle has been restored to normal, the function of the muscle will not improve and symptoms will not be alleviated.

Morphology	Quantity	Loss of muscle mass (or bulk)
	Site	Localised to legs or general abnormality Orientation and fibre position
	Quality	Atrophy, damage and/or necrosis Change of fibre type
Function		Weakness and/or increased fatigue
Blood flow		ml/min reduced, ml/min/100ml variable
Metabolism		An inevitable consequence of atrophy and damage, or a specific change

Clark AL, Poole-Wilson PA, Coats AJ JACC 1996;28:1092-1102
Harrington D, Coats AJS Eur Heart J 1997;18:1865-1872
Poole-Wilson PA, Ferrari R J Mol Cell Cardiol 1996;28:2275-2285

Figure 5-11. Skeletal muscle in heart failure

THE ORIGINS OF HEART FAILURE

A fundamental issue in heart failure is not what happens in heart failure but what is the cause. There is certainly early activation of the sympathetic system and the release of atrionatiuretic peptides. However many hormonal systems (Fig. 5-12) are activated only in severe heart failure.[28] This is accompanied by weight loss and the syndrome of cachexia. One possibility is that the response in early heart

	Controls	All HF	Non-cachetic	Cachetic
Sodium mmol/ℓ	139.9	137.7*	138.6	135.6*
Potassium mmol/ℓ	3.9	4.0	4.0	3.9
Creatinine lmol/ℓ	92	125*	121	134
Aldosterone pmol/ℓ	279	699**	552	1039*
PRA ng/ml/h	1.3	11.7*	9.2	17**
TSH µiu/ℓ	1.5	2.1	2.1	2.2
Reverse T_3 nmol/ℓ	0.31	0.52*	0.48	0.62
Norepinephrine nmol/ℓ	1.94	3.41**	2.58	5.31*
Epinephrine nmol/ℓ	0.51	1.29	0.68	2.7*
TNF-α pg/m	7.0	9.5	6.9	15.3*
Cortisol nmol/ℓ	372	415	379	498*
Testosterone nmol/ℓ	9.9	11.2	11.5	10.5
Estradiol pmol/ℓ	45.4	69.2	62.6	84.6
DHEA nmol/ℓ	15.3	10.4**	11.3	8.3
Basal insulin pmol/ℓ	40.6	77.8*	81.7	68
hGH ng/mℓ	1.1	1.8	0.9	3.8*
IGF-1 ng/mℓ	148	146	150	137

*P<0.01, **P<0.001   Anker et al Circulation 1997;96:526-534

Figure 5-12. Hormonal changes in heart failure and cachexia

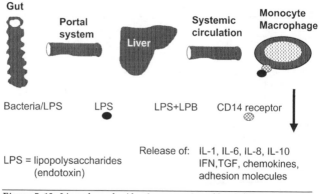

Figure 5-13. Lipopolysaccharides & progression of heart failure

failure is initiated by a fall of blood pressure consequent upon damage to the myocardium.[29,30] In more severe heart failure immunological and inflammatory systems are activated.[28,31,32] The reasons are not clear and could be related to long term activation of the sympathetic system, damage to the myocardium itself, hypoxia or the release of bacteria or bacterial products from the gut (Fig. 5-13).

TREATMENTS FOR HEART FAILURE

With this background it is not unexpected that there are many options in the treatment of heart failure (Fig. 5-14). The conventional drug treatment is based on diuretics, ACE inhibitors and beta-blockers. Many new interventions are being investigated. A large number of trials (Fig. 5-15) have demonstrated a reduction in the annual mortality from heart failure.[15-23,33] The magnitude of this reduction is very considerable compared to trials which may have wider applicability in the population but which identify patients with multiple risk factors for coronary heart disease or raised lipids.

1. Drugs
- *Diuretics Loop, thiazide, K⁺ sparing, metolazone, spironolactone or combination*
- *ACE inhibitors*
- *Beta-blockers*
- *Digoxin*
- *Aspirin, statins, anticoagulants*
- *Angiotensin II receptor inhibitors*
- *Nitrates, hydralazine, antiarrhythmics*
- *IV inotropes*

2. Surgery, CABG or valve surgery

3. Implantable cardioverter-defibrillator - ICD, pacing

4. Haemofiltration, peritoneal dialysis or haemodialysis

5. Aortic balloon pump, ventricular assist devices cardiomyoplasty, volume reduction, transplantation

Figure 5-14. Options in the treatment of heart failure

Annual mortality (%)

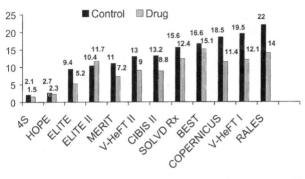

Figure 5-15. Annual mortality in recent trials in heart failure

A new trial in relation to the use of diuretics is the RALES study.[33] This showed that giving spironolactone to patients with NYHA 3 or 4 heart failure was beneficial (Fig. 5-16). The authors would wish to claim this was a consequence of spironolactone inhibiting the tendency of aldosterone to promote fibrosis in the myocardium. A simpler explanation is that it was a consequence of a diuretic interaction with loop diuretic. This could have been tested by evaluating spironolactone against a small dose of a thiazide diuretic. The DIG study[23] (Fig. 5-17) demonstrated that digoxin had no effect on mortality in a large number of patients or in any sub-group of the population. The primary endpoint was negative. Regrettably this study has been misinterpreted and emphasis has been placed on the benefit in the group who had a cardiovascular death due to worsening heart failure. That argument is invalid since inevitably cardiovascular deaths from other cardiac causes must have increased and did so significantly (Fig. 5-17). Essentially the DIG study failed to demonstrate that digoxin was beneficial in patients in sinus rhythm. The drug should be used cautiously in those with moderate to severe heart failure if at all.

Angiotensin converting enzyme (ACE) inhibitors are one of the cornerstones of treatment of heart failure in conjunction with diuretics. The CONSENSUS trial has now reported a

	Placebo		Spironolactone	
All cause mortality	386/841	284/822	0.70 (0.60-0.82)	0.001
Total hospitalisation			0.83	
Total death & hosp.			0.78 (0.70-0.88)	0.0001
Hosp. Cardiac cause	336	260	0.70 (0.59-0.82)	0.001
Hosp. Progr. HF	300	215	0.65 (0.54-0.77)	0.001
Sudden death	110	82	0.71 (0.54-0.95)	0.02
Hyperkalaemia in 0.5% and gynecomastia in 9%. Ann. mortality 22%				

Presented at the AHA, November 1998 & Pitt et al NEJM 1999:341;709-717

1663 patients, NYHA III (72%) or IV, EF<35%, 65y, 73% male, >50% IHD, 11 % on beta-blocker, on loop diuretic, ACEi & digoxin spironolactone 25 or 50 mg od v placebo. Mean follow-up 24 months

Figure 5-16. RALES: randomised aldactone evaluation study

	Digoxin n = 3397	Placebo n = 3403	Absol. risk (%)	RR (95% CI)	P
Total mortality	1181 35%	1194 35%	-0.4	0.99 (0.91-1.07)	ns
Cardiovascular death	1016	1004	+0.4	1.01 (0.93-1.10)	ns
Worsening HF	394	449	-1.6	0.88 (0.77-1.01)	0.06
Other cardiac	508	444	1.9	1.14 (1.01-1.30)	0.04
No. pat. hospitalised	2184	2282	-2.8	0.92 (0.87-0.98)	0.006
No. Hospitalisations	6356	6777			
Withdrawal from drug	29.2%	32.1%			
Little effect of initial EF, CTR, NYHA class, aetiology or previous use of digoxin from N.Engl.J.Med 1997;336:525-533					

CHF, EF < 0.45, 63 years, 22% female, 82% on diuretics, 94% on ACE inhibitors median digoxin dose 0.25 mg per day, average follow-up 37 months

Figure 5-17. DIG trial: results excluding those with EF > 0.45

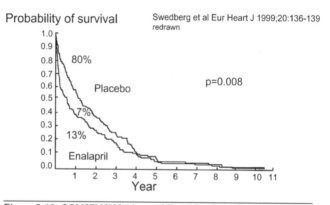

Probability of survival   Swedberg et al Eur Heart J 1999;20:136-139 redrawn

80%

Placebo   p=0.008

7%

13%

Enalapril

Figure 5-18. CONSENSUS 10 year follow-up. All randomized patients

ten-year follow up by which time almost all the patients have died.[34] This is a key study because for the first time it is possible to see the total overall benefit achieved. The number of patient years alive increased by approximately 50 % (Fig. 5-18). On the other hand it is also possible to see what an awful prognosis heart failure has and what needs to be done in the future. The ELITE II study[16] failed to demonstrate that losartan was superior to captopril in the treatment of heart failure. It remains probable though that

3 152 patients, 288 centres from 45 countries, recruitment stopped

Primary endpoint:	All cause mortality
Secondary endpoints:	Sudden death, tolerability and safety

Age over 60y, NYHA II-IV, EF<0.40, not on ACE inhibitors
70% history of IHD
<25% receiving a beta-blocker

Assume mortality in placebo group 9.4% pa
90% power, a=0.43, to detect 25% reduction in mortality

Driven by endpoints. Number needed is 510

Figure 5-19. ELITE II Evaluation of Losartan In The Elderly study

angiotensin II receptor antagonist may be similar to ACE inhibitors and could provide an additional drug class available to physicians (Figure 5-19).

Several trials CIBIS,[21] MERIT[20] and COPERNICUS have demonstrated the benefit of beta-blockers (Figs. 5-20 and 5-21).

	Placebo	Metoprolol CR/XL	RR (95% CI)	P
Deaths total	217/2001	145/1990	0.66 (0.53-0.81)	0.006
Cardiov. deaths	203	128	0.62 (0.50-0.78)	0.0003
Sudden death	132	79	0.59 (0.45-0.78)	0.0002
Wors. HF, death	58	30	0.51 (0.33-0.79)	0.002
At 6 months HR	-3	-12 beats/ min	–	–
SBP	-3.5	-2 mm Hg	–	0.013
Drug stopped	15.3%	13.9%	0.90 (0.77-1.06)	ns
Annual mortality	11.0%	7.2%	0.66 (0.53-0.81)	0.006
RR= relative risk, CI = confidence intervals. (Lancet 1999;353:2001-2007)				

3991 patients, 64 y, 78% male, 66% ischaemic, NYHA II 41%, NYHA III 55%, mean ejection fraction 28%, mean follow-up 1 y, trial stopped early

Figure 5-20. MERIT-HF trial

Primary endpoint was mortality:		
	Placebo	Carvedilol
Deaths	190/1133 (16.8 %)	130/1156 (11.2 %)
Hazard ratio	0.65 (0.52-0.81)	adjusted p<0.0014
Annual mortality	18.5%	11.4%

2 289 patients, 334 sites, 63 y, 80% male, EF 20%, 67% ischaemic, 65% in hospital in preceding year. No patient lost to follow-up. Mean follow-up 316 days. Target dose 25 mg bd, achieved in 74%

Figure 5-21. COPERNICUS trial

In the past beta-blockers have been regarded as contraindicated in heart failure and are a known cause of heart failure in some patients. These recent studies have shown benefit because the beta blockers were used carefully (initial use of a low dose and slow titration of dose) in selected patients. Importantly the COPERNICUS study has shown that benefit occurs in patients with more severe heart failure (NYHA 3). Beta-blockers probably still should not be used in those in hospital with unstable severe heart failure (NYHA 4). The reason for this benefit remains unclear. It would be pleasing to believe that beta blockade was inhibiting a key pathway in heart failure namely activation of the sympathetic system. Some data[35] (Fig. 5-22) show that not only does the ejection fraction increase (to be expected as the resting heart rate falls) but that the end diastolic volume is reduced indicating a fundamental remodelling of the myocardium. Several studies in the past (Fig. 5-23) showed that regardless of whether heart failure was present, beta-blockers were beneficial after infarction. The effect was greater in those with heart failure because events were more common. This would suggest that the benefit of beta-blockers is not necessarily intrinsically related to the process of heart failure but maybe a consequence of the benefit which they bring to ischaemic myocardium.

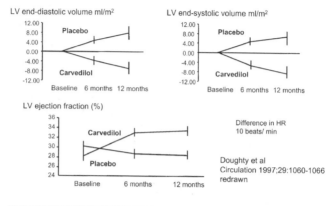

Figure 5-22. Carvedilol and LV function

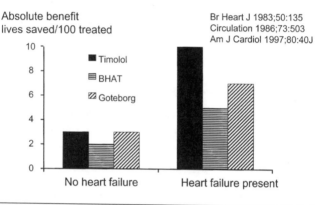

Figure 5-23. Beta blockade after myocardial infarction

Other treatments are being considered. There is currently considerable interest in new left ventricular assist devices. There has also been concern about the selection of patients for transplantation (Fig. 5-24). In one study[36] there appeared to be little advantage of transplantation except in patients at high risk. This is key point for a physician because often patients are turned down for transplantation because they are too sick.

For the future, the clinical application of genetics and the possibilities of cell transplantation and the application of

	n	One year mortality (%)		
		Listed	On waiting list	After transplant
High risk	107	51	32	36
Medium risk	360	32	20	24
Low risk	422	29	19	25
Total	889	33	–	29

Ejection fraction 22%, peak O_2 15.8 ml/min/kg, Na^+ 138 mmol/l, NYHA 3.3
Deng et al BMJ 2000;321:540-545

Figure 5-24. Outcome from heart transplantation

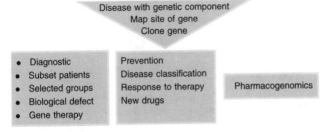

Figure 5-25. The clinical application of genetics

knowledge from molecular biology will be crucial (Figs. 5-25, 5-26).

Genetics may improve diagnosis and allow the subsetting of patients particularly with regard to particular treatments. Cell transplantation may allow, at last, the physician to have the ability to promote the growth of myocardium or to restore new tissue. It is still heresy to suggest that the myocyte in adult myocardium may be induced to divide but at least cells which are multinucleate might be persuaded to separate thus increasing the total population of myocardial cells. Alternatively myocytes might be derived from circulating primitive cells derived from bone marrow or from as yet undetected myoblasts in cardiac muscle.

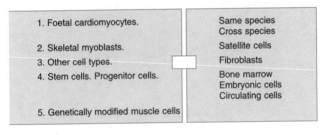

Figure 5-26. Opportunities for cell transplantation

A current view of the progression of heart failure is given in Fig. 5-27. The prevention of heart failure is essentially the prevention of coronary heart disease. Numerous paths for the progression of heart failure are indicated and the pathophysiology of those pathways is different. That leads to the important conclusion (Fig. 5-28) that the treatment of heart failure will vary with time and will vary according to the particular characteristics of an individual patient. Pleasing but misleading generalisations on the treatment of patients with heart failure should be cast aside and placed

1. Proliferation of remaining myocytes and migration to infarct area
2. Conversion of fibroblasts to muscle cells in ischaemic area
3. Induction of angiogenesis to support new myocytes
4. Cell transplantation
5. Cell growth of myocytes from embryonic cells or stem cells
6. Division and growth of adult mammalian cardiac myocytes
7. Vaccines for infection and inflammation in arteries
8. Pharmacological control of smooth muscle cell

Figure 5-27 Molecular biology - probable advances

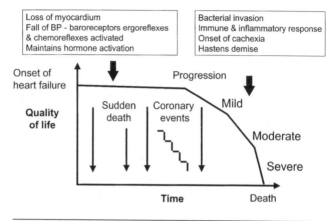

Figure 5-28. *Progression of heart failure*

in history books. The future for the management of the patient with heart failure will be more precise diagnosis and the selection of particular treatments for identified patients.

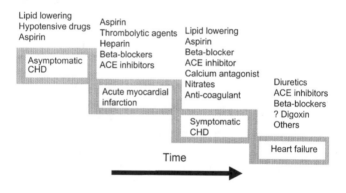

Figure 5-29. *Drugs and time in the treatment of CHD*

SUMMARY

Heart failure is a clinical syndrome, an increasing health problem in ageing populations and a medical condition still in search of an effective treatment. Many new concepts have emerged in the last few decades. New drugs have been introduced which delay death, reduce hospitalisation and improve the quality of life. But the enthusiasm engendered by these advances obscures the less agreeable fact that the overall benefit remains limited. More radical solutions are needed. The key will be the ability to regenerate cardiac muscle in the living human heart.

REFERENCES

1. McKenzie J. Diseases of the heart. 3 ed. Oxford: Oxford Medical Publications, 1913.

2. Lewis T. Diseases of the heart. London, New York: MacMillan, 1933.

3. Wood P. Diseases of the heart and circulation. 1 ed. London: Eyre and Spottiswoode, 1950.

4. Braunwald E. Heart Disease. A textbook of Cardiovascular Medicine. 3 ed. Philadelphia, London, Toronto: W.B.Saunders, 1988.

5. Poole-Wilson PA. Heart failure. Med.Int. 1985; 2:866-871.

6. Poole-Wilson PA. Chronic heart failure: cause, pathophysiology, prognosis, clinical manifestations, investigations. In: Julian DG, Camm AJ, Fox KF, Hall RJC, Poole-Wilson PA, editors. Diseases of the Heart. 1 ed. London: Balliere-Tindall, 1989:24-36.

7. The Task Force on Heart Failure of the European Society of Cardiology. Guidelines for the diagnosis of heart failure. Eur.Heart J. 1995; 16:741-751.

8. Purcell IF, Poole-Wilson PA. Heart failure: why and how to define it? Eur J Heart Failure 1999; 1:7-10.

9. Cowie MR, Mosterd A, Wood DA, Deckers JW, Poole-Wilson PA, Sutton GC, et al. The epidemiology of heart failure. [Review] [160 refs]. Eur.-Heart J. 1997; 18:208-225.

10. Cowie MR. Annotated references in epidemiology. Eur J Heart Failure 1999; 1:101-107.

11. Murdoch DR, Love MP, Robb SD, McDonagh TA, Davie AP, Ford I, et al. Importance of heart failure as a cause of death. Changing contribution to overall mortality and coronary heart disease mortality in Scotland 1979-1992. Eur Heart J 1998; 19:1829-1835.

12. McMurray JJ, Petrie MC, Murdoch DR, Davie AP. Clinical epidemiology of heart failure: public and private health burden. Eur Heart J 1998; 19 Suppl P:9-16.

13. Cowie MR, Wood DA, Coats AJS, Thompson SG, Poole-Wilson PA, Suresh V, et al. Incidence and aetiology of heart failure. A population-based study. Eur.Heart J. 1999; 20:421-428.

14. Cowie MR, Wood DA, Coats AJ, Thompson SG, Suresh V, Poole-Wilson PA, et al. Survival of patients with a new diagnosis of heart failure: a population based study. Heart 2000; 83:505-510.

15. The CONSENSUS Trial Study Group. Effects of enalapril on mortality in severe congestive heart failure. Results of the Cooperative North Scandinavian Enalapril Survival Study (CONSENSUS). The CONSENSUS Trial Study Group. N.Engl.J.Med. 1987; 316:1429-1435.

16. Pitt B, Poole-Wilson P, Segal R, Martinez FA, Dickstein K, Camm AJ, et al. Effects of losartan versus captopril on mortality in patients with symptomatic heart failure: rationale, design, and baseline characteristics of patients in the losartan heart failure survival study - ELITE II. J Card Fail 1999; 5:146-154.

17. The SOLVD Investigators. Effect of enalapril on survival in patients with reduced left ventricular ejection fractions and congestive heart failure. N.Engl.J.Med. 1991; 325:293-302.

18. The SOLVD investigators. Effect of enalapril on mortality and the development of heart failure in asymptomatic patients with reduced left ventricular ejection fractions. N.Engl.J.Med. 1992; 327:685-691.

19. Cohn JN, Johnson G, Ziesche S, Cobb F, Francis GS, Tristani F, et al. A comparison of enalapril with hydralazine-isosorbide dinitrate in the treatment of chronic congestive heart failure. N.Engl.J.Med. 1991; 325:302-310.

20. MERIT-HF Study Group. Effect of metoprolol CR/XL in chronic heart failure: Metoprolol CR/XL Randomised Intervention Trial in Congestive Heart Failure (MERIT-HF). Lancet 1999; 353:2001-2007.

21. CIBIS-II Investigators and Committees. The Cardiac Insufficiency Bisoprolol Study II (CIBIS-II): a randomised trial. Lancet 1999; 353:9-13.

22. Garg R, Yusuf S. Overview of randomized trials of angiotensin-converting enzyme inhibitors on mortality and morbidity in patients with heart failure. Collaborative Group on ACE Inhibitor Trials. J.Am.Med.Assoc. 1995; 273:1450-1456.

23. The Digitalis Investigation Group. The effect of digoxin on mortality and morbidity in patients with heart failure. N.Engl.J.Med. 1997; 336:525-533.

24. Clark AL, Poole-Wilson PA, Coats AJ. Exercise limitation in chronic heart failure: central role of the periphery. [Review] [173 refs]. J.Am.Coll.Cardiol. 1996; 28:1092-1102.

25. Harrington D, Anker SD, Chua TP, Webb-Peploe KM, Ponikowski PP, Poole-Wilson PA, et al. Skeletal muscle function and its relation to exercise tolerance in chronic heart failure. J.Am.Coll.Cardiol. 1997; 30:1758-1764.

26. Poole-Wilson PA, Ferrari R. Role of skeletal muscle in the syndrome of chronic heart failure. [Review] [120 refs]. J.Mol.Cell.Cardiol. 1996; 28:2275-2285.

27. Coats AJ, Clark AL, Piepoli M, Volterrani M, Poole-Wilson PA. Symptoms and quality of life in heart failure: the muscle hypothesis. [Review] [32 refs]. Br.Heart J. 1994; 72:S36-S39

28. Anker SD, Chua TP, Ponikowski P, Harrington D, Swan JW, Kox WJ, et al. Hormonal Changes and Catabolic/Anabolic Imbalance in Chronic Heart Failure and Their Importance for Cardiac Cachexia. Circulation 1997; 96:526-534.

29. Harris P. Congestive cardiac failure: central role of the arterial blood pressure. Br.Heart J. 1987; 58:190-203.

30. Harris P. Evolution and the cardiac patient. Cardiovasc.Res. 1983; 17:373-378.

31. Anker SD, Egerer KR, Volk HD, Kox WJ, Poole-Wilson PA, Coats AJ. Elevated soluble CD14 receptors and altered cytokines in chronic heart failure. Am.J.Cardiol. 1997; 79:1426-1430.

32. Niebauer J, Volk HD, Kemp M, Dominguez M, Schumann RR, Rauchhaus M, et al. Endotoxin and immune activation in chronic heart failure: a prospective cohort study. Lancet 1999; 353:1838-1842.

33. Pitt B, Zannad F, Remme WJ, Cody R, Castaigne A, Perez A, et al. The effect of spironolactone on morbidity and mortality in patients with severe heart failure. N.Engl.J.Med. 1999; 341:709-717.

34. Swedberg K, Kjekshus J, Snapinn S. Long-term survival in severe heart failure in patients treated with enalapril. Ten year follow-up of CONSENSUS I [see comments]. Eur Heart J 1999; 20:136-139.

35. Doughty RN, Whalley GA, Gamble G, MacMahon S, Sharpe N. Left ventricular remodeling with carvedilol in patients with congestive heart failure due to ischemic heart disease. Australia-New Zealand Heart Failure Research Collaborative Group. J.Am.Coll.Cardiol. 1997; 29:1060-1066.

36. Deng MC, De Meester JM, Smits JM, Heinecke J, Scheld HH. Effect of receiving a heart transplant: analysis of a national cohort entered on to a waiting list, stratified by heart failure severity. Comparative Outcome and Clinical Profiles in Transplantation (COCPIT) Study Group [see comments]. Br.Med.J. 2000; 321:540-545.

CHAPTER 6

Apoptosis: Its Relevance to Cardiology?

Martin R Bennett

Apoptosis or programmed cell death is a process through which multicellular organisms dispose of cells efficiently. Much has been discovered about the molecular control of apoptosis since its initial description as a series of morphological events.[1] The regulation of cell death is critical for the maintenance of tissue homeostasis and may play a role in several cardiovascular diseases (Table 6-1). Moreover, it is apparent that all cells are programmed to die, and cell death is their default state, which can be suppressed through the expression or presence of intracellular and extracellular survival factors. Although it may seem strange that cells can be lost so easily from tissues, for long lived multicellular organisms it makes biological sense to have an efficient mechanism of disposal of cells that, for whatever reason, may be of no use or potentially harmful.

THE MODE OF CELL DEATH

Apoptosis defines a type of cell death distinct from the more conventional necrotic death, on the basis of characteristic morphological features (Figure 6-1). Specifically, these features are condensation of nuclear chromatin, at first

TABLE 6-1: DISEASES IN WHICH APOPTOSIS HAS BEEN IMPLICATED

Cardiac (myocyte)
Idiopathic dilated cardiomyopathy
Ischaemic cardiomyopathy
Acute myocardial infarction
Arrhythmogenic right ventricular dysplasia
Myocarditis

Cardiac (conducting tissues)
Pre-excitation syndromes
Heart block, Congenital complete atrioventricular heart block, long QT syndromes)

Vascular
Atherosclerosis
Restenosis after angioplasty/stenting
Vascular graft rejection
Arterial aneurysm formation

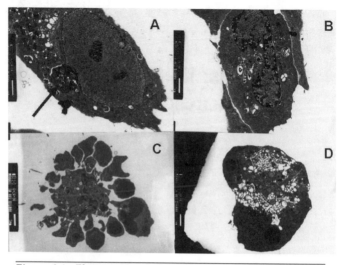

Figure 6-1. Electron microscopic appearances of a human vascular smooth muscle cell undergoing apoptosis in culture. (A) Normal appearance of a human vascular smooth muscle cell. Vascular smooth muscle cell also contains an apoptotic body (arrow) (B) Peripheral condensation of nuclear chromatin (C) Intense membrane blebbing and vesicle formation in apoptosis, with condensation of the nuclear chromatin into clumps. (D) An apoptotic body, the end product of apoptosis.

around the inner face of the nuclear membrane, and then clumping of the chromatin. Apoptosis is also associated with loss of cell-cell contact and cell shrinkage and fragmentation, with formation of membrane–bound processes and vesicles containing fragments of nuclear material or organelles. Adjacent cells (Figure 6-1) may then phagocytose the end product, the apoptotic body. The whole process occurs with minimal disruption of membrane integrity or release of lysosomal enzymes, with consequently little inflammatory reaction. In addition, organelle structure and function appear to be maintained until late into the process.

In contrast, necrosis actually describes the morphological stigmata of a cell when it has passed the point of no return, i.e. when it has committed to die. However, necrosis now more commonly describes cell death characterised by cell swelling, without the chromatin condensation seen in apoptosis, but with organelle dysfunction early in the process, loss of membrane integrity, and release of lysosomal enzymes with consequent inflammation.

Although the terms are frequently used synonymously, programmed cell death and apoptosis are not interchangeable. Programmed cell death, in its truest sense, is cell death occurring at defined times in embryogenesis. This is clearly "physiological" cell death that is initiated by a specific genetic program. In addition, programmed cell death can be considered to occur in adult organisms during regression of a variety of hyperplastic tissues, in particular, the hormone–dependent regression of breast or uterine tissues. Death in this instance is also a physiological response, but the factor triggering death may be intrinsic or exogenous, for example removal of a trophic stimulus. Within the vasculature, true programmed cell death (which occurs via an apoptotic morphology) can be said to occur in closure of the ductus arteriosus, and in many of the changes in vessel calibre and wall thickness which occur as an adaptation to blood flow in the neonate (see below).

APOPTOSIS IN THE HEART

The adult cardiomyocyte is a terminally differentiated cell that cannot divide. Therefore, by definition, apoptosis within the adult heart cannot be physiological, as no turnover of myocytes is possible. Indeed, apoptosis is observed very infrequently in adult hearts.[2-7] In contrast, cardiomyocyte apoptosis in development plays a critical role in formation of the heart.

Apoptosis in cardiac development. During development, organs and tissues are remodelled using the processes of cell division, cell migration and cell death. Most if not all of this cell death occurs through apoptosis. Thus, apoptosis is seen when the notochord fuses in the developing spinal cord and apoptosis causes the breakdown of interdigital webs to sculpt the fingers. Within the heart, cell death may be involved in the formation of septa between cardiac chambers or of valves, suggesting that defects in apoptosis can result in congenital heart disease.[8, 9] Major foci of apoptosis include the atrioventricular cushions and their zones of fusion, the bulbar cushions and their zones of fusion, and the aortic and pulmonary valves.[9] Indeed, apoptosis has been found in the developing rat bulbus cordis within mesenchymal cells.[10] Most of the apoptosis seen is in non–myocytes, although in midgestation there is focal myocyte apoptosis in the interventricular septum close to the atrioventricular valves.[10] Apoptosis of right ventricular and interventricular septal myocytes is also seen immediately after birth, where it may contribute to RV remodelling as part of the transition from foetal to adult circulations. The conducting tissue also undergoes apoptosis, and both increased or decreased apoptosis have been implicated in the pathogenesis of congenital heart block and long QT syndrome[11-13] or the persistence of accessory pathways respectively.[12]

Apoptosis in ischaemia/reperfusion. Ischaemia is now a well-characterised inducer of myocyte apoptosis *in vitro*. Deprivation of oxygen alone, or in addition to serum withdrawal and deprivation of glucose induces neonatal myocyte apoptosis that does not require protein synthesis, i.e. the machinery for executing apoptosis is already functional.[14,15]

Reperfusion is the mainstay of treatment for acute myocardial infarction, as demonstrated by numerous thrombolysis trials demonstrating improved left ventricular function and reduced mortality following successful reperfusion. However, reperfusion is also associated with myocyte death,[16] and neutrophil accumulation, inflammation, calcium overload and oxidative stress for example have all been implicated in the pathogenesis of reperfusion injury.[17-21] Reperfusion has been shown to increase apoptosis, and apoptosis therefore may represent the underlying mechanism of reperfusion injury. Ischaemia alone can induce apoptosis in the ischaemic territory *in vivo*, and this may be reduced by reperfusion. However, although reperfusion may limit ischaemia-induced apoptosis, it may accelerate the appearance of apoptosis in the reperfused regions.[2,22,23] *In vitro*, hypoxia is mostly associated with death through non–apoptotic mechanisms, although re–oxygenation potently induces apoptosis.[24]

Apoptosis in myocardial infarction. Myocardial infarction has been considered to be a *prima facie* example of necrotic cell death, due to the breakdown of cellular energy metabolism. However, there is increasing evidence that apoptosis of cardiomyocytes may occur in a temporally and spatially specific manner. Thus, the acute stage of myocardial infarction may be associated with both forms of cell death.[25-28] In particular apoptotic myocytes are apparent at the hypoperfused 'border' zones, between a central area of necrosis and the viable myocardium.[27-29] However, apoptosis may occur in the central, unperfused region of an infarct,[5,7,23] particularly within the first 6 hours after infarction. Although apoptosis increases in a time–dependent manner reaching maximal levels 18–48 hours after the onset of ischaemia in mouse models,[7] between 6–24 hours necrosis may be more common than apoptosis, and may be due to secondary necrosis of apoptotic myocytes.[5] Apoptosis also occurs in the remote non-infarcted myocardium, where it may be partly responsible for myocardial remodelling and dilatation after MI,[29,30] and may be amenable to treatment.[31] In human autopsy specimens, apoptosis of cardiomyocytes has been observed 12 hours to several days following the onset of MI.[25]

Apoptosis in heart failure. One of the most exciting advances in recent years has been the finding that cardiomyocyte apoptosis occurs in the end-stage human heart and may contribute to heart failure in a variety of situations.[32,33] Thus, in models of heart failure induced by either pacing or coronary microemboli, cardiomyocyte death is associated with TUNEL-positive cells,[3] which is particularly marked at the border zones of infarcts.[6] Ageing is also associated with myocardial cell loss in both human and animal hearts, and cardiomyocyte apoptosis has been suggested to be the mechanism of the gradual deterioration in cardiac function in ageing.[34,35] In humans undergoing transplantation, apoptosis can be observed,[33,36] with some studies suggesting higher levels in ischaemic versus idiopathic dilated cardiomyopathy.[32] The transition from compensated to decompensated hypertrophy is also associated with myocyte apoptosis in animals.[37] and high levels of apoptosis are seen in arrhythmogenic right ventricular dysplasia, a condition characterised by myocardial replacement with fibrofatty material.[38] Finally, there is increasing evidence that toxic cardiomyopathies, such as that induced by doxorubicin (adriamycin), are associated with cardiomyocyte apoptosis.[39]

Although the evidence that apoptosis directly contributes to heart failure is persuasive, the present problem is defining by how much. Vastly different rates of apoptosis have been reported in both human and animal heart failure, with reported rates of up to 35.5%.[32] Whilst, these rates of death may be seen only in very localised areas, given that apoptosis takes <24 hours to complete, such rates would result in rapid involution of the whole heart. The variable and prolonged period of time over which heart failure develops and the gradual cell drop out in failing hearts would suggest that very few myocytes would be undergoing apoptosis at any one time. More recently rates of <0.5% have been consistently reported in end stage heart failure, which make far more physiological sense.[3,33] Unfortunately, whilst such low rates implicate apoptosis in disease, they make detecting any differences after therapeutic manoeuvres very difficult.

Thus, although the evidence for apoptosis in heart failure is convincing, the role of apoptosis *per se* in unknown. In end stage heart failure necrotic cells are still (up to 7x) more likely to be found than apoptotic cells.[36]

APOPTOSIS IN THE VESSEL WALL

Vascular smooth muscle cells within the vessel wall are able to proliferate, migrate, and synthesise and degrade extracellular matrix upon receiving appropriate stimuli. The normal adult artery shows very low levels of vascular smooth muscle cell turnover, and apoptotic and mitotic indices are low in this tissue.[40] In diseased tissue additional factors are present both locally, such as inflammatory cytokines, inflammatory cells and the presence of modified cholesterol, and systemically, such as blood pressure and flow. These factors can substantially alter the normal balance of cell proliferation and apoptosis, although the degree to which they are altered is dependent upon the vascular disease under study.

Remodelling. Vessel wall remodelling defines a condition in which alterations in luminal size can occur through processes that do not necessarily require large changes in overall cell number or tissue mass. Thus, redistribution of cells, either towards or away from the lumen, through processes such as selective cell proliferation/apoptosis or matrix synthesis/degradation can significantly alter lumen dimensions. Physiological remodelling by cell proliferation/apoptosis occurs in closure of the ductus arteriosus,[41] and reduction in lumen size of infra-umbilical arteries after birth.[42,43] Surgical reduction in flow also results in compensatory vascular smooth muscle cell apoptosis.[44,45] Remodelling also occurs in primary atherosclerosis, after angioplasty and in angioplasty restenosis. Although apoptosis undoubtedly occurs in all of these conditions (see below), the role of vascular smooth muscle cell apoptosis in determining the outcome of remodelling is unclear.

Arterial injury. Acute arterial injury, such as that occurring at angioplasty, is followed by rapid induction of medial cell apoptosis, at least in animal models. Thus, in rat or rabbit vessels, balloon overstretch injury results in medial cell apoptosis from 30 minutes – 4 hours after injury.[46-48] In pigs, apoptotic cells occur within the media at 6 hours with peaks in the media, adventitia, and neointima at 18 hours, 6 hours, and 7 days after PTCA, respectively.[49] Although we have no direct evidence, the consistency of this response in animal models suggests that human vessels may behave similarly. Repair of the vessel after injury is also associated with vascular smooth muscle cell apoptosis, both in the media and in the intima, and in the rat occurs 8–21 days after injury.[50] In humans, restenosis after angioplasty has been reported to be associated with either an increase,[51] or decrease[52] in vascular smooth muscle cell apoptosis. Thus, the role of vascular smooth muscle cell apoptosis in either the initial injury or the remodelling process in restenosis is again unclear in human vessels.

Aneurysm formation. The commonest form of arterial aneurysm in humans is associated with advanced atherosclerosis, and is characterised by a loss of vascular smooth muscle cells from the vessel media, with fragmentation of elastin and matrix degradation, leading to progressive dilatation and eventually rupture. Apoptosis of vascular smooth muscle cells is increased in aortic aneurysms[53-55] compared with normal aorta, associated with an increase in expression of a number of pro-apoptotic molecules, such as death receptors and p53.[53,55] Macrophages and T-lymphocytes are found in aneurysmal lesions, suggesting that inflammatory mediators released by these cells may promote vascular smooth muscle cell apoptosis. Moreover, the production of tissue metalloproteinases by macrophages may accelerate cell death by degrading the extracellular matrix from which vascular smooth muscle cells derive survival signals (see below). This evidence suggests that vascular smooth muscle cell apoptosis is a major cause of the development of arterial aneurysms.

Atherosclerosis. Rupture of atherosclerotic plaques is associated with a thinning of the vascular smooth muscle cell-rich fibrous cap overlying the core. Rupture occurs particularly at the shoulder regions of plaques, which are noted for their lack of vascular smooth muscle cells and the presence of macrophages and other inflammatory cells. Apoptotic vascular smooth muscle cell are evident in advanced human plaques,[51,56,57] including the shoulder regions, prompting the suggestion that vascular smooth muscle cell apoptosis may hasten plaque rupture. Indeed, increased vascular smooth muscle cell apoptosis occurs in unstable versus stable angina lesions.[52]

Although loss of vascular smooth muscle cells would be

expected to promote plaque rupture, there is no direct evidence of the effect of apoptosis *per se* in advanced human atherosclerosis. Most apoptotic cells in histological sections are found in advanced lesions next to the lipid core,[58] and most of these apoptotic cells are macrophages, not vascular smooth muscle cells. Loss of macrophages from atherosclerotic lesions is likely to promote plaque stability rather than rupture, since macrophages can promote vascular smooth muscle cell apoptosis by both direct interactions[59] and by release of cytokines.[60] Of interest, apoptosis also occurs in early stages of atherosclerosis induced by cholesterol feeding in animals, at the fatty streak stage of before morphological evidence of lesion formation.[61] Again, the effect of apoptosis at this early stage of lesion development is unknown.

Vascular smooth muscle apoptosis. The effect of vascular smooth muscle cell apoptosis is clearly context-dependent. Thus, vascular smooth muscle cell apoptosis in advanced atherosclerotic plaques would be expected to promote plaque rupture, and medial atrophy in aneurysm formation. In neointima formation post injury, vascular smooth muscle cell apoptosis of both the intima and media can limit neointimal formation[47,48,62] at a defined time point, although long term studies have not been performed to ensure that the neointima is not simply delayed. It is not yet known whether such inhibition of neointimal formation in an animal model can translate into suppression of restenosis following angioplasty or stenting.

Therapeutic induction of apoptosis in the vessel wall may also be limited by important sequelae. In contrast to the dogma that apoptosis is silent (that is, it does not elicit an immune response) a number of deleterious effects of apoptotic cells have emerged within the vasculature. In particular, exposure of phosphatidylserine on the surface of apoptotic cells provides a potent substrate for the generation of thrombin and activation of the coagulation cascade.[63,64] Apoptotic cells can also release membrane-bound microparticles into the circulation, which remain pro-coagulant and are increased in patients with unstable versus stable coronary syndromes.[65,66] Although apoptotic cells are not the only source of circulating microparticles, such micro-particles may contribute to the increased pro-coagulant state in these syndromes. Finally, there is increasing evidence that induction of vascular smooth muscle cell apoptosis may be directly pro-inflammatory, with release of chemoattractants and cytokines form inflammatory cells.[67]

REGULATION OF APOPTOSIS

Apoptosis via death receptors. Many stimuli can trigger apoptosis in cells, but in vascular disease it is likely that specific alterations within the cell itself elicit sensitivity to a particular stimulus that is disease-associated. Thus, remodelling may trigger apoptosis following reduction in blood flow, and the major stimulus may therefore be flow-dependent stimuli such as nitric oxide or shear stress. In contrast, apoptosis in atherosclerosis or aneurysm formation may be due to the surrounding influences of inflammatory cells that express death ligands on their surface or secrete pro-apoptotic cytokines. Whatever the stimulus, many of the downstream pathways by which the apoptotic stimuli are transmitted are similar.

The regulation of apoptosis within the cell can be simplified into two major pathways (Figures 6-2 and 6-3). First, membrane-bound death receptors of the tumour necrosis receptor family (TNF-R), such as Fas (CD95), TNF-R1, death receptor (DR)-3, DR4 and DR5 bind their trimerised ligands causing receptor aggregation, and subsequent recruitment of a number of adapter proteins through protein: protein interactions[68] (see Figure 6-2). For example, binding of agonistic anti-Fas monoclonal antibody or its natural ligand Fas-ligand to its cognate receptor induces receptor trimerisation, with subsequent recruitment of adapter molecules such as FADD and RIP to the receptor complex.[69-71] In turn, FADD and RIP recruit cell death cysteine proteases (caspases) such as caspase 8 (FLICE) and caspase 2 to the complex.[72] Within the complex of Fas, FADD and caspase 8 (known as the death-inducing signalling complex (DISC)), caspase 8 becomes proteolytically activated by oligomerisation.[73] This facilitates the subsequent activation of terminal effector caspases such as caspases 3, 6 and 7[74-78] responsible for cleavage of intracellular substrates required for cellular survival, architecture and metabolic function.[79, 80] Caspase

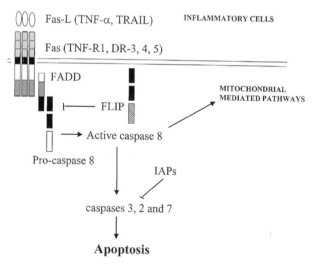

Figure 6-2. Schematic of Fas death signalling pathways. Fas, the prototypic member of the TNF death receptor family binds to its cognate ligand. Recruitment of the adapter molecule FADD and pro-caspase 8 results in activation of the latter. Caspase 8 activation directly activates downstream caspases, (3, 6 and 7) which results in DNA fragmentation and cleavage of cellular proteins. This pathway is thought to occur in type I cells and does not involve mitochondrial pathways. Caspase 8 activation also results in cleavage of Bid, which translocates and interacts with other Bcl–2 family members (see Figure 3).

activation is also responsible for many of the hallmarks of apoptosis, such as DNA fragmentation, chromatin condensation and apoptotic body formation.[81-83] The major active caspases in Fas-mediated apoptosis are caspases 8, 3, 6 and 7,[83] with stepwise appearance of active caspases suggesting a caspase cascade. Cells in which caspase 8 is expressed in abundance, recently termed type I cells, use this pathway of direct caspase 3 activation. Moreover, in these cells, Fas mediated cell death cannot be inhibited by anti-apoptotic factors such as Bcl-2 and Bcl-X$_L$ since the pathway does not require amplification by pro-apoptotic factors released by mitochondria.[84]

Apoptosis via mitochondrial amplification. In contrast, cells in which caspase 8 is not abundantly expressed cannot activate caspase 3 and other downstream caspases directly. Instead, in these cells termed type II cells,[84] caspase 8 activation causes cleavage of proteins of the bcl-2 family such as bid[85] (see Figure 6-3). Bcl-2 family members are characterised as either pro-apoptotic (Bax, Bid, Bik, Bak) or anti-apoptotic (Bcl-2, Bcl-X$_L$). Activation of pro-apoptotic Bcl-2 family members causes their translocation to mitochondria, where they interact with anti-apoptotic members that are components of the mitochondrial membrane. This interaction causes changes in voltage-dependent mitochondrial channels and releases mitochondrial mediators of apoptosis such as cytochrome c[86] and Smac/DIABLO.[87, 88] In turn the

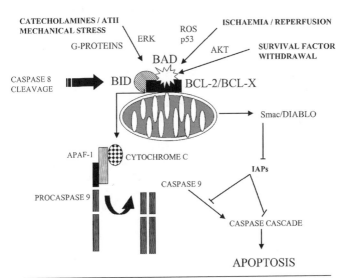

Figure 6-3. *Schematic of mitochondrial death signalling pathways. Anti–apoptotic members of the Bcl-2 family, such as Bcl-2 and Bcl-X are located on the mitochondrial outer membrane. Here they act to prevent the release of apoptogenic factors from the inner mitochondrial space. Binding of the pro-apoptotic proteins Bid (after cleavage by caspase 8) or Bad (after dephosphorylation) to Bcl-2 mitigates the protective effect of Bcl-2 and triggers release of cytochrome c and Smac/DIABLO. Cytochrome c, in concert with the adapter protein apaf-1 and caspase 9 activates caspase 3 and the downstream caspase cascade. Smac/DIABLO inhibits IAPs, which in turn inhibit caspase activities, thus propagating apoptosis. Stimuli such as growth factor withdrawal or activation of p53 and Fas activation in type II cells act through this mitochondrial pathway.*

association of cytochrome c with an adapter molecule apaf-1 and caspase 9 activates caspase 3, and the caspase cascade. In contrast, Smac/DIABLO promotes apoptosis by directly antagonising IAP proteins.[87, 88] Thus, death induced by Fas signalling may or may not be inhibitable by Bcl-2 family members suggesting that high levels of expression of anti-apoptotic Bcl-2 family members do not automatically correlate with suppression of cell death. The classification of human vascular smooth muscle cells into type I or type II cells has yet to be made, however, the kinetics of cell death in response to anti-Fas antibodies suggests that they are type II cells.

Fas-induced apoptosis can also be blocked by expression of several intracellular proteins, including FLIPs (FLICE inhibitory protein) and IAPs (inhibitor of apoptosis) (see Figure 6-2). FLIPs are similar to caspase molecules, having the same pro-domain structure as caspase 8, but not the active caspase site within the C-terminus. The pro-domain of caspase 8 has two protein: protein interaction motifs called death effector domains (DEDs) that are also found in FADD. These DEDs facilitate the binding of FADD to caspase 8 and the binding of FLIP to FADD. Caspase 8 is activated upon binding to FADD via a series of cleavage reactions. FLIP undergoes the first of these cleavages, but not the second, preventing the activation of caspase 8.[89] In contrast, IAPs can inhibit the enzymatic activity of downstream caspases[90-92] (see below), or they can mediate anti-apoptotic signalling pathways through the activation of nuclear transcription factor B (NF-κβ).

Regulation of cardiomyocyte apoptosis. The stimulus for cardiomyocyte apoptosis clearly depends upon the clinical or experimental setting and on a variety of signalling paths (Table 6-2). Ischaemia is associated with many changes in the intracellular and extracellular milieu of cardiomyocytes, many of which are potent stimuli to apoptosis. Hypoxia is associated with cardiomyocyte apoptosis, both *in vitro* and *in vivo*,[14,93] although the effectors of this pathway are unknown. p53 may promote both hypoxia-induced apoptosis,[93] or apoptosis related to inhibition of the vacuoalar ATPase (see below)[94] but is not an absolute requirement for apoptosis post-myocardial infarction.[7] Ischaemia/reperfusion and hypoxia/re-oxygenation is associated with increased expression of Fas,[5,95] although there is no direct evidence of Fas/Fas-L-induced apoptosis in cardiomyocytes. Decreased serum and glucose concentrations do trigger cytochrome c release from mitochondria in cardiomyocytes,[96] suggesting that the effects of ischaemia may be mediated by mitochondrial amplification of apoptosis signals.

In ischaemia/reperfusion models reactive oxygen species may promote apoptosis,[97] again by triggering pathways involving mitochondria with release of cytochrome c and activation of caspases.[24] In addition, prolonged hypoxia and depletion of high-energy phosphates may inhibit the

ATP-dependent vacuolar proton pump ATPase, resulting in intracellular acidification and apoptosis.[94,98]

In heart failure, a huge variety of initial stimuli have been propounded. *In vitro*, mechanical stretch can induce apoptosis, indicating a possible role for volume overload and raised ventricular end diastolic pressure.[4] This study also directly implicated reactive oxygen species in the induction of stretch-induced apoptosis. Pressure overload following aortic banding can also induce early myocyte apoptosis, before significant hypertrophy, emphasising the role of mechanical stimuli,[99] and there is increased myocyte apoptosis in hearts of spontaneously hypertensive rats.[100] In models of chronic heart failure, such as following microembolisation of coronary arteries in dogs, apoptotic myocytes tend to cluster in peri-infarct zones, also suggesting that ongoing ischaemia or mechanical stress is responsible.[6] Four weeks of rapid ventricular pacing also induces myocyte apoptosis in dogs associated with heart failure, suggesting that catecholamine responses may be directly toxic to myocytes.[3] Indeed, *in vitro* data suggest that catecholamines are potent inducers of cardiomyocyte apoptosis.

A large number of circulating factors have also been implicated in cardiomyocyte apoptosis in heart failure, including both angiotensin II[101] and ANF, both of which increase apoptosis in cultured cardiomyocytes. In contrast, intraperitoneally- administered IGF-1 may limit ischaemia/reperfusion-induced apoptosis.[22]

Regulation of vascular smooth muscle cell apoptosis. Human vascular smooth muscle cells express both Fas and TNF-R1,[102] and given the widespread occurrence of TRAIL-Rs are also likely to express these receptors. T-lymphocytes and macrophages within the atherosclerotic plaque express Fas ligand and TNF-α and interaction between membrane-bound ligands on T-cells and macrophages and receptors on vascular smooth muscle cell may induce the death of vascular smooth muscle cells. Vascular smooth muscle cells can also express Fas-L and TNF-α which exist as membrane-bound or soluble forms. The soluble forms are cleaved from the membrane-bound forms by a metalloproteinase of the ADAM family. Interestingly, a recent study of the tissue inhibitors of metalloproteinases (TIMPs), indicates that TIMP-3 can induce vascular smooth muscle cell apoptosis *in vitro* and *in vivo*,[103] which may be acting by stabilising expression of the more potent membrane forms of death ligands on the vascular smooth muscle cell surface.

Although overexpression of FADD can induce vascular smooth muscle cell apoptosis *in vitro* and *in vivo*,[67] soluble ligand binding to death receptors is a very weak inducer of apoptosis in vascular smooth muscle cells,[60,104] and does not induce apoptosis in the absence of 'priming' of the cell, usually with cycloheximide. Some of this resistance can be explained by the observation that death receptors are sequestered intracellularly in vascular smooth muscle cells,[104] and priming may be associated with increased surface expression. Physiologically, increased death receptor expression can be achieved via combination of cytokines such as IL-1-βIFN-γ and TNF-α,[102,105,106] possibly via NO and p53 stabilisation,[60,106-108] or via direct activation of p53.[104] Free radicals and NO can also induce apoptosis which may be independent of p53 but associated with caspase 3 activation,[109-114] but not associated with death receptor signalling. In contrast, efficient death receptor-mediated apoptosis of vascular smooth muscle cells can be achieved by high level expression of death ligands such as Fas-L,[62] possibly by increasing expression of membrane-bound forms of these ligands. Thus, DNA damage induced by nitric oxide, anoxia or free radical formation for instance may stabilise p53, effectively priming vascular smooth muscle cells to death receptor mediated apoptosis.

Irrespective of the local environment, vascular smooth muscle cells derived from atherosclerotic plaques show increased rates of apoptosis in culture compared with cells from normal vessels, reflecting an intrinsic sensitivity to apoptosis.[115] This appears to be a stable property, and is part of the phenotype of plaque vascular smooth muscle cells that includes slow proliferation and early senescence. Heterogeneity of sensitivity to apoptosis within vascular smooth muscle cells in the vessel wall has also been demonstrated in animal vessels after injury,[116] and in medial vascular smooth muscle cells from normal human arteries.[117] This is likely to reflect differences in expression of pro-and anti-apoptotic molecules, specifically those regulating signalling from survival cytokines, cell:cell and cell: matrix interactions and members of the *bcl-2* family. Indeed, Insulin-like growth factor 1 (IGF-1) is a potent survival factor for normal vascular smooth muscle cells, although IGF-1 cannot completely inhibit plaque vascular smooth muscle cell apoptosis *in vitro* after serum withdrawal.[115] Similarly, inhibition of bFGF binding induces vascular smooth muscle cell apoptosis *in vitro*[118,119] and *in vivo*,[120] possibly by induction of the oncogene *mdm2*, which inactivates p53.[121]

Evidence suggesting the critical role of *bcl-2* family members in regulating vascular smooth muscle cell apoptosis has come from both *in vitro* and *in vivo* studies. Human vascular smooth muscle cells express low levels of Bcl-2,[115,122] but Bax is seen particularly in atherosclerotic plaques, both in human and animal models of atherosclerosis and injury.[122-124] In addition, spontaneous and growth-factor withdrawal-induced apoptosis can be inhibited by overexpression of *bcl-2*.[115] *In vivo*, rat vascular smooth muscle cells express minimal Bcl-2, but high levels of Bcl-X can be found after injury.[124] Indeed, inhibition of Bcl-X can dramatically induce apoptosis of vascular smooth muscle cells after balloon injury[47] and differences in expression of Bcl-X may account for differences in sensitivity to apoptosis after injury of intimal versus medial vascular smooth muscle cells.[48] The reduced levels of vascular smooth muscle cells apoptosis seen after cholesterol lowering in rabbit models of atherosclerosis is also associated with a loss of Bax immunoreactivity,[123] arguing for a pro-apoptotic role of this protein in vascular smooth muscle cell apoptosis. However, it should be noted that excessive reliance on immunocyto-chemistry of one member of the bcl-2 family to ascertain a role for that protein *in vivo* should be avoided. Although Bcl-X is upregulated after injury, in rats it is the short $Bcl-x_s$ or pro-apoptotic form that appears to predominate.[124]

Regulation of sensitivity to apoptosis in vascular smooth muscle cells is also mediated by expression of IAP proteins[125] and individual caspases,[117,126] and it is likely that there are marked differences in expression of multiple proteins that regulate vascular smooth muscle cell apoptosis of individual vascular smooth muscle cells in response to specific stimuli. This may underlie observations that despite (apparently) the same stimulus for apoptosis, vascular smooth muscle cell apoptosis in the either the normal or diseased vessel wall is highly localised.

THERAPEUTIC OPTIONS FOR APOPTOSIS TREATMENT

From the above discussion, prevention of cardiomyocyte apoptosis would appear to be a very important therapeutic aim. Although the mechanisms of induction of apoptosis and the precise significance of apoptosis in the development of each disease entity are unclear, it would seem obvious that a live myocyte is better than a dead one. However, critical to determining therapeutic benefit of any treatment is not just inhibiting markers of apoptosis at a single defined time point, but of improving cardiac function. Many agents may prevent the development of the morphological appearance of an apoptotic cell or a defined biochemical marker (for example DNA fragmentation) without inhibiting cell death. The ability to delay death may serve no useful purpose and may be deleterious if that cell is destined to undergo necrosis at a later time point, with concomitant inflammation.

In contrast, some studies have indicated that inhibition of apoptosis improves ventricular remodelling and contractility after infarction.[31,127] For example, in a rat model of myocardial infarction (ischaemia/reperfusion), treatment with the caspase inhibitor zVAD.fmk reduced infarct size, with an improvement in acute myocardial function.[128] The long-term effects of this inhibitor are however, unknown, and prevention of apoptosis may simply delay death, but not prevent it.

Apoptosis can be interrupted at many points in the signalling pathway. Prevention of apoptotic myocyte death may be directed at (1) inhibiting/preventing the apoptotic stimulus, (2) inhibiting the regulatory mechanisms determining the decision to die, or (3) inhibiting the effector pathways executing apoptosis. The cascade of events leading to cardiomyocyte apoptosis, and also the point at which a cell is irreversibly committed to die crucially determine the approach to inhibiting apoptosis. Clearly, a multitude of signalling pathways are activated in complex pathophysiological states such as ischaemia and heart failure. Interruption of a single pathway would therefore be predicted not to inhibit apoptosis if there are multiple, redundant pathways inducing apoptosis. Such arguments would indicate that mediators that act beyond convergence of multiple signalling pathways would be better targets to inhibit apoptosis. However, many of the identified downstream mediators are enzymes required for effective disintegration and packaging of the cell, and as such, are beyond the point at which the cell is committed to die. Inhibition at these points would prevent the cellular appearances and markers of apoptosis, but the cell would still die. In addition, these molecules are critical to apoptosis in many tissues and such non-cardiac specificity may be unwelcome. From this argument, inhibiting the stimulus to apoptosis, particularly if specific to the heart at one point in time, would be more effective. The timing and delivery of therapy is also dependent upon the clinical situation. Clearly, it is easier to inhibit apoptosis transiently in an acute situation such as myocardial infarction, than with chronic therapy in diseases such as heart failure.

Inhibiting/preventing the pro-apoptotic stimulus. Ischaemia/reperfusion, hypertrophy due to increased afterload, and myocardial remodelling following infarction all are associated with myocyte apoptosis.[14, 25-27,29,99] This suggests that current therapy of proven benefit in these diseases may already act by inhibition of apoptosis. The beneficial effects of β-blockers in chronic heart failure and ischaemic heart disease may counteract the pro-apoptotic effect of excess catecholamines. Indeed, carvedilol can inhibit ischaemia/reperfusion induced apoptosis of myocytes,[95] and ACE inhibitors would be predicted to protect against angiotensin II-induced apoptosis.[101] Clearly, approaches aimed at reducing myocardial stretch, or oxidative stress, or improving myocardial perfusion would be predicted to have the same effect. Finally, many pathways leading to apoptosis are triggered by specific death ligands, with either apoptosis or the disease entity being associated with upregulation of death receptors or transgenic expression of the death ligand directly inducing the disease.[14,95,129,130] Inhibition of delivery of death ligands, for example by scavenging ligands through soluble receptors or receptor antagonists would be predicted to reduce apoptosis mediated though these pathways.

Protection against apoptosis. The expression of many molecules protects cells from apoptosis, including anti-apoptotic members of the Bcl-2 family, IAPs, decoys for death receptors etc. Although many of these agents are promiscuous enough to inhibit apoptosis mediated by a variety of stimuli, and may therefore be clinically useful, at present they cannot be selectively expressed without gene transfer into the heart, with all its inherent problems. More promising is the potential administration of soluble survival factors following the apoptotic stimulus. Many growth factors, including IGF-1, cardiotrophin-1 and the neuregulins inhibit apoptosis following ischaemia, serum withdrawal, myocyte stretch and cytotoxic drugs.[22,31,131-134] Overexpression of IGF-1 can reduce apoptosis in non-infarcted remote zones and promote favourable remodelling post MI.[31] and a single intraperitoneal injection of IGF-1 can inhibit ischaemia/reperfusion–induced apoptosis in the rat by 50%.[22] Activation of the cardiotrophin-1 receptor also inhibits cardiac dilatation following aortic banding, suggesting that reduced cardiomyocyte apoptosis can be translated into improved function.[135] These agents signal though the AKT and ERK pathways respectively, that are known to be anti-apoptotic in many cell types. Inhibition of the ERK kinase signalling pathway increases ischaemia/reperfusion-induced apoptosis and worsens reperfusion injury, so those agents that increase signalling through this pathway may be beneficial.[95,136] These agents could be given either locally or systemically at the time of infarction. Stimulation of the MKK/p38α pathway also causes cardiomyocyte apoptosis[137,138] as does overexpression of Gsα or Gqα. Antagonists to these more 'classical' myocyte signalling pathways may therefore of benefit.

In contrast, a number of agents have been suggested as potential therapeutics for long term administration. Heart failure is characterised by increased plasma levels of catecholamines and TNF-α. The beneficial effects of β-blockers in heart failure may therefore be by prevention of myocyte apoptosis, and licensed inhibitors of TNF-α are now available. Evidence identifying the Type 2 AT–II receptor as inducing apoptosis in many cell types, including the myocardium, especially in models of heart failure, has suggested that inhibition of this receptor may also be beneficial.

Preventing the execution of apoptosis. Execution of apoptosis and cellular disintegration and packaging requires the activation of downstream signalling pathways, including mitochondrial amplification and activation of caspases. Augmentation of endogenous inhibitors of caspases, such as the IAPs, could therefore inhibit apoptosis induced by a variety of stimuli. Pharmacological inhibition of caspases using cell permeable analogues of caspase cleavage sites can inhibit myocyte apoptosis over the short term. However, the long-term benefits of such drugs are unknown, as it may be that cells that are destined to die do so anyway, and delaying apoptosis may not provide long-term benefit. In addition, some inducers of apoptosis may absolutely require caspases for execution of cell death.[139]

OUTSTANDING QUESTIONS

There are many unresolved questions regarding anti-apoptotic therapeutics in cardiovascular disease, in particular relating to myocardial apoptosis.

1. There is considerable debate as to the role and amount

that apoptosis contributes to cardiovascular disease, particularly in disease entities that are characterised by complex pathophysiology. For example, heart failure is characterised by impairments of excitation-contraction coupling, alterations in intracellular filaments, interstitial fibrosis, side-side slippage of myocytes and neurohormonal deregulation. How much myocyte apoptosis contributes to this complex situation is unknown. Clearly, anti-apoptotic therapy may inhibit only a very small part of such a complex pathophysiology.

2. It is presently unknown whether inhibition of apoptosis prevents or simply delays disease progression. Although many studies have shown reduced apoptosis after therapy, few have shown that this translates into improved left ventricular function, and none that has been demonstrated to be maintained long term and associated with increased survival.

3. The specificity of action of any therapy is unknown. Many of the apoptotic/anti-apoptotic signalling pathways have many other functions, and given the conserved nature of apoptosis signalling, no pathway is likely to be cardiac-specific. Whilst this may not be important for myocardial salvage after infarction where short-term therapy is planned, it is a critical consideration for long term therapy in heart failure. It must be remembered that apoptosis is a vital element in the prevention and destruction of tumours, and any long-term therapy has to be examined for tumourigenicity. Apoptosis is also crucial to such physiological functions as normal fertility, shedding of the skin and gut lining, and deletion of leukocytes. Inhibition of normal apoptosis may therefor cause sterility and autoimmune disease such as haemolytic anaemia, and thrombocytopaenia in addition. Genetic knockout of many of many components of the apoptotic machinery is also lethal in the embryonic period. It is therefore possible that targeting apoptosis is directly teratogenic.

Furthermore, although apoptosis is signalled by death receptors, other signals also emanate from these receptors. For example, Fas activation reduces the membrane potential and induces afterdepolarisations in cardiac myocytes. Thus, therapy inhibiting Fas-induced apoptosis may allow escape of other Fas-signalling, promoting arrhythmias.[140] Similarly, interrupting TNF-α-induced apoptosis may still allow the negatively inotropic effect of this cytokine.

SUMMARY

Vascular smooth muscle cell apoptosis occurs in the vasculature in both physiological and pathological contexts. These deaths are regulated by specific proteins that serve to either induce or protect against apoptosis. We are now beginning to understand the complex biology observed in lesions such as atherosclerosis and to identify potential pro-apoptotic factors that may lead to the loss of cells from the vasculature. Sensitivity to apoptosis is determined by expression of cell death receptors and ligands, and by multiple protein species below receptor level. In addition, sensitivity to apoptosis is determined by the presence and response to survival cytokines, mitogens, and local cell and matrix interactions, and by the growth status of the cell. Although, much of this research has been carried out *in vitro*, future studies in animal models should help to identify which of the pro- and anti-apoptotic factors that are effective *in vitro* are also relevant *in vivo*. Moreover, a closer examination of the population dynamics of vascular cells within the vessel wall will aid the understanding of the timing and triggers of vascular smooth muscle cell apoptosis in disease.

In contrast, in the adult cardiomycoyte apoptosis is almost always pathological. Apoptosis of cardiac myocytes is part of many disease states including myocardial infarction and heart failure. At present, the precise role of cardiac myocyte apoptosis in the pathogenesis of these diseases is unknown, and therefore the likely benefit from anti-apoptotic therapy is unproven. Prevention of cardiomycoyte apoptosis may involve inhibiting both the pro-apoptotic stimulus and apoptosis signalling within the cell. Given the lack of cardiac specificity of apoptosis signalling such strategies are far more likely to be beneficial in short-lived insults, such as myocardial infarction or unstable angina, rather than chronic administration in heart failure. However, it is also highly likely that proven conventional therapy for heart failure works at least in part by inhibiting apoptosis.

REFERENCES

1. Kerr, J F, Wyllie, A H and Currie, A R. Apoptosis: a basic biological phenomenon with wide-ranging implications in tissue kinetics. *Br J Cancer.* 1972; 26:239–57.

2. Gottlieb, R A, Burleson, K O, Kloner, R A, Babior, B M and Engler, R L. Reperfusion injury induces apoptosis in rabbit cardiomyocytes. *J Clin Invest.* 1994; 94:1621–8.

3. Liu, Y, Cigola, E, Cheng, W, Kajstura, J, Olivetti, G, Hintze, T and Anversa, P. Myocyte nuclear mitotic division and programmed myocyte cell death characterize the cardiac myopathy induced by rapid ventricular pacing in dogs. *Lab Invest.* 1995; 73:771–787.

4. Cheng, W, Li, B, Kajstura, J, Li, P, Wolin, M S, Sonnenblick, E H, Hintze, T H, Olivetti, G and Anversa, P. Stretch-induced programmed myocyte cell death. *J Clin Invest.* 1995; 96:2247–59.

5. Kajstura, J, Cheng, W, Reiss, K, Clark, W, Sonnenblick, E, Krajewski, S, Reed, J, Olivetti, G and Anversa, P. Apoptotic and necrotic myocyte cell deaths are independent contributing variables of infarct size in rats. *Lab Invest.* 1996; 74:86–107.

6. Sharov, V G, Sabbah, H N, Shimoyama, H, Goussev, A V, Lesch, M and Goldstein, S. Evidence of cardiocyte apoptosis in myocardium of dogs with chronic heart failure. *Am J Pathol.* 1996; 148:141–9.

7. Bialik, S, Geenen, D L, Sasson, I E, Cheng, R, Horner, J W, Evans, S M, Lord, E M, Koch, C J and Kitsis, R N. Myocyte apoptosis during acute myocardial infarction in the mouse localizes to hypoxic regions but occurs independently of p53. *Journal Of Clinical Investigation.* 1997; 100:1363–1372.

8. Krstic, R and Pexieder, T. Ultrastructure of cell death in bulbar cushions of chick embryo heart. *Z Anat Entwicklungsgesch.* 1973; 140:337–50.

9. Pexieder, T. Cell death in the morphogenesis and teratogenesis of the heart. *Adv Anat Embryol Cell Biol.* 1975; 51:3–99.

10. Takeda, K, Yu, Z X, Nishikawa, T, Tanaka, M, Hosoda, S, Ferrans, V J and Kasajima, T. Apoptosis and DNA fragmentation in the bulbus cordis of the developing rat heart. *J Mol Cell Cardiol*. 1996; 28:209–15.

11. James, T N, Terasaki, F, Pavlovich, E R and Vikhert, A M. Apoptosis and pleomorphic micromitochondriosis in the sinus nodes surgically excised from five patients with the long QT syndrome. *J Lab Clin Med*. 1993; 122:309–23.

12. James, T N. Normal and abnormal consequences of apoptosis in the human heart. From postnatal morphogenesis to paroxysmal arrhythmias. *Circulation*. 1994; 90:556–73.

13. James, T N, St. Martin, E, Willis, P W, 3rd and Lohr, T O. Apoptosis as a possible cause of gradual development of complete heart block and fatal arrhythmias associated with absence of the AV node, sinus node, and internodal pathways. *Circulation*. 1996; 93:1424–38.

14. Tanaka, M, Ito, H, Adachi, S, Akimoto, H, Nishikawa, T, Kasajima, T, Marumo, F and Hiroe, M. Hypoxia induces apoptosis with enhanced expression of Fas antigen messenger RNA in cultured neonatal rat cardiomyocytes. *Circ Res*. 1994; 75:426–33.

15. Umansky, S, Cuenco, G, Khutzlan, S and al, e. Post ischemic apoptotic death of rat neonatal cardiomyocytes. *Cell Death Differentiation*. 1995; 2:235.

16. Braunwald, E and Kloner, R. Myocardial reperfusion: a double-edged sword? *J Clin Invest*. 1985; 76:1713.

17. Zweier, J, Flaherty, J and Weisfeldt, M. Direct measurement of radical generation following reperfusion of ischemic myocardium. *Proc Natl Acad Sci USA*. 1987; 84:1404.

18. Nayler, W, Panagiotopoulos, S, Elz, J and Daly, M. Calcium mediated damage during post ischemic reperfusion. *J Molec Cell Cardiol*. 1988; 20:41.

19. Smith, E F d, Egan, J W, Bugelski, P J, Hillegass, L M, Hill, D E and Griswold, D E. Temporal relation between neutrophil accumulation and myocardial reperfusion injury. *Am J Physiol*. 1988; 255:H1060–8.

20. Litt, M R, Jeremy, R W, Weisman, H F, Winkelstein, J A and Becker, L C. Neutrophil depletion limited to reperfusion reduced myocardial infarct size after 90 minutes of ischemia: Evidence for neutrophil-mediated reperfusion injury. *Circulation*. 1989; 80:1816–27.

21. Entman, M and Smith, C. Postreperfusion inflammation: A model for reaction to injury in cardiovascular disease. *Cardiovasc Res*. 1994; 28:1301.

22. Buerke, M, Murohara, T, Skurk, C, Nuss, C, Tomaselli, K and Lefer, A. Cardioprotective effect of insulin-like growth factor I in myocardial ischaemia followed by reperfusion. *Proc Natl Acad Sci USA*. 1995; 92:8031–8035.

23. Fliss, H and Gattinger, D. Apoptosis in ischemic and reperfused rat myocardium. *Circ Res*. 1996; 79:949–56.

24. Kang, P M, Haunstetter, A, Aoki, H, Usheva, A and Izumo, S. Morphological and molecular characterization of adult cardiomyocyte apoptosis during hypoxia and reoxygenation [In Process Citation]. *Circ Res*. 2000; 87:118–25.

25. Itoh, G, Tamura, J, Suzuki, M, Suzuki, Y, Ikeda, H, Koike, M, Nomura, M, Jie, T and Ito, K. DNA fragmentation of human infarcted myocardial cells demonstrated by the nick end labeling method and DNA agarose gel electrophoresis. *Am J Pathol*. 1995; 146:1325–31.

26. Bardales, R H, Hailey, L S, Xie, S S, Schaefer, R F and Hsu, S M. In situ apoptosis assay for the detection of early acute myocardial infarction. *Am J Pathol*. 1996; 149:821–9.

27. Saraste, A, Pulkki, K, Kallajoki, M, Henriksen, K, Parvinen, M and Voipio-Pulkki, L. Apoptosis in human acute myocardial infarction. *Circulation*. 1997; 95:320–323.

28. Takemura, G, Ohno, M, Hayakawa, Y, Misao, J, Kanoh, M, Ohno, A, Uno, Y, Minatoguchi, S, Fujiwara, T and Fujiwara, H. Role of apoptosis in the disappearance of infiltrated and proliferated interstitial cells after myocardial infarction. *Circ Res*. 1998; 82:1130–8.

29. Olivetti, G, Quaini, F, Sala, R, Lagrasta, C, Corradi, D, Bonacina, E, Gambert, S R, Cigola, E and Anversa, P. Acute myocardial infarction in humans is associated with activation of programmed myocyte cell death in the surviving portion of the heart. *J Mol Cell Cardiol*. 1996; 28:2005–16.

30. Cheng, W, Kajstura, J, Nitahara, J A, Li, B, Reiss, K, Liu, Y, Clark, W A, Krajewski, S, Reed, J C, Olivetti, G and Anversa, P. Programmed myocyte cell death affects the viable myocardium after infarction in rats. *Exp Cell Res*. 1996; 226:316–27.

31. Li, Q, Li, B, Wang, X, Leri, A, Jana, K P, Liu, Y, Kajstura, J, Baserga, R and Anversa, P. Overexpression of insulin-like growth factor-1 in mice protects from myocyte death after infarction, attenuating ventricular dilation, wall stress, and cardiac hypertrophy. *J Clin Invest*. 1997; 100:1991–9.

32. Narula, J, Haider, N, Virmani, R, DiSalvo, T G, Kolodgie, F D, Hajjar, R J, Schmidt, U, Semigran, M J, Dec, G W and Khaw, B A. Apoptosis in myocytes in end-stage heart failure. *N Engl J Med.* 1996; 335:1182–9.

33. Olivetti, G, Abbi, R, Quaini, F, Kajstura, J, Cheng, W, Nitahara, J A, Quaini, E, Di Loreto, C, Beltrami, C A, Krajewski, S, Reed, J C and Anversa, P. Apoptosis in the failing human heart. *N Engl J Med.* 1997; 336:1131–41.

34. Anversa, P, Hiler, B, Ricci, R, Guideri, G and Olivetti, G. Myocyte cell loss and myocyte hypertrophy in the aging rat heart. *J Am Coll Cardiol.* 1986; 8:1441–8.

35. Olivetti, G, Giordano, G, Corradi, D, Melissari, M, Lagrasta, C, Gambert, S R and Anversa, P. Gender differences and aging: effects on the human heart. *J Am Coll Cardiol.* 1995; 26:1068–79.

36. Guerra, S, Leri, A, Wang, X, Finato, N, Di Loreto, C, Beltrami, C A, Kajstura, J and Anversa, P. Myocyte death in the failing human heart is gender dependent. *Circ Res.* 1999; 85:856–66.

37. Li, Z, Bing, O H, Long, X, Robinson, K G and Lakatta, E G. Increased cardiomyocyte apoptosis during the transition to heart failure in the spontaneously hypertensive rat. *Am J Physiol.* 1997; 272:H2313–9.

38. Mallat, Z, Tedgui, A, Fontaliran, F, Frank, R, Durigon, M and Fontaine, G. Evidence of apoptosis in arrhythmogenic right ventricular dysplasia. *New Eng J Med.* 1996; 335:1190–1196.

39. Nakamura, T, Ueda, Y, Juan, Y, Katsuda, S, Takahashi, H and Koh, E. Fas-mediated apoptosis in adriamycin-induced cardiomyopathy in rats: In vivo study [In Process Citation]. *Circulation.* 2000; 102:572–8.

40. Gordon, D, Reidy, M A, Benditt, E P and Schwartz, S M. Cell proliferation in human coronary arteries. *Proc Natl Acad Sci U S A.* 1990; 87:4600–4.

41. Slomp, J, GittenbergerdeGroot, A C, Glukhova, M A, vanMunsteren, J C, Kockx, M M, Schwartz, S M and Koteliansky, V E. Differentiation, dedifferentiation, and apoptosis of smooth muscle cells during the development of the human ductus arteriosus. *Arterioscler Thromb Vasc Biol.* 1997; 17:1003–1009.

42. Cho, A and Langille, B L. Arterial Smooth-Muscle Cell Turnover During the Postnatal-Period In Lambs. *Faseb Journal.* 1993; 7:A 756–a 756.

43. Cho, A, Courtman, D and Langille, L. Apoptosis (programmed cell death) in arteries of the neonatal lamb. *Circ Res.* 1995; 76:168–175.

44. Cho, A, Mitchell, L, Koopmans, D and Langille, B L. Effects of changes in blood flow rate on cell death and cell proliferation in carotid arteries of immature rabbits. *Circ Res.* 1997; 81:328–337.

45. Kumar, A and Lindner, V. Remodeling with neointima formation in the mouse carotid artery after cessation of blood flow. *Arterioscler Thromb Vasc Biol.* 1997; 17:2238–2244.

46. Perlman, H, Maillard, L, Krasinski, K and Walsh, K. Evidence for the rapid onset of apoptosis in medial smooth muscle cells after balloon injury. *Circulation.* 1997; 95:981–987.

47. Pollman, M J, Hall, J L, Mann, M J, Zhang, L N and Gibbons, G H. Inhibition of neointimal cell bcl-x expression induces apoptosis and regression of vascular disease. *Nature Medicine.* 1998; 4:222–227.

48. Pollman, M J, Hall, J L and Gibbons, G H. Determinants of vascular smooth muscle cell apoptosis after balloon angioplasty injury – Influence of redox state and cell phenotype. *Circ Res.* 1999; 84:113–121.

49. Malik, N, Francis, S E, Holt, C M, Gunn, J, Thomas, G L, Shepherd, L, Chamberlain, J, Newman, C M H, Cumberland, D C and Crossman, D C. Apoptosis and cell proliferation after porcine coronary angioplasty. *Circulation.* 1998; 98:1657–1665.

50. Bochatonpiallat, M, Gabbiani, F, Redard, M, Desmouliere, A and Gabbiani, G. Apoptosis participates in cellularity regulation during rat aortic intimal thickening. *Am J Path.* 1995; 146:1059–1064.

51. Isner, J, Kearney, M, Bortman, S and Passeri, J. Apoptosis in human atherosclerosis and restenosis. *Circulation.* 1995; 91:2703–2711.

52. Bauriedel, G, Schluckebier, S, Hutter, R, Welsch, U, Kandoff, R, Lderitz, B and Prescott, M. Apoptosis in restenosis versus stable-angina atherosclerosis. *Arterioscler Thromb Vasc Biol.* 1998; 18:1132–1139.

53. LopezCandales, A, Holmes, D R, Liao, S X, Scott, M J, Wickline, S A and Thompson, R W. Decreased vascular smooth muscle cell density in medial degeneration of human abdominal aortic aneurysms. *Am J Pathol.* 1997; 150:993–1007.

54. Thompson, R W, Liao, S X and Curci, J A. Vascular smooth muscle cell apoptosis in abdominal aortic aneurysms. *Cor Art Dis.* 1997; 8:623–631.

55. Henderson, E L, Gang, Y J, Sukhova, G K, Whittemore, A D, Knox, J and Libby, P. Death of smooth muscle cells and expression of mediators of apoptosis by T lymphocytes in human abdominal aortic aneurysms. *Circulation.* 1999; 99:96–104.

56. Han, D, Haudenschild, C, Hong, M, Tinkle, B, Leon, M and Liau, G. Evidence for apoptosis in human atherosclerosis and in a rat vascular injury model. *Am J Path*. 1995; 147:267–277.

57. Geng, Y and Libby, P. Evidence for apoptosis in advanced human atheroma: colocalization with interleukin-1b converting enzyme. *Am J Path*. 1995; 147:251–266.

58. Kockx, M M. Apoptosis in the atherosclerotic plaque – Quantitative and qualitative aspects. *Arterioscler Thromb Vasc Biol*. 1998; 18:1519–1522.

59. Boyle, J, Bennett, M, Proudfoot, D, Bowyer, D and Weissberg, P. Human monocyte/macrophages induce human vascular smooth muscle cell apoptosis in culture. *J Pathol*. 1998; 184:A13 (Abstract).

60. Geng, Y, Wu, Q, Muszynski, M, Hansson, G and Libby, P. Apoptosis of vascular smooth-muscle cells induced by in vitro stimulation with interferon-gamma, tumor necrosis factor- alpha, and interleukin-1-beta. *Arterioscler Thromb Vasc Biol*. 1996; 16:19–27.

61. Hasdai, D, Sangiorgi, G, Spagnoli, L G, Simari, R D, Holmes, D R, Kwon, H M, Carlson, P J, Schwartz, R S and Lerman, A. Coronary artery apoptosis in experimental hypercholesterolemia. *Atherosclerosis*. 1999; 142:317–325.

62. Sata, M, Perlman, H R, Muruve, D A, Silver, M, Ikebe, M, Libermann, T A, Oettgen, P and Walsh, K. Fas ligand gene transfer to the vessel wall inhibits neointima formation and overrides the adenovirus-mediated T cell response. *Proc Natl Acad Sci USA*. 1998; 95:1213–1217.

63. Flynn, P, Byrne, C, Baglin, T, Weissberg, P and Bennett, M. Thrombin generation by apoptotic vascular smooth muscle cells. *Blood*. 1997; 89:4373–4384.

64. Bombeli, T, Karsan, A, Tait, J F and Harlan, J M. Apoptotic vascular endothelial cells become procoagulant. *Blood*. 1997; 89:2429–2442.

65. Mallat, Z, Benamer, H, Hugel, B, Steg, P, Freyssinet, J and Tedgui, A. Elevated plasma levels of shed membrane microparticles in patients with acute coronary syndromes. *Circulation*. 1998; 98:I–172 (Abstract).

66. Mallat, Z, Hugel, B, Ohan, J, Leseche, G, Freyssinet, J M and Tedgui, A. Shed membrane microparticles with procoagulant potential in human atherosclerotic plaques – A role for apoptosis in plaque thrombogenicity. *Circulation*. 1999; 99:348–353.

67. Schaub, F J, Han, D K, Conrad Liles, W, Adams, L D, Coats, S A, Ramachandran, R K, Seifert, R A, Schwartz, S M and Bowen-Pope, D F. Fas/FADD-mediated activation of a specific program of inflammatory gene expression in vascular smooth muscle cells. *Nat Med*. 2000; 6:790–6.

68. Ashkenazi, A and Dixit, V. Death receptors: Signalling and modulation. *Science*. 1998; 281:1305–1308.

69. Chinnaiyan, A, O'Rourke, K, Tewari, M and Dixit, V. FADD, a novel death domain-containing protein, interacts with the death domain of fas and initiates apoptosis. *Cell*. 1995; 81:505.

70. Chinnaiyan, A, Tepper, C, Seldin, M, O'Rourke, K, Kischkel, F, Hellbardt, S, Krammer, P, Peter, M and Dixit, V. FADD/mort1 is a common mediator of CD95 (Fas/Apo-1) and tumor necrosis factor receptor induced apoptosis. *J Biol Chem*. 1996; 271:4961–4965.

71. Stanger, B Z, Leder, P, Lee, T H, Kim, E and Seed, B. Rip – a Novel Protein Containing a Death Domain That Interacts With Fas/Apo-1 (Cd95) in Yeast and Causes Cell-Death. *Cell*. 1995; 81:513–523.

72. Cohen, G M. Caspases: the executioners of apoptosis. *Biochem J*. 1997; 326:1–16.

73. Muzio, M, Chinnaiyan, A, Kischkel, F, O'Rourke, K, Shevchenko, A, Ni, J, Scaffidi, C, Bretz, J, Zhang, M, Gentz, R, Mann, M, Krammer, P, Peter, M and Dixit, V. FLICE, a novel FADD-homologous ice/ced-3-like protease, is recruited to the CD95 (Fas/Apo-1) death-inducing signaling complex. *Cell*. 1996; 85:817–827.

74. Fernandes-Alnemri, T, Litwack, G and Alnemri, E. Mch2, a new member of the apoptotic ced-3/ice cysteine protease gene family. *Cancer Res*. 1995; 55:2737–2742.

75. Enari, M, Talanian, R, Wong, W and Nagata, S. Sequential activation of ICE-like and CPP32-like proteases during Fas-mediated apoptosis. *Nature*. 1996; 380:723–726.

76. Srinivasula, S, Ahmad, M, Fernandes-Alnemri, T, Litwack, G and Alnemri, E. Molecular ordering of the fas-apoptotic pathway: the fas/APO-1 protease mch-5 is a CrmA-inhibitable protease that activates multiple Ced-3/ICE-like cysteine proteases. *Proc Natl Acad Sci USA*. 1996; 93:14486–14491.

77. Muzio, M, Salvesen, G S and Dixit, V M. FLICE induced apoptosis in a cell-free system – Cleavage of caspase zymogens. *J Biol Chem*. 1997; 272:2952–2956.

78. Takahashi, A, Hirata, H, Yonehara, S, Imai, Y, Lee, K K, Moyer, R W, Turner, P C, Mesner, P W, Okazaki, T, Sawai, H, Kishi, S, Yamamoto, K, Okuma, M and Sasada, M. Affinity labeling displays the stepwise activa-

tion of ICE-related proteases by Fas, staurosporine, and CrmA-sensitive caspase-8. *Oncogene.* 1997; 14:2741–2752.

79. Dixit, V. The cell-death machine. *Curr Biol.* 1996; 6:555–562.

80. Krammer, P. The CD95 (Apo-1/Fas) receptor/ligand system-death signals and diseases. *Cell Death Differ.* 1996; 3:159–160.

81. Enari, M, Sakahira, H, Yokoyama, H, Okawa, K, Iwamatsu, A and Nagata, S. A caspase-activated DNase that degrades DNA during apoptosis and its inhibitor ICAD. *Nature.* 1998; 391:43–50.

82. Janicke, R U, Sprengart, M L, Wati, M R and Porter, A G. Caspase-3 is required for DNA fragmentation and morphological changes associated with apoptosis. *J Biol Chem.* 1998; 273:9357–9360.

83. Hirata, H, Takahashi, A, Kobayashi, S, Yonehara, S, Sawai, H, Okazaki, T, Yamamoto, K and Sasada, M. Caspases are activated in a branched protease cascade and control distinct downstream processes in Fas-induced apoptosis. *J Exp Med.* 1998; 187:587–600.

84. Scaffidi, C, Fulda, S, Srinivasan, A, Friesen, C, Li, F, Tomaselli, K J, Debatin, K M, Krammer, P H and Peter, M E. Two CD95 (APO-1/Fas) signaling pathways. *EMBO J.* 1998; 17:1675–1687.

85. Li, H L, Zhu, H, Xu, C J and Yuan, J Y. Cleavage of BID by caspase 8 mediates the mitochondrial damage in the Fas pathway of apoptosis. *Cell.* 1998; 94:491–501.

86. Shimizu, S, Narita, M and Tsujimoto, Y. Bcl-2 family proteins regulate the release of apoptogenic cytochrome c by the mitochondrial channel VDAC. *Nature.* 1999; 399:483–487.

87. Du, C, Fang, M, Li, Y, Li, L and Wang, X. Smac, a mitochondrial protein that promotes cytochome c-dependent caspase activation by eliminating IAP inhibition. *Cell.* 2000; 102:33–42.

88. Verhagen, A, Ekert, P, Pakusch, M, Silke, J, Connolly, L, Reid, G, Moritz, R, Simpson, R and Vaul, D. Identification of DIABLO, a mammalian protein that promotes apoptosis by binding to and antagonising IAP proteins. *Cell.* 2000; 102:43–53.

89. Irmler, M, Thome, M, Hahne, M, Schneider, P, Hofmann, B, Steiner, V, Bodmer, J L, Schroter, M, Burns, K, Mattmann, C, Rimoldi, D, French, L E and Tschopp, J. Inhibition of death receptor signals by cellular FLIP. *Nature.* 1997; 388:190–195.

90. Liston, P, Roy, N, Tamai, K, Lefebvre, C, Baird, S, ChertonHorvat, G, Farahani, R, McLean, M, Ikeda, J E, MacKenzie, A and Korneluk, R G. Suppression of apoptosis in mammalian cells by NAIP and a related family of IAP genes. *Nature.* 1996; 379:349–353.

91. Deveraux, Q L, Takahashi, R, Salvesen, G S and Reed, J C. X-linked IAP is a direct inhibitor of cell-death proteases. *Nature.* 1997; 388:300–304.

92. Deveraux, Q L, Roy, N, Stennicke, H R, VanArsdale, T, Zhou, Q, Srinivasula, S M, Alnemri, E S, Salvesen, G S and Reed, J C. IAPs block apoptotic events induced by caspase-8 and cytochrome c by direct inhibition of distinct caspases. *EMBO J.* 1998; 17:2215–2223.

93. Long, X L, Boluyt, M O, Hipolito, M D, Lundberg, M S, Zheng, J S, Oneill, L, Cirielli, C, Lakatta, E G and Crow, M T. p53 and the hypoxia-induced apoptosis of cultured neonatal rat cardiac myocytes. *J Clin Invest.* 1997; 99:2635–2643.

94. Long, X, Crow, M T, Sollott, S J, O'Neill, L, Menees, D S, de Lourdes Hipolito, M, Boluyt, M O, Asai, T and Lakatta, E G. Enhanced expression of p53 and apoptosis induced by blockade of the vacuolar proton ATPase in cardiomyocytes. *J Clin Invest.* 1998; 101:1453–61.

95. Yue, T L, Ma, X L, Wang, X, Romanic, A M, Liu, G L, Louden, C, Gu, J L, Kumar, S, Poste, G, Ruffolo, R R, Jr. and Feuerstein, G Z. Possible involvement of stress-activated protein kinase signaling pathway and Fas receptor expression in prevention of ischemia/reperfusion-induced cardiomyocyte apoptosis by carvedilol. *Circ Res.* 1998; 82:166–74.

96. Bialik, S, Cryns, V L, Drincic, A, Miyata, S, Wollowick, A L, Srinivasan, A and Kitsis, R N. The mitochondrial apoptotic pathway is activated by serum and glucose deprivation in cardiac myocytes. *Circ Res.* 1999; 85:403–14.

97. Jeroudi, M O, Hartley, C J and Bolli, R. Myocardial reperfusion injury: role of oxygen radicals and potential therapy with antioxidants. *Am J Cardiol.* 1994; 73:2B–7B.

98. Karwatowska-Prokopczuk, E, Nordberg, J A, Li, H L, Engler, R L and Gottlieb, R A. Effect of vacuolar proton ATPase on pHi, Ca2+, and apoptosis in neonatal cardiomyocytes during metabolic inhibition/recovery. *Circ Res.* 1998; 82:1139–44.

99. Teiger, E, Than, V D, Richard, L, Wisnewsky, C, Tea, B S, Gaboury, L, Tremblay, J, Schwartz, K and Hamet, P. Apoptosis in pressure overload-induced heart hypertrophy in the rat. *J Clin Invest.* 1996; 97:2891–2897.

100. Hamet, P, Richard, L, Dam, T, Teiger, E, Orlov, S, Gaboury, L, Gossard, F and Tremblay, J. Apoptosis in target organs of hypertension. *Hypertension.* 1995; 26:642–648.

101. Kajstura, J, Cigola, E, Malhotra, A, Li, P, Cheng, W, Meggs, L and Anversa, P. Angiotensin II induces apoptosis of adult ventricular myocytes in vitro. *J Mol Cell Cardiol.* 1997; 29:859–870.

102. Geng, Y J, Henderson, L E, Levesque, E B, Muszynski, M and Libby, P. Fas is expressed in human atherosclerotic intima and promotes apoptosis of cytokine-primed human vascular smooth muscle cells. *Arterioscler Thromb Vasc Biol.* 1997; 17:2200–2208.

103. Baker, A H, Zaltsman, A B, George, S J and Newby, A C. Divergent effects of tissue inhibitor of metalloproteinase-1, -2, or -3 overexpression on rat vascular smooth muscle cell invasion, proliferation, and death in vitro – TIMP-3 promotes apoptosis. *J Clin Invest.* 1998; 101:1478–1487.

104. Bennett, M, Macdonald, K, Chan, S-W, Simari, R, Luzio, J and Weissberg, P. Cell surface trafficking of Fas: a rapid mechanism of p53-mediated apoptosis. *Science.* 1998; 282:290–293.

105. Fukuo, K, Nakahashi, T, Nomura, S, Hata, S, Suhara, T, Shimizu, M, Tamatani, M, Morimoto, S, Kitamura, Y and Ogihara, T. Possible participation of Fas-mediated apoptosis in the mechanism of atherosclerosis. *Gerontology.* 1997; 43:35–42.

106. Hoffmann, G, Kenn, S, Wirleitner, B, Deetjen, C, Frede, S, Smolny, M, Rieder, J, Fuchs, D, BaierBitterlich, G and Schobersberger, W. Neopterin induces nitric oxide-dependent apoptosis in rat vascular smooth muscle cells. *Immunobiology.* 1998; 199:63–73.

107. Fukuo, K, Hata, S, Suhara, T, Nakahashi, T, Shinto, Y, Tsujimoto, Y, Morimoto, S and Ogihara, T. Nitric oxide induces up regulation of fas and apoptosis in vascular smooth muscle. *Hypertension.* 1996; 27:823–826.

108. Boyle, J J, Bowyer, D E, Weissberg, P L and Bennett, M R. Interactions between TNF alpha and nitric oxide in human macrophage-induced vascular smooth muscle cell apoptosis. *J Pathol.* 1999; 187:A12.

109. Pollman, M J, Yamada, T, Horiuchi, M and Gibbons, G H. Vasoactive substances regulate vascular smooth-muscle cell apoptosis – countervailing influences of Nitric-Oxide and Angiotensin-Ii. *Circ Res.* 1996; 79:748–756.

110. Zhao, Z H, Francis, C E, Welch, G, Loscalzo, J and Ravid, K. Reduced glutathione prevents nitric oxide-induced apoptosis in vascular smooth muscle cells. *Biochim et Biophys Acta.* 1997; 1359:143–152.

111. Li, P F, Dietz, R and vonHarsdorf, R. Differential effect of hydrogen peroxide and superoxide anion on apoptosis and proliferation of vascular smooth muscle cells. *Circulation.* 1997; 96:3602–3609.

112. Nishio, E and Watanabe, Y. NO induced apoptosis accompanying the change of oncoprotein expression and the activation of CPP32 protease. *Life Sci.* 1997; 62:239–245.

113. Iwashina, M, Shichiri, M, Marumo, F and Hirata, Y. Transfection of inducible nitric oxide synthase gene causes apoptosis in vascular smooth muscle cells. *Circulation.* 1998; 98:1212–1218.

114. Wang, H and Keiser, J A. Molecular characterization of rabbit CPP32 and its function in vascular smooth muscle cell apoptosis. *Am J Physiol.* 1998; 43:H1132–H1140.

115. Bennett, M R, Evan, G I and Schwartz, S M. Apoptosis of human vascular smooth muscle cells derived from normal vessels and coronary atherosclerotic plaques. *J Clin Invest.* 1995; 95:2266–2274.

116. Bochaton-Piallat, M-L, Ropraz, P, Gabbiani, F and Gabbiani, G. Phenotypic heterogeneity of rat aortic smooth muscle cell clones. *Arterioscler Thromb Vasc Biol.* 1996; 16:815–820.

117. Chan, S, Weissberg, P and Bennett, M. Heterogeneity of caspase regulation of human vascular smooth muscle cell apoptosis. *Heart.* 1998; 71:12 (Abstract).

118. Fox, J and Shanley, J. Antisense inhibition of basic fibroblast growth factor induces apoptosis in vascular smooth muscle cells. *J Biol Chem.* 1996; 271:12578–12584.

119. Miyamoto, T, Leconte, I, Swain, J L, Fox, J C, Jain, R K, Safabakhsh, N, Sckell, A, Chen, Y, Jiang, P, Benjamin, L, Yuan, F and Keshet, E. Autocrine FGF signaling is required for vascular smooth muscle cell survival in vitro. *J Cell Physiol.* 1998; 177:58–67.

120. Neschis, D G, Safford, S D, Hanna, A K, Fox, J C and Golden, M A. Antisense basic fibroblast growth factor gene transfer reduces early intimal thickening in a rabbit femoral artery balloon injury model. *J Vascr Surg.* 1998; 27:126–134.

121. Shaulian, E, Resnitzky, D, Shifman, O, Blandino, G, Amsterdam, A, Yayon, A and Oren, M. Induction of Mdm2 and enhancement of cell survival by bFGF. *Oncogene.* 1997; 15:2717–2725.

122. Konstadoulakis, M M, Kymionis, G D, Karagiani, M, Katergianakis, V, Doundoulakis, N, Pararas, V, Koutselinis, A, Sehas, M and Peveretos, P. Evidence of apoptosis in human carotid atheroma. *J Vasc Surg.* 1998; 27:733–739.

123. Kockx, M M, DeMeyer, G Y, Buyssens, N, Knaapen, M W M, Bult, H and Herman, A G. Cell composition, replication, and apoptosis in athero-

sclerotic plaques after 6 months of cholesterol withdrawal. *Circ Res.* 1998; 83:378–387.

124. Igase, M, Okura, T, Kitami, Y and Hiwada, K. Apoptosis and Bcl-xs in the intimal thickening of balloon-injured carotid arteries. *Clin Sci.* 1999; 96:605–612.

125. Erl, W, Hansson, G, de Martin, R, Draude, G, Weber, K and Weber, C. Nuclear factor-kb regulates induction of apoptosis and inhibitor of apoptosis protein-1 expression in vascular smooth muscle cells. *Circ Res.* 1999; 84:668–677.

126. Krajewska, M, Wang, H G, Krajewski, S, Zapata, J M, Shabaik, A, Gascoyne, R and Reed, J C. Immunohistochemical analysis of in vivo patterns of expression of CPP32 (Caspase-3), a cell death protease. *Cancer Res.* 1997; 57:1605–1613.

127. Goussev, A, Sharov, V G, Shimoyama, H, Tanimura, M, Lesch, M, Goldstein, S and Sabbah, H N. Effects of ACE inhibition on cardiomyocyte apoptosis in dogs with heart failure. *Am J Physiol.* 1998; 275:H626–31.

128. Yaoita, H, Ogawa, K, Maehara, K and Maruyama, Y. Attenuation of ischemia/reperfusion injury in rats by a caspase inhibitor. *Circulation.* 1998; 97:276–281.

129. Torre-Amione, G, Kapadia, S, Lee, J, Bies, R, Lebovitz, R and Mann, D. Expressson and functional significance of tumor necrosis factor receptors in human myocardium. *Circulation.* 1995; 92:1487–1493.

130. Kubota, T, McTiernan, C, Frye, C, Slawson, S, Lemster, B, Koretsky, A, Demetris, A and Feldman, A. Dilated cardiomyopathy in transgenic mice with cardiac-specific overexpression of tumor necrosis factor-a. *Circ Res.* 1997; 81:627–635.

131. Sheng, Z, Knowlton, K, Chen, J, Hoshijima, M, Brown, J and Chien, K. Cardiotrophin 1 (CT-1) inhibition of cardiac myocyte apoptosis via a mitogen-activated protein kinase-dependent pathway: Divergence from downstream CT-1 signals for myocardial cell hypertrophy. *J Biol Chem.* 1997; 272:

132. Wang, L, Ma, W Q, Markovich, R, Chen, J W and Wang, P H. Regulation of cardiomyocyte apoptotic signaling by insulin-like growth factor I. *Circ Res.* 1998; 83:516–522.

133. Zhao, Y Y, Sawyer, D R, Baliga, R R, Opel, D J, Han, X, Marchionni, M A and Kelly, R A. Neuregulins promote survival and growth of cardiac myocytes. Persistence of ErbB2 and ErbB4 expression in neonatal and adult ventricular myocytes. *J Biol Chem.* 1998; 273:10261–10269.

134. Leri, A, Liu, Y, Claudio, P P, Kajstura, J, Wang, X W, Wang, S L, Kang, P, Malhotra, A and Anversa, P. Insulin-like growth factor-1 induces Mdm2 and down-regulates p53, attenuating the myocyte renin-angiotensin system and stretch-mediated apoptosis. *American Journal of Pathology.* 1999; 154:567–580.

135. Hirota, H, Chen, J, Betz, U A, Rajewsky, K, Gu, Y, Ross, J, Jr., Muller, W and Chien, K R. Loss of a gp130 cardiac muscle cell survival pathway is a critical event in the onset of heart failure during biomechanical stress. *Cell.* 1999; 97:189–198.

136. Yue, T L, Wang, C, Gu, J L, Ma, X L, Kumar, S, Lee, J C, Feuerstein, G Z, Thomas, H, Maleeff, B and Ohlstein, E H. Inhibition of extracellular signal-regulated kinase enhances Ischemia/Reoxygenation-induced apoptosis in cultured cardiac myocytes and exaggerates reperfusion injury in isolated perfused heart. *Circ Res.* 2000; 86:692–699.

137. Wang, Y, Huang, S, Sah, V P, Ross, J, Jr., Brown, J H, Han, J and Chien, K R. Cardiac muscle cell hypertrophy and apoptosis induced by distinct members of the p38 mitogen-activated protein kinase family. *J Biol Chem.* 1998; 273:2161–2168.

138. Zechner, D, Craig, R, Hanford, D S, McDonough, P M, Sabbadini, R A and Glembotski, C C. MKK6 activates myocardial cell NF-kappaB and inhibits apoptosis in a p38 mitogen-activated protein kinase-dependent manner. *J Biol Chem.* 1998; 273:8232–8239.

139. Susin, S A, Lorenzo, H, Zamzami, N, Marzo, I, Snow, B, Brothers, G, Mangion, J, Jacotet, E, Constantini, P, Loeffler, M, Larochette, N, Goodlett, D, Aebersold, R, Siderovski, D, Penninger, J and Kroemer, G. Molecular characterization of mitochondrial apoptosis-inducing factor. *Nature.* 1999; 397:441–446.

140. Felzen, B, Shilkrut, M, Less, H, Sarapov, I, Maor, G, Coleman, R, Robinson, R B, Berke, G and Binah, O. Fas (CD95/Apo-1)-mediated damage to ventricular myocytes induced by cytotoxic T lymphocytes from perforin-deficient mice: a major role for inositol 1,4,5-trisphosphate. *Circ Res.* 1998; 82:438–450.

CHAPTER 7

The Limits of Exercise for the Heart — a New Hypothesis

T D (Tim) Noakes

In the early 1920s, Archibald Vivian Hill, Nobel Laureate in Medicine and former Professor of Physiology at the University College, London, together with his colleagues C.N.H. Long and Hartley Lupton, developed the concept that the heart has a limiting maximum capacity, which is reached during maximal all-out exercise lasting between 3–7 minutes. This limiting cardiac output determines the peak exercise capacity by establishing the peak rate of oxygen delivery to the exercising muscles. This theory has been the single most enduring feature of the exercise sciences for the past 75 years.

But perhaps the more remarkable realisation is that, on the basis of a minimum of data and a surfeit of interpretation, Hill and his colleagues developed a model of cardiac function during exercise that included both the exceptionally clever and the profoundly incorrect. Worse, that part of the theory which is probably the most incorrect, is the one that has survived. Their more revolutionary concept has been forgotten. These ideas, dormant for 75 years, provide a completely novel understanding of how the heart's function may be limited during maximum exercise, specifically to ensure that myocardial ischaemia cannot develop, at least in health. Hill's concept can be extended to provide a novel understanding of the physiological basis of fatigue during exercise under a variety of conditions.

THE ORIGINAL STUDIES OF A.V. HILL

The legacy of Hill and his colleagues arises from a series of experiments undertaken between 1923 and 1925, shortly after Hill had assumed the Chair of Physiology at the University College, London. In these experiments Hill, and his associates, Hartley Lupton and Henry Long, repeatedly measured the oxygen consumption of subjects who ran for 3 minutes at different speeds on a circular grass track, 85 m in circumference; the use of laboratory treadmills was still in its infancy. On the basis of these experiments, the authors concluded: "Considering the case of running there is clearly some critical speed for each individual above which, the maximum oxygen intake is inadequate, lactic acid accumulating, a continuously increasing oxygen debt being incurred, fatigue and exhaustion setting in".[1]   Hill[2] further concluded that: "The oxygen intake may attain its maximum and remain constant merely because it cannot go any higher owing to the limitations of the circulatory and respiratory systems."

The Hill hypothesis. Hence the enduring hypothesis[3-7] proposed by Hill and his colleagues was that, during exercise, there is a workrate, the whole body oxygen demand of which exceeds the heart's capacity to supply. As a result, oxygen consumption (VO_2) "plateaus" at that workrate, defining the maximum whole body oxygen consumption (VO_2 max). Increasing the workrate beyond the VO_2 max requires an increasing "anaerobic" metabolism. Ultimately exercise terminates when the metabolic by-products of anaerobic metabolism, especially lactate and H^+, interfere with both energy production and muscle contractile activity, terminating exercise. Or in the words of a contemporary: "the valuable glycogen inside the muscle-fibres is turned into poisonous lactic acid, the muscles become stiff and tired, dwindle in power, and finally refuse to function until the lactic acid has been turned back into glycogen during the recuperative process of rest".[8] Hence this model predicts that rising muscle and blood lactate concentrations and falling pH, act to terminate or "constrain" further exercise.

Furthermore, Hill and his colleagues believed there to be an absolute and universal VO_2 max of 4L.min^{-1} that occurred at a running speed of 13 km.hr^{-1} [9] (Figure 7-1). This inter-

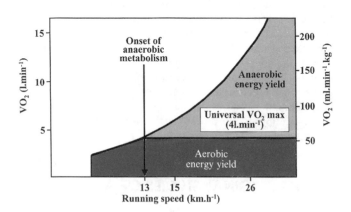

Redrawn from A.V. Hill and H. Lupton
Quarterly Journal of Medicine 16; 157, 1923.

Figure 7-1. Hill and his colleagues believed that oxygen consumption (VO₂) rose as an exponential function of running speed and comprised aerobic and anaerobic components. The aerobic component peaked at 13 km.h⁻¹ which constituted the "universal" maximum oxygen consumption (VO₂ max) of 4 L.min⁻¹. Anaerobic metabolism increased at running speeds above 13 km.h⁻¹ and was the predominant energy source for all running speeds above about 18 km.h⁻¹.

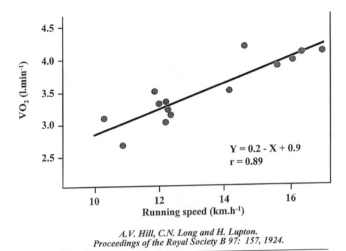

A.V. Hill, C.N. Long and H. Lupton.
Proceedings of the Royal Society B 97: 157, 1924.

Figure 7-2. In contrast to their theoretical prediction (Figure 7-1), the actual data for all experiments on A.V. Hill show that his oxygen consumption rose linearly to the highest running speed of which he was capable (17 km.h⁻¹). This anomaly between Figures 7–1 and 7–2 was not recognised in Hill's lifetime.

pretation was made even though none of their studies actually showed an unambiguously identified VO_2 "plateau".[9-12] In fact their most frequently studied subject, Hill himself, showed a progressive linear increase in VO_2 even at the highest running speed of which he was capable without rapid exhaustion (17 km.hr⁻¹) (Figure 7-2). In as much as a continuously rising VO_2 must indicate a progressive rise in cardiac output, these early findings cannot be interpreted as conclusive evidence that the cardiac output reaches a limiting maximum during peak exercise such that a further increase in workrate could not elicit any further rise in cardiac output.

In 1955, a section of Hill's work was selectively rediscovered and incorrectly interpreted as proof that there is "an upper limit to the capacity of the combined respiratory and cardiovascular system to transport oxygen to the muscles. Further increases in workload merely result in an increase in oxygen debt and a shortening of the time in which the work can be performed".[13] Hence by 1955, the work of Hill and his colleagues had been interpreted as proof that maximal exercise of short duration (3–15 minutes) is constrained by a *limiting* capacity for oxygen transport in the body due, most likely, to the attainment of a limiting, maximum cardiac output.

In fact, Hill and his colleagues did not ever show conclusively that VO_2 "plateaus" during maximum exercise,[9-12] nor did they even believe that VO_2 rises as a linear function of an increasing workrate. Rather this was described as an exponential function[14] as shown in Figure 7-1. The reasons for his error have been detailed previously.[9]

By 1955 a linear relationship between VO_2 and (submaximal) exercising workrate had been established.[15] Perhaps as a result, the first diagrams representing what Hill and his colleagues were supposed to have found, took the charac-

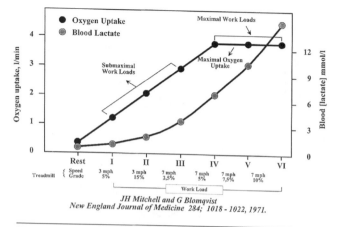

JH Mitchell and G Blomqvist
New England Journal of Medicine 284; 1018 - 1022, 1971.

Figure 7-3. On the basis of Taylor et al's[13] 1955 interpretation of Hill's work, the more modern interpretation of the "plateau phenomenon" is shown in this figure. Note that oxygen consumption increases linearly up to a "plateau" value of 4 L.min^{-1}; further increases in workrate do not cause any further increase in VO$_2$. The exponential increase in blood lactate concentrations with increasing workrate has been interpreted to indicate the onset of "anaerobic" metabolism even during submaximal exercise. This contrasts with Hill's original teaching that "anaerobic" metabolism began only after the VO$_2$ max had been reached (Figure 7-1).

teristics of that shown in Figure 7-3.[16] Here VO$_2$ rises linearly up to a clearly defined "plateau" (contrast to Figure 7-1). Note that the VO$_2$ max in this 1972 diagram is 4L.min^{-1}, perhaps revealing the subliminal influence of the universal 4L.min^{-1} VO$_2$ max concept formulated nearly 50 years earlier by Hill and his colleagues.

Role of the heart. But this 1955 re-interpretation of work completed 30 years earlier, ignored two of the core tennants of Hill's evolving (Cardiovascular/Anaerobic) model of exercise physiology. The first was his realisation that if the rate of oxygen delivery to skeletal muscle does indeed reach a maximum that can be sustained for some variable time – the "plateau" shown in Figure 7-3 – then this must result from some form of cardiac failure that prevents any further rise in cardiac output during the "anaerobic" exercise that occurs at workrates requiring more than the VO$_2$ max. Thus he proposed that: "The enormous output of the heart of an able-bodied man, maintained for considerable periods during vigorous exercise, requires a large contemporary supply of oxygen to meet the demands for energy. When the oxygen supply becomes inadequate, it is probable that the heart rapidly begins to diminish its output, so avoiding exhaustion."[17] This interpretation was not confined exclusively to the hallowed lecture halls of the University College, London but crossed the North Atlantic to be included in the writings of Arlie Bock and David Dill co-founders of the Harvard Fatigue Laboratory in Cambridge, Massachusetts:[18] "The blood supply to the heart, in many men, may be the weak link in the chain of circulatory adjustments during muscular exercise, and as the intensity of muscular exertion increases, a point is probably reached in most individuals at which the supply of oxygen to the heart falls short of its demands, and the continued performance of work becomes difficult or impossible."[18] As a result: "The heart, as a rule, reaches the limit of its powers earlier than the skeletal muscles, and determines a man's capability for exertion."[18]

Perhaps the reason why this interpretation has been ignored is because most now accept the converse; that is, that cardiac fatigue or failure does not develop during maximum exercise,[19] even at extreme altitude under conditions of profound hypoxia.[20,21] But none appear willing to have asked the question: If not, why not?

Plateau phenomenon. For logic demands that if cardiac output and oxygen consumption reach maximum values at the VO_2 plateau, then so too must muscle blood flow and total peripheral resistance. In other words, if the "plateau phenomenon" is real, a mechanism must exist that allows the active skeletal muscles to increase their work output (stage V and VI in Figure 7-3) without any further alteration in central or peripheral circulation. For any such alteration, for example, either a rise or fall in total peripheral resistance, will increase myocardial oxygen demand by increasing either the cardiac pre- or afterload. But, by definition, myocardial oxygen consumption cannot increase when the exercising workrate rises beyond the "VO_2 max". Hence any alteration in central or peripheral circulation during exercise at intensities beyond the VO_2 max "plateau" must cause an imbalance between myocardial oxygen demand and oxygen supply, inducing myocardial ischaemia, according to the very definition of the "plateau" phenomenon which requires that the workrate should increase without any further rise in myocardial or skeletal muscle VO_2.

Interestingly, one of the original diagrams depicting the expected cardiovascular changes during exercise at workrates up to, and beyond those eliciting the "plateau phenomenon", included information on changes in heart rate, stroke volume and cardiac output, only up to the workrate eliciting the VO_2 max. Figure 7-4 has been redrawn from the classic paper of Mitchell and Blomqvist.[16] It shows the clearly defined plateau in oxygen consumption in this subject when the work rate exceeds stage 4 of the test corresponding to Hill's universal VO_2 max of 4 L.min^{-1}. During the submaximal portions of the exercise test (stages 1 to 4), increases in work rate cause essentially linear increases in cardiac output, stroke volume, and heart rate. When the VO_2 plateaus at stages 5 and 6, these variables must also level off, hence proving that the pumping capacity of the heart limits the VO_2 max.

Surprisingly, Mitchell and Blomqvist[16] did not provide data for these cardiovascular measures once the VO_2 max has been reached (Figure 7-4). A more recent review by Mitchell of that paper[22] also lacks such data. Perhaps as serious scientists they were correctly reluctant to speculate on what they had not measured. Or perhaps they realized the

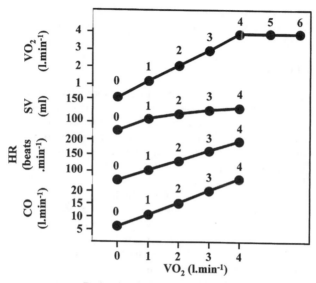

Redrawn from J.H. Mitchell and G. Blomqvist.
New England Journal of Medicine 284: 1018 - 1022, 1971.

Figure 7-4. An original diagram depicting the plateau phenomenon in VO₂ (top panel; also Figure 7-3), included predicted changes in stroke volume (SV), heart rate (HR) and cardiac output (CO). Note that although the plateau in VO₂ at 4 L.min⁻¹ was identified with no further increases during workrate stages 5 and 6, no data are included for predicted changes in SV, HR, and CO during work stages 5 and 6, "beyond the plateau phenomenon". Logic suggests that, if the "plateau phenomenon" is real, then cardiac output should begin to fall shortly after the attainment of VO₂ max, as a consequence of myocardial ischaemia. A.V. Hill and others believed that myocardial ischaemia develops during maximum exercise (for details, see text).

dilemma that such a conclusion posed, especially for the heart.

For the issue that must ultimately be addressed is: What are the consequences of the cardiovascular/anaerobic model for the heart itself? Or, alternatively, if the cardiac output limits the VO_2 max, what limits the cardiac output? For the heart is also a muscle. The cardiovascular/anaerobic model predicts that (skeletal) muscle function fails when its oxygen supply is inadequate. Hence if logic is to be preserved, this failure of the heart's pumping capacity, in Rowell's words "to raise the cardiac output" at the VO_2 max,[23] must result from an inadequate (myocardial) oxygen supply. Hence coronary blood flow must plateau sometime before the cardiac output levels off at the VO_2 max. This limiting coronary blood flow induces myocardial "fatigue", causing the plateau in cardiac output and hence in the VO_2 max, leading only thereafter to skeletal muscle anaerobiosis. Thus by this logic, the coronary blood flow must be the first physiological function to show a "plateau phenomenon" during progressive exercise to exhaustion.

Proposed "governor". When Hill and his colleagues realised that myocardial ischaemia must occur if the "plateau phenomenon" is real, they proposed a genuinely novel con-

Hill's original "governor" of heart function:

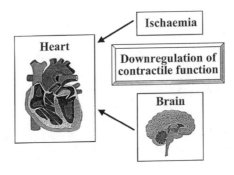

Figure 7-5. Hill proposed the need for a "governor", in either the heart or the brain, to reduce the extent to which myocardial ischaemia would develop during maximum exercise. This governor would act directly on the heart itself, to reduce its contractile state, thereby reducing myocardial oxygen demand and protecting the heart from damage during a developing "oxygen debt".

cept that has escaped the critical attention of subsequent generations of cardiologists and exercise physiologists: "It would seem probable that the heart is able to regulate its output, to some extent, in accordance with the degree of saturation of the arterial blood, either of that which reaches it through the coronary vessels or by some reflex in other organs produced by a deficient oxygen supply. From the point of view of a well co-ordinated mechanism, some such arrangement is imminently desirable; it would clearly be useless for the heart to make an excessive effort if by so doing it nearly produced a far lower degree of saturation of the arterial blood; and we suggest that, in the body (either in the heart muscle itself or in the nervous system), there is some mechanism which causes a slowing of the circulation as soon as a serious degree of unsaturation occurs, and vice versa. This mechanism would tend to act as a "governor", maintaining a high degree of saturation of blood".[17]

Thus, the physiological model of cardiovascular function during maximum exercise developed by A.V. Hill and his colleagues, requires that a limiting maximum cardiac output is reached sometime before the onset of fatigue and the termination of exercise. This causes a plateau in blood flow to the exercising muscles inducing skeletal muscle anaerobiosis. Such anaerobiosis then causes metabolic changes in the exercising muscles which lead to the rapid termination of exercise.

Myocardial ischaemia vs skeletal muscle anaerobiosis.
But, with respect to maximal cardiac function, the far more interesting point is that the plateau in cardiac output necessary to induce skeletal muscle anaerobiosis, must cause myocardial ischaemia to develop *before* skeletal muscle anaerobiosis. Hill and his colleagues as well as their proteges at the Harvard Fatigue Laboratory, David Dill and Arlie Bock, did indeed teach that cardiac fatigue or failure must develop during maximum exercise at workrates be-

yond the VO_2 max. But the novel insight of Hill and his colleagues was their proposal that some controlling mechanism – a "governor" – must exist in either the heart or the brain to limit the extent of this myocardial ischaemia (Figure 7-5).

In contrast, the major contribution for which Hill and his colleagues have been remembered is to the effect that "there is an upper limit to the capacity of the combined respiratory and cardiovascular system to transport oxygen to the muscle. Further increases in workload beyond this point merely result in an increase in oxygen debt and a shortening of the time in which the work can be performed.".[13]

The consequence of this interpretation has been that exercise physiologists have, for the past 75 years, favoured the belief that oxygen transport and its use exclusively determine maximum exercise capacity in humans and other mammals and any alteration thereof, whether due to disease, training, or other interventions.[3,13,16,24-26] This interpretation has recently been reaffirmed.[4-7] Indeed, for the past 50 years the focus of argument has not been to test the fundamental veracity of this hypothesis. Rather the debate has centered on the factors that determine the oxygen limitation this is supposed to occur at the VO_2 "plateau" – either the inability of the heart to increase oxygen delivery to the muscles[27] or a limiting capacity for oxygen uptake by the maximally exercising skeletal muscles.[28]

But not only did Hill and his colleagues fail to provide the experimental evidence underpinning any hypothesis that an oxygen limitation develops during exercise causing fatigue[9-12] but they understood the implications, at least for the heart, of this model. What is more, they proposed a unique controller, a governor, that would limit the extent to which myocardial ischaemia would develop, once the VO_2 "plateau" had been reached.

CHALLENGES POSED BY THIS INTERPRETATION OF THE WORK OF HILL

A number of important intellectual challenges arise from this interpretation of what Hill and his colleagues actually believed. The first is whether or not there is any evidence that cardiac output reaches a "plateau" or maximum value during intensive exercise, prior to the onset of fatigue, as predicted in Figure 7-4. This is an essential component of the traditional model.[1-7,13,14,16-18] Yet, to my knowledge, no study has yet actively evaluated this prediction of the model, which is surprising.

A number of studies have measured changes in cardiac output with increasing workrate up to those that elicit the VO_2 max.[29-34] These show that cardiac output rises linearly with increasing workrate and none suggest any evidence for the plateau in cardiac output predicted by the original model of A.V. Hill and his colleagues (Figure 7-4). However, no study has looked specifically for a plateau in cardiac output that might occur, for example, in the last few minutes of exercise of progressively increasing intensity to exhaustion. Perhaps the really interesting question is why none have yet actively searched for the presence or absence of this phenomenon, given the centrality of this postulate to the Hill model.

The second intellectual challenge is to establish whether or not there is any published evidence suggesting the presence of either a cardiac or neural "governor". I propose that this evidence can be found in the phenomenon of the "lactate paradox" that develops in healthy humans during maximum exercise at increasing altitude but also during maximum exercise at sea level in patients with various chronic diseases of the heart or lungs.[9,10] Especially the "lactate paradox" at altitude provides the unambiguous test (a) of which organ, either heart or skeletal muscle, is at greatest risk for developing anaerobiosis or ischaemia during maximum exercise and (b) for the possible existence of a cardiac "governor".

For if, according to Hill's original model, myocardial ischaemia develops as the necessary precursor for skeletal muscle anaerobiosis during maximum exercise, then maximum exercise at altitude should identify this response even more readily than exercise at sea level. Three findings from a series of studies of cardiorespiratory and metabolic responses during maximal exercise at extreme altitude would appear to provide the definitive answer to these speculations.

Maximal exercise at extreme altitudes. Thus it has been found that peak muscle and blood lactate concentrations *fall* at increasing altitude[35-37] such that "above an altitude of 7500 m, no blood lactate is predicted even for maximal exercise. If this extrapolation held good, a well-acclimatized climber who reached the summit of Mount Everest without supplementary oxygen would have no blood lactate. This is a paradox indeed, because such a climber is apparently more hypoxic during maximal exercise than is any other known situation".[36] This phenomenon is paradoxical because blood and muscle lactate concentrations should, according to the traditional Cardiovascular/Anaerobic Model of Exercise Physiology,[12] increase under the conditions of increasing hypoxia or anaerobiosis that would be expected during maximum exercise at increasing altitude when arterial PO_2 is substantially reduced.

The most obvious explanation for the "lactate paradox" is simply the very low workrates achieved at extreme altitude. Skeletal muscle lactate production is most clearly related to the external workrate[38] so that any reduction in work rate would be expected to produce lower muscle and blood lactate concentrations. Nevertheless the lactate paradox at altitude must indicate (a) that skeletal muscle anaerobiosis is not present and (b) that something other than skeletal muscle hypoxia or anaerobiosis "constrains" the work output of the skeletal muscles at extreme altitude. But as the traditional model also requires that lactate or other metabolic by-products of "anaerobic" metabolism be the "constrainer" that limits maximal exercise, so that old model is quite unable to explain this additional paradox, which is therefore conveniently ignored.[5-7] Yet something other than elevated blood lactate concentrations or tissue hypoxia act to "constrain" maximum exercise at increasing altitude. Could this be the elusive governor proposed by Hill?

The second crucial finding is that, with acclimatisation, the maximum cardiac output *falls* during maximum exercise at altitude.[39] This is the opposite of the expected result.

Figure 7-6 shows that a reduction in the arterial PO_2 will have 2 effects on oxygen transport during exercise. The first has been the more readily grasped by exercise physiologists – a reduced capacity for oxygen delivery to the exercising skeletal muscles. Hence it has been assumed that the principal effect of a reduced arterial PO_2 will be to increase *skeletal muscle* anaerobiosis/hypoxia during exercise.[40]

But this interpretation has ignored the second obvious effect which is a simultaneous reduction in the capacity for oxygen transport to the heart itself (Figure 7-6). Hence when the arterial PO_2 is reduced, there is also an increased probability that myocardial anaerobiosis, hypoxia or ischemia may also develop.

As a result, the model of maximum exercise at altitude provides the test of whether it is the heart or skeletal muscles that is protected during exercise in an hypoxic environment. Thus if the traditional (Cardiovascular/Anaerobic) model is correct, then the oxygen demands of skeletal muscles will

Does the oxygen supply to the exercising muscles or to the heart limit exercise at altitude?

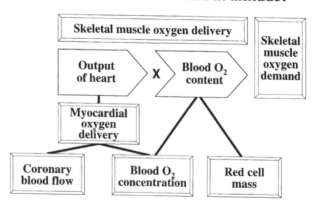

Figure 7-6. During ascent to increasing altitude, the arterial oxygen tension falls. Exercise physiologists have consistently assumed that the crucial effect of this would be to reduce the potential for oxygen delivery to the exercising muscles. An equally relevant effect is also to reduce myocardial oxygen delivery. If myocardial ischaemia is likely to develop during maximum exercise, then maximum exercise at altitude will increase the probability that this will happen unless alternate control mechanisms exist to terminate exercise before myocardial ischaemia develops.

Does the oxygen supply to the exercising muscles or to the heart limit exercise at altitude?

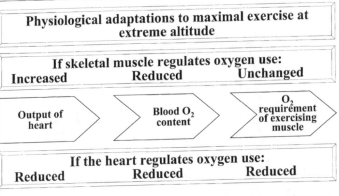

Figure 7-7. Maximum exercise at extreme altitude offers the opportunity to determine whether or not oxygen delivery to the exercising skeletal muscles drives cardiovascular function during such exercise. This would be the case if the cardiac output rises as the arterial oxygen tension falls (in order to maximise oxygen delivery to the exercising muscles). In contrast, if oxygen delivery to the heart determines the maximum (allowed) cardiac output during exercise, then the cardiac output during maximum exercise will fall at increasing altitude, as the arterial oxygen tension and, hence, maximum myocardial oxygen delivery falls.

take primacy during maximum exercise under conditions of hypoxia. As a result, cardiac output must always be the same or greater during maximum exercise at increasing altitude with progressively lower arterial PO_2 (Figure 7-7).

In contrast, if some other mechanism exists, for example if it is a limiting myocardial oxygen delivery that "constrains" myocardial function according to the proposal of Hill and his colleagues, then maximum cardiac output will fall as the arterial PO_2 is reduced at increasing altitude (Figure 7-7).

Hence the finding that the maximum cardiac output falls with increasing altitude[39] establishes that, when the arterial PO_2 is reduced, the skeletal muscles are unable to maximize their potential oxygen supply by forcing the heart to achieve its maximum (sea level) cardiac output (Figure 7-8). Rather the progressively lower maximum cardiac outputs achieved during maximum exercise at increasing altitude suggest that whatever "constrains" skeletal muscle activity at altitude, also "constrains" cardiac function, probably as a direct consequence.

The lower maximal cardiac outputs at altitude are also not the result of a myocardial ischaemia that could develop during maximum exercise at altitude.[20,21] For example, from their study showing that left ventricular systolic function measured either as the ejection fraction or as the ratio of the peak left ventricular systolic pressure to the end systolic volume, was the same during peak exercise and at altitude (7620 m), Suarez et al.[21] concluded that: "Left ventricular systolic function is not a limiting factor in compromising the exercise capacity of normal humans on ascent to high altitude, even to the peak of Mount Everest".

Does the oxygen supply to the exercising muscles or to the heart limit exercise at altitude?

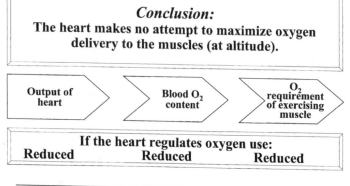

Figure 7-8. The finding that the maximum cardiac output falls with progressive reductions in arterial oxygen tension at increasing altitude, proves that oxygen delivery to organs other than skeletal muscle determines the maximum oxygen consumption and peak workrate achieved during exercise (at altitude).

Hence the conclusions from these studies are that:

Maximum exercise at extreme altitude is terminated before anaerobiosis develops in either heart or skeletal muscle.

The heart makes no attempt to increase cardiac output and therefore maximize O_2 delivery to skeletal muscle during maximum exercise at extreme altitude.

Hence something other than tissue hypoxia and the by-products of "anaerobic" metabolism in the exercising muscles "constrains" maximum exercise at extreme altitude.

What prevents muscle anaerobiosis? Hence the third intellectual challenge posed by this novel interpretation is: What acts to "constrain" both cardiac and skeletal muscle function at extreme altitude such that neither organ becomes anaerobic, hypoxic or ischaemic during maximum exercise under those extreme conditions? The allied question is whether the same "constrainer" also acts during maximum exercise at sea level.

The study of Kayser et al[41] suggests, in my view, the most reasonable solution. They showed that skeletal muscle electromyographic (EMG) activity was lower at exhaustion during maximum exercise at moderate altitude compared to sea level. Furthermore, when subjects inhaled 100% oxygen during maximum exercise at altitude, the peak exercise workrate and muscle EMG activity increased but still did not reach sea level values. This suggests that the variable constraining skeletal muscle recruitment at altitude responds to alterations in the oxygen tension either of the inhaled air or, as a result, of one or more of the tissues involved in the exercise response.

The findings of these studies can best be explained by the mechanisms proposed in Figure 7-9.

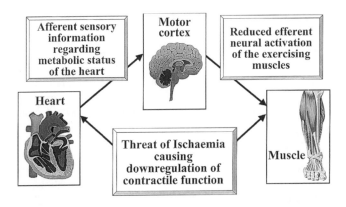

Figure 7-9. *A postulated model in which governors in the brain and the active muscles act to ensure that neither cardiac nor skeletal muscle anaerobiosis develops during maximum exercise. Postulated receptors in the heart anticipating perhaps the onset of myocardial ischaemia, act to reduce the central, neural recruitment of the exercising muscles, thereby preventing any further increase in the oxygen demands of the active skeletal muscles and, consequently, the heart.*

ROLE OF GOVERNORS

It is postulated that one "governor" exists in the brain. The function of that governor is to prevent the development of myocardial ischemia whenever a limiting myocardial oxygen delivery is approached. This might occur, for example, at the very high cardiac outputs (and coronary flows) achieved during maximum exercise, or the expectedly high and perhaps limiting coronary flows achieved under conditions of exercise at low arterial PO_2 as occurs at extreme altitude. Alternatively, at extreme altitude, an added or perhaps primary function of the governor may be to prevent hypoxia of the brain.

Afferent input to the governor may arise from oxygen-sensitive receptors in the heart, either in the myocardium or the coronary vessels, in the brain, and perhaps also in skeletal muscle. Alternatively, these receptors may monitor changes in intracellular metabolites, perhaps the phosphagens. These governors would forestall the development of hypoxia or ischemia in heart, brain or muscle by reducing the central (neural) recruitment of the exercising muscle mass whenever a limiting myocardial or cerebral oxygen delivery is approached. Reduced skeletal muscle recruitment would prevent further increases in peripheral and, as a consequence, also myocardial oxygen demands. At extreme altitude, reduced skeletal muscle recruitment would prevent arterial PO_2 from falling to levels that would induce cerebral hypoxia and unconsciousness.

The action of these neural governors would explain why the peak cardiac output is "constrained" whenever the arterial PO_2 is reduced[39,42,43] and alternatively why cardiac output increases when this constraint is removed as occurs, for example, when patients with chronic obstructive lung disease exercise whilst inhaling oxygen that increases the arterial PO_2.[44]

This model would also explain why there is as yet no evidence that (i) either cardiac output[16] or skeletal muscle blood flow[45] reach limiting "plateau" values during maximum exercise at sea level or (ii) that skeletal muscle anaerobiosis develops during maximum exercise at sea level,[43, 46-49] or (iii) that skeletal muscle or myocardial anaerobiosis develops during maximum exercise at extreme altitude.[20,21,35-37,39] Indeed the fundamentally more interesting question is why (and how) the intracellular PO_2 remains constant despite large changes in the external workrates of both skeletal muscle and heart.[43,47-49] But the action of the governor would ensure this outcome.

Figure 7-9 also suggests the existence of another governor, foreseen by Hill and his colleagues, and localised to both myocardium and skeletal muscle. This "governor" clearly established by the studies of Heyndrickx et al.[50] in cardiac muscle and by Spriet et al[51] and Hogan et al[52] in skeletal muscle, can explain why the contractile function of these organs is reduced wherever the arterial PO_2 in the blood perfusing those tissues is reduced.

RELEVANCE OF MODEL TO THE TEACHING OF MODERN CARDIOLOGY

Factors limiting maximum exercise performance. This new model proposed here predicts that the maximum cardiac output is only the indirect determinant of the maximum exercise capacity, at least at sea-level. Rather, this theory postulates that it is the maximum capacity for oxygen delivery to the myocardium that determines the mass of skeletal muscle that can be activated and hence the peak workrate that can be achieved, during maximum exercise of short duration. The actual cardiac output that will be achieved at this limiting myocardial oxygen delivery will be determined by the contractility of the heart and its efficiency with respect to oxygen use. Similarly the actual external workrate (running speed or cycling velocity, for example) that is achieved will be determined by the contractility and efficiency of the mass of active skeletal muscles that receives the limiting, maximum oxygen delivery at the maximum cardiac output.

If this model is correct, it suggests that the peak coronary blood flow is the most important physiological variable measured during maximum exercise. It is interesting, for example, that the peak workload achieved during exercise is one of the most accurate predictors of further life expectancy in persons with myocardial dysfunction, secondary to coronary artery disease. Could this be because the peak workload achieved by this group of patients is determined directly by the extent of their coronary vascular disease?

Similarly this model predicts that the subjects with the

highest VO_2 max values should have the greatest capacity for coronary blood flow as well as superior cardiac and skeletal muscle contractility and efficiency. If coronary blood flow is such an important determinant of ultimate athletic ability, the question that arises is whether this is a genetic attribute, fixed at birth, or whether heavy athletic training, early in life, might increase the coronary capacity and hence determine the ultimate athletic ability. This might explain why young swimmers, especially, train so intensively from a young age, a training for which, otherwise, there appears to be little physiological logic,

In addition, if this model is correct, it could help explain one of the most interesting phenomena in exercise physiology. Which is that during very high intensity exercise of short duration, the work output falls within the first few seconds and well before metabolite accumulation could begin to limit exercise. This model would predict that the governor can anticipate that the maintenance of such a high workrate would rapidly induce damage, either to the heart or skeletal muscle. As a result, the (subconscious) decision is taken to reduce the excessively high workrate, well before any such damage could occur.

Similarly, the traditional argument that the exercise intensity that can be sustained falls after 1–2 minutes because of an inability to generate ATP sufficiently rapidly, may simply reflect the action of the governor to reduce muscle activation specifically to ensure that myocardial ischaemia does not develop.

***Prevention of myocardial ischaemia during maximum exercise in patients with coronary artery disease**.* It is perhaps surprising that patients with coronary artery disease develop myocardial ischaemia relatively infrequently. It is surprising because their muscles are presumably healthy and hence potentially able to generate a large power output, greater than that with which their damaged hearts can cope. The presence of the governor would ensure that maintained muscle function would not risk overtaxing the capacity of the damaged heart in patients with an impaired coronary blood flow.

Causes of fatigue in skeletal muscle disorders, including McArdle's syndrome. Patients with McArdle's syndrome are unable to produce lactate during exercise because of the absence of one or more of the glycogenolytic/glycolytic enzymes. Yet the exercise tolerance of these patients is profoundly impaired. This is inexplicable according to the traditional model. Furthermore, despite a reduced capacity to generate ATP, patients with this condition do not develop skeletal muscle rigor during maximum exercise.

The "governor" theory adequately explains why a reduced muscle recruitment in response to afferent sensory information resulting from the abnormal skeletal muscle metabolism would terminate exercise before the onset of skeletal muscle rigor.

SUMMARY

In summary, this chapter provides circumstantial evidence for the existence of the "governors" proposed by A.V. Hill and his colleagues. Such governors act to "constrain" exercise via central, neural mechanisms in order to prevent the development of myocardial ischaemia during those forms of exercise that elicit a maximum cardiac output. In contrast, the paradoxically low muscle and blood lactate concentrations together with an absence of acidosis, during maximal exercise at extreme altitude or during exhausting exercise in patients with chronic cardiorespiratory diseases, indicates that the traditional Hill (Cardiovascular/Anaerobic) model cannot explain what constrains exercise under these conditions. Rather it is likely that the same "governor" must be active, perhaps responding also to a reduced PO_2 in the cerebral circulation.

Thus, perhaps the most remarkable feature of the enduring 75-year influence that A.V. Hill and his colleagues have exerted on cardiology and exercise physiology,[3-7,9-13,16] has been their immortalisation for that which they neither taught nor believed and which may be incorrect.[9-12] But their truly innovative ideas were that (a) it is the heart, not skeletal muscle, that is at greatest risk of anaerobiosis or ischemia during maximal exercise at sea level so that (b) a governor must exist to limit (their model) or prevent (the model presented here Figure 7-9) myocardial ischemia during maximum exercise.[9-12]

It is a theory ripe for investigation.

ACKNOWLEDGEMENTS

The author's research is funded by the dedicated financial support of the University of Cape Town, the Medical Research Council of South Africa, Discovery Health, the Foundation for Research and Development, the Founding Donors of the Sports Science Institute of South Africa, Bromor Foods, and a variety of nutritional and pharmaceutical companies.

REFERENCES

1.   Hill, A. V., C.N.H. Long and H. Lupton (1924). Muscular exercise, lactic acid, and the supply and utilization of oxygen: parts IV-VI. Proc. Roy. Soc. B. 97, 84–138.

2.   Hill, A.V. (1925). Muscular Activity. London: Bailliere, Tindall and Cox, pp. 1–115.

3.   Bassett, D.R. and E.T. Howley (1997). Maximal oxygen uptake: "classical" versus "contemporary" viewpoints. Med. Sci. Sports Exerc. 29, 591–603.

4. Dempsey, J.A. and P.D. Wagner (1999). Exercise-induced arterial hypoxemia. J. Appl. Physiol. 87, 1997–2005.

5. Bassett. D.R. and E.T. Howley (2000). Limiting factors for maximum oxygen uptake and determinants of endurance performance. Med. Sci. Sports Exerc. 32, 70–84.

6. Bergh, U., B. Ekblom, and P-O. Astrand (2000). Maximal oxygen uptake "classical" versus "contemporary" viewpoints. Med. Sci. Sports Exerc. 32(1), 85–88/

7. Wagner, P.D. (2000). New ideas on limitations to VO_2 max. Exerc. Sport Sci. Rev. 28, 10–14.

8. Webster, F.A.M. (1948). The science of athletics. Nicholas Kaye, London.

9. Noakes, T.D. (1998). Maximal oxygen uptake: "classic" versus "contemporary" viewpoints: a rebuttal. Med. Sci. Sports Exerc. 30, 1381–1398.

10. Noakes, T.D. (1997). Challenging beliefs: ex Africa semper aliquid novi. Med. Sci. Sports Exerc. 29, 571–590.

11. Noakes, T.D. (1988). Implications of exercise testing for prediction of athletic performance: a contemporary perspective. Med. Sci. Sports Exerc. 20, 319–330.

12. Noakes, T.D. (2000). Physiological methods to understand exercise fatigue and the adaptations that predict or enhance athletic performance. Scand. J. Med. Sci. Sports 10, 123–145.

13. Taylor, H.L., E. Buskirk, and A. Henschel (1955). Maximal oxygen intake as an objective measure of cardio-respiratory performance. J. Appl. Physiol. 8, 73–80.

14. Hill, A. V. and H. Lupton (1923). Muscular exercise, lactic acid, and the supply and utilization of oxygen. Q. J. Med. 16, 135–171.

15. Astrand, P.O. (1952). Experimental studies of physical working capacity in relation to sex and age. Ejnar Munksgaard, Copenhagen, pp. 1–171.

16. Mitchell, J.H. and G. Blomqvist (1971). Maximal oxygen uptake. New Engl. J. Med. 284, 1018–1022.

17. Hill, A.V., C.N.H. Long, and H. Lupton (1924). Muscular exercise, lactic acid, and the supply and utilization of oxygen: parts I-III. Proc. Royal Soc. Bri. 97, 438–475.

18. Bainbridge, F.A. (1931). The physiology of muscular exercise. Third edition; Bock AV, Dill DB (eds). Longmans, Green and Co., London, pp. 1–272.

19. Raskoff, W.J., S. Goldman, and K. Cohn (1976). The "Athletic Heart". Prevalence and physiological significance of left ventricular enlargement in distance runners. JAMA 236, 158–162.

20. Reeves, J.T., B.M. Groves, J.R. Sutton, P.D. Wagner, A. Cymerman, M.K. Malconian, P.B. Rock, P.M. Young, and C.S. Houston (1987). Operation Everest II: preservation of cardiac function at extreme altitude. J. Appl. Physiol. 63, 531–539.

21. Suarez, J., J.K. Alexander, and C.S. Houston (1987). Enhanced left ventricular systolic performance at high altitude during Operation Everest II. Amer. J. Cardiol. 60, 137–142.

22. Mitchell, J.H. and P.B. Raven (1994). Cardiovascular adaptation to physical activity. In: Physical Activity, Fitness and Health. C. Bouchard, R.J. Shephard and T. Stephens (Eds). Champaign, IL: Human Kinetics, pp. 286–301.

23. Rowell, L.B. (1993). Human Cardiovascular Control. New York: Oxford University Press, pp. 1–500.

24. Wasserman, K. and M.B. McIlroy (1964). Detecting the threshold of anaerobic metabolism in cardiac patients during exercise. Am. J. Cardiol. 14, 844–852.

25. Wasserman, K., W.L. Beaver, and B.J. Whipp (1990). Gas exchange theory and the lactic acidosis (anaerobic) threshold. Circulation 81 (Suppl. 2), 14–27.

26. Wasserman, K., B.J. Whipp, S.N. Koyal, and W.L. Beaver (1973). Anaerobic threshold and respiratory gas exchange during exercise. J. Appl. Physiol. 35, 236–243.

27. Wagner, P.D. (1992). Gas exchange and peripheral diffusion limitation. Med. Sci. Sports Exerc. 24(1), 54–58.

28. Jobsis, F.F. and W.N. Stainsby (1986). Oxidation of NADH during contractions of circulated mammalian skeletal muscle. Respir. Physiol. 45, 2937–2941.

29. Riley, R.L., A. Himmelstein, H.L. Motley, H.M. Weiner, and A. Cournand (1948). Studies of the pulmonary circulation at rest and during exercise in normal individuals and in patients with chronic pulmonary disease. Am. J. Physiol. 152, 372–382.

30. Hamilton, W.F., R.L. Riley, A.M. Attyah, A. Cournand, D.M. Fowell, A. Himmelstein, R.P. Noble, J.W. Pemington, D.W. Richards, N.C. Wheeler, and A.C. Witham (1948). Comparison of the Fick and the dye injection methods of measuring the cardiac output in man. Am. J. Physiol. 153, 309–321.

31. Chapman, C.B., J.N. Fischer, and B.J. Sproule (1960). Behaviour of stroke volume at rest and during exercise in human beings. J. Clin. Invest. 39, 1208–1213.

32. Wang, Y. (1961). Cardiac response to exercise in unconditioned young men and athletes. Circulation 24, 1064.

33. strand, P-O, T.E. Cuddy, B. Saltin, and J. Stenberg (1964). Cardiac output during submaximal and maximal work. J. Appl. Physiol. 19, 268–274.

34. Barker, R.C., S.R. Hopkins, N. Kellogg, I.M. Olfert, T.D. Brutsaert, T.P. Gavin, P.L. Entin, A.J. Rice, and P.D. Wagner (1999). Measurement of cardiac output during exercise by open-circuit acetylene uptake. J. Appl. Physiol. 87, 1506–1512.

35. Christensen, E.H. and W.H. Forbes (1937). Skand. Arch. Physiol. 76, 75. Quoted in: Dill DB. Life, heat and altitude. Cambridge, MA: Harvard University Press, p. 168, 1938.

36. West, J.B. (1986). Lactate during exercise at extreme altitude. Fed. Proc. 45, 2953–2957.

37. Green, H.J., J.R. Sutton, P. Young, A. Cymerman, and C.S. Houston (1989). Operation Everest II: muscle energetics during maximal exhaustive exercise. J. Appl. Physiol. 66, 142–150.

38. MacRae, H. S-H., S.C. Dennis, A.N. Bosch, and T.D. Noakes (1992). Effects of training on lactate production and removal during progressive exercise in humans. J. Appl. Physiol. 72, 1649–1656.

39. Sutton, J.R., J.T. Reeves, P.D. Wagner, et al. (1988). Operation Everest II: oxygen transport during exercise at extreme simulated exercise. J. Appl. Physiol. B64, 1309–1321.

40. Green, H.J., J.R. Sutton, A. Cymerman, P.M. Young and C.S. Houston (1989). Operation Everest II: adaptations in human skeletal muscle. J. Appl. Physiol. 66(5), 2454–2461.

41. Kayser, B., M. Narici, T. Binzoni, B. Grassi, and P. Cerretelli (1994). Fatigue and exhaustion in chronic hypobaric hypoxia: influence of exercising and muscle mass. J. Appl. Physiol. 76, 634–640.

42. Pugh, L.G.C.E. (1964). Cardiac output in muscular exercise at 5,800m (19,000 ft). J. Appl. Physiol. 19, 441–447.

43. Richardson, R.S., E.A. Noyszewski, J.S. Leigh, and P.D. Wagner (1998). Lactate efflux from exercising human skeletal muscle: role of intracellular PO_2. J. Appl. Physiol. 85, 627–634.

44. Maltais, F., M. Simon, J. Desmeules, M.J. Sullivan, M. Belanger and P. Le Blanc (2001). Oxygen, leg blood flow, and O_2 uptake during exercise in mildly hypoxemic COPD. Med. Sci. Sports Exerc. (in press).

45. Richardson, R.S., B. Kennedy, D.R. Knight, and P.D. Wagner (1995). High muscle blood flows are not attenuated by recruitment of additional muscle mass. Am. J. Physiol. 269 (Heart Circ. Physiol. 38), H1545–H1552.

46. Graham, T.E. and B. Saltin (1989). Estimation of the mitochondrial redox state in human skeletal muscle during exercise. J. Appl. Physiol. 66, 561–566.

47. Hochachka, P.W. (1999). The metabolic implications of intracellular circulation. Proc. Natl. Acad. Sci. 96, 12233–12239.

48. Richardson, R.S., E.A. Noyszewski, K.F. Kendrick, J.S. Leigh, and P.D. Wagner (1996). Myoglobin O_2 desaturation during exercise. Evidence of limited O_2 transport. J. Clin. Invest. 96, 1916–1926.

49. Hochachka, P.W. and G.B. McClelland (1997). Cellular metabolic homeostasis during large scale change in ATP turnover rates in muscles. J. Exp. Biol. 200, 381–386.

50. Heyndrickx, G.R., Millard, R.W., McRitchie, R.J. et al. (1975). Regional myocardial function and electrophysiological alterations after brief coronary artery occlusion in conscious dogs. J. Clin. Invest. 56, 978–985.

51. Spriet, L.L., K. Soderlund, M. Bergstrom, and E. Hultman (1987). Anaerobic energy release in skeletal muscle during electrical stimulation in men. J. Appl. Physiol. 62, 511–615.

52. Hogan, M.C., B. Gladden, B. Grassi, C.M. Stary and M. Samaja (1998). Bioenergetics of contracting skeletal muscle after partial reduction of blood flow. J. Appl. Physiol. 84, 1882–1888.

CHAPTER 8

Therapeutic Angiogenesis for Coronary Artery Disease

Saul B. Freedman, Jeffrey M. Isner

INTRODUCTION

The development of collateral vessels following coronary artery occlusion has been familiar to clinicians for many years. These collateral vessels appear in relation to a gradually developing high grade stenosis or occlusion, growing at the interface between normal and ischemic tissue. Collateral coronary flow may be sufficient to preserve wall motion and prevent ischemia at rest and may reduce or prevent ischemia during stress. It is therefore potentially attractive to emulate and/or enhance this process by delivery of growth factors to promote neovascularization.

The therapeutic and pathological implications of neovascularization due to angiogenic growth factors were identified in the pioneering work of Folkman almost 30 years ago.[1] Work from his laboratory documented the dependence of tumor growth on neovascularization, and subsequently, the role of angiogenic growth factors in this process. More recently, therapeutic angiogenesis[2] has emerged as a complementary strategy for the treatment of vascular insufficiency. Proof of concept for this approach in human subjects was established in severely symptomatic patients with critical limb ischemia.[3,4] Shortly thereafter, clinical investigations were extended to involve severely symptomatic patients with occlusive coronary artery disease unsuitable for conventional revascularization; this patient population has been estimated to comprise up to 12% of individuals presenting to interventional referral centers.[5] This update will first discuss in brief the biology of angiogenesis that forms the basis for these clinical studies, and then summarize what has been learned thus far in clinical trials of therapeutic angiogenesis.

ANGIOGENESIS, VASCULOGENESIS AND ARTERIOGENESIS

Angiogenesis and vasculogenesis comprise a duet of

mechanisms responsible for the development of the vascular system in the embryo.[6] Vasculogenesis is the process of *in situ* formation of blood vessels from endothelial progenitor cells (EPCs) or angioblasts.[7] There is functional similarity and proximity between hematopoietic stem cells and endothelial progenitor cells EPCs in the embryo, and both may derive from a common hemangioblast precursor.[8,9] In the process of vasculogenesis, solitary EPCs migrate and fuse with other angioblasts and capillaries, and differentiate into endothelial cells (ECs) while forming new vessels *in situ*.[7] In contrast, angiogenesis involves extension of the already formed primitive vasculature by the sprouting of new capillaries through migration and proliferation of previously differentiated ECs.

Until recently, vasculogenesis was considered restricted to embryonic development, while angiogenesis, recognized to occur in the embryo as well, was considered to be solely responsible for neovascularization in the adult. The demonstration that bone marrow derived EPCs circulate in peripheral blood,[10] home to and incorporate into foci of neovascularization in adult animals,[11] are increased in number in response to tissue ischemia,[12] and can augment collateral development following *ex vivo* expansion and transplantation[13] revised the paradigm for postnatal neovascularization. These studies established that neovascularization in the adult is not restricted to angiogenesis but recapitulates both embryonic mechanisms.

A third mechanism that likely contributes to collateral vessel development is an increase in size and caliber of pre-existing arteriolar collateral connections by remodeling, termed arteriogenesis.[14] The presence and number of these native collaterals varies widely within and among species. When an occlusion occurs, such pre-existing collaterals are subject to an increase in the velocity of blood flow and a consequent increase in shear stress within the lumen, ultimately contributing to maturation of collateral conduits. Arteriogenesis has been suggested[14] to represent a particularly prominent mechanism for development of those medium-sized collaterals that are large enough to be recognized by conventional angiography.[3,4]

Hypoxia and angiogenic factors. Hypoxia or ischemia resulting from arterial occlusion is the natural biological stimulus for endogenous angiogenesis.[15] The oxygen sensor, most likely a heme protein, increases production of the transcription factor hypoxia inducible factor (HIF-1).[16,17] Under normoxic conditions, the alpha subunit of HIF-1 is degraded, but under hypoxic conditions, degradation of HIF-1 alpha is dramatically reduced. Upregulated HIF-1 binds to the hypoxia-response element of the promoter of the vascular endothelial growth factor (VEGF) gene, enhancing its expression.[18] Hypoxia also stabilizes the mRNA encoding VEGF, via a sequence in its 3'-untranslated region.[15,16,19] There may be additional stabilization of VEGF mRNA at its 5'-untranslated region, and/or increased protein production via an internal ribosome entry site that permits cap-independent translation by ribosomal scanning of VEGF mRNA.[15,20]

The VEGF family and VEGF receptors. The VEGFs are a family of glycoproteins, of which VEGF (also called VEGF-1 or VEGF-A) has been studied most extensively in pre-clinical and clinical trials of therapeutic angiogenesis. The others, which share structural homology with VEGF-1, include VEGF-C or VEGF-2, VEGF-B or VEGF-3, VEGF-D, VEGF-E, and placental growth factor. Four species of VEGF-1, each the result of alternative splicing, have been identified with 121, 165, 189, and 206 amino acids (VEGF$_{121}$, VEGF$_{165}$, VEGF$_{189}$ and VEGF$_{206}$ respectively). VEGF$_{121}$, VEGF$_{165}$, and VEGF$_{189}$ have been shown to have similar angiogenic potency in a rabbit model of hindlimb ischemia.[21] The isoforms differ in their heparin binding capacity: VEGF$_{121}$ does not bind to heparin, and is thus the most soluble, while VEGF$_{165}$, and VEGF$_{189}$ bind heparin avidly and therefore remain more closely bound to either the cell surface or to heparan sulfate in the extracellular matrix. Importantly, all VEGF-1 isoforms as well as the other VEGF family members contain a secretory signal sequence that permits their active secretion from intact cells transfected by the VEGF gene.

The principal cellular target of VEGF is the EC. The common EC receptor for VEGF-1 and VEGF-2 (VEGF-C) is KDR or VEGF receptor 2 (VEGFR-2),[22,23] VEGFR-2 is generally regarded as the VEGF receptor which transduces signals required for angiogenesis. Controversy, however, persists as to the role of VEGFR-1 (Flt-1)[24] in mediating angiogenesis. VEGFR-3 (Flt-4) principally mediates lymphangiogenesis.[25] Hypoxia appears to upregulate KDR expression on ECs[26,27] in addition to increasing EC production of VEGF,[28] consistent with an autocrine loop. The presence of an autocrine loop activated by hypoxia, and the proliferation of ECs following this stimulus may serve to amplify and protract the response of ECs to administered VEGF. An important additional role for VEGF is augmentation of circulating EPC numbers, documented in mice and humans following VEGF gene transfer.[29-31]

Other cytokines – The FGF family. Although a variety of cytokines other than VEGF have been shown to promote angiogenesis,[32-34] only a small number have thus far been tested in clinical trials (Table 8-1). Apart from VEGF, the fibroblast growth factor (FGF) family has been most widely studied in both experimental animals and patients with advanced coronary disease. Acidic FGF (aFGF or FGF-1) and basic FGF (bFGF or FGF-2) are potent EC mitogens, but in addition, serve as ligands for other cell types including smooth muscle cells and fibroblasts. The FGFs utilize cell surface heparan sulphate proteoglycans to facilitate binding to their tyrosine kinase receptors; such binding underlies the rapid extraction of injected FGF from the circulation, particularly in the lungs, and its localization on cells and extracellular matrix, similar to VEGF. The FGFs, like VEGF, also stimulate EC synthesis of proteases including plasmi-

TABLE 8-1.   ANGIOGENIC CYTOKINES AND GENES USED IN
              CLINICAL ANGIOGENESIS TRIALS

Cytokine	Protein	Gene Ph	Gene Ad	EC specific	Pleiotro-pic	Secretory sequence
VEGF165	✓	✓		✓		✓
VEGF 121			✓	✓		✓
VEGF-2 (VEGF-C)		✓		✓		✓
HIF-1α			✓			
FGF-1 (aFGF)	✓				✓	
FGF-1 modified		✓			✓	✓
FGF-2 (bFGF)	✓				✓	
FGF-4			✓		✓	✓

VEGF = Vascular endothelial growth factor, HIF = Hypoxia inducible factor,
FGF = Fibroblast growth factor, a=acidic, b=basic, Ph = Plasmid human, Ad
= Adenoviral vector

nogen activator and metalloproteinases, important for extracellular matrix digestion in the process of angiogenesis.[35]
Unlike VEGF, the common forms of FGF (FGF-1 and 2)
lack a secretory signal sequence; clinical trials of FGF gene
transfer have consequently required either modification of
the FGF gene[36] or use of another of the FGF gene family
with a signal sequence.[37,38]

RATIONALE FOR THERAPEUTIC
ANGIOGENESIS IN PATIENTS WITH
OCCLUSIVE VASCULAR DISEASE

While ischemia from vascular occlusion upregulates expression of angiogenic growth factors, the fact that certain
patients present with disabling angina indicates that such
natural compensatory processes are not always sufficient.
There are two possible explanations for this: either the production of angiogenic cytokines is inadequate, or patients'
response to them is attenuated. It has been shown that
angiogenesis is impaired in older versus younger animals,[39]
secondary to reduced VEGF expression. Similar reductions
in VEGF expression were observed in non-obese diabetic
mice[40] and in hypercholesterolemic mice.[41] These limitations in VEGF expression can be overcome in part by VEGF
supplementation.[40,41] Patients with advanced coronary disease are often older, and may have diabetes, hypercholesterolemia, or other undetermined characteristics limiting
their capacity to upregulate angiogenic cytokines in
response to ischemia, but may nevertheless respond to exogenous angiogenic cytokines. Significantly higher VEGF
production in response to hypoxia was recently demonstrated in monocytes harvested from patients with angio-
graphically visible collaterals, compared to those with
reduced collaterals, suggesting that individual differences in
cytokine expression may constitute yet another basis for
variations in the magnitude of collateral development.[42]

Reduced expression of angiogenic cytokines is not the only factor contributing to the heterogeneous response to collateral vessel development. Marked genetic heterogeneity in the response to growth factor-stimulated angiogenesis has been observed in different strains of inbred mice.[43] Age-related reduction in endothelial cell viability has also recently been demonstrated.[39] Endothelial dysfunction accompanies many of the known coronary risk factors, and may reduce endothelial responsiveness to angiogenic growth factors. Also, the responsiveness of EPCs to hypoxic stimuli may well be deficient and potentially limit therapeutic angiogenesis. Strategies to increase EC responsiveness and to enhance EPC production or availability are therefore reasonable targets for therapeutic angiogenesis.[15,44,45]

Angiogenic protein versus gene therapy. Angiogenic cytokines may be administered as the natural recombinant human protein, or by gene transfer. Recombinant protein is a more conventional approach and typically displays a more precise dose-response relationship than gene transfer. Recombinant protein is usually administered systemically, and is therefore limited by potential adverse effects of the high plasma concentrations required to achieve adequate myocardial uptake. These include hypotension and edema with VEGF,[46,47] and anemia, thrombocytopenia and renal toxicity for FGF[48,49]. Data regarding the kinetics of recombinant protein circulation suggests that intravenous delivery is unlikely to result in sufficient myocardial uptake and/or residence time to achieve important biological effects; intracoronary delivery constitutes an alternative route of parenteral administration.[50]

The ideal regimen for therapeutic angiogenesis would be a single administration providing a sustained but transient (2-3 weeks) increase in local angiogenic protein concentration at foci of myocardial ischemia. A limited rise in systemic VEGF levels would be expected to reduce the potential for distant, unwanted side-effects. Currently available gene therapy strategies approach this ideal. Both naked DNA and adenoviral vectors produce only transient transfection, ideal for the timescale required for angiogenesis. The principal challenge is that optimal transfection in the case of naked DNA is best achieved by intramyocardial injection, although intracoronary administration may be sufficient for adenoviral gene transfer.[37] Unlike viral vectors, plasmid DNA does not induce inflammation. While naked DNA gene transfer is less efficient than viral-mediated transduction, uptake of naked DNA is augmented in muscle,[51] particularly ischemic or inflamed muscle.[52,53]

Routes of administration. Angiogenic cytokines and genes have been administered via a wide variety of routes. Injection sites include intravenous, selective pulmonary artery, left atrium, intracoronary, selective intracoronary, transepicardial intramyocardial at time of bypass surgery or via thoracotomy, transendocardial intramyocardial by electromechanical catheter, peri-adventitial at time of bypass surgery or by thoracotomy, and intra-pericardial. Because local delivery of recombinant protein or gene may be considered ideal,[54] trials in patients have favored the intracoronary (adenovirus) or intramyocardial (naked DNA or adenovirus) route. Though not an issue if performed as a part of a coronary bypass procedure, the attendant risk of surgery is otherwise a limitation of the transepicardial route; in the future, this may be averted by the catheter-based transendocardial approach (Fig. 8-1) discussed below.

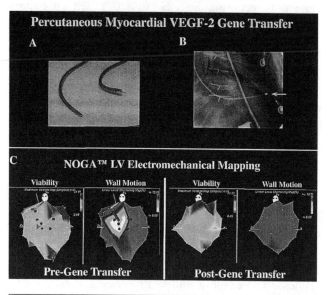

Figure 8-1. Catheter gene transfer of VEGF. Composite illustration of gene transfer of VEGF-2. Panel A shows catheter on the left, with the 27G needle advanced on the right. Panel B shows position of the catheter tip (arrow) in the left ventricle. A combination of electromechanical mapping and fluoroscopy is used to guide catheter positioning within the ventricle. Panel C shows 4 electromechanical maps: two before and two after VEGF-2 gene transfer. Pre-gene transfer, the left map ("viability") comprises the maximum unipolar voltage electrical endocardial map, with viable areas color coded from green through blue to purple, indicating that hypocontractile areas were viable. The points chosen for gene transfer are marked in brown. The next panel ("wall motion"), shows the linear local shortening map before gene transfer, with an area of hypo-contractility indicated by the red, yellow, green, and blue colors in the anterolateral wall. Surrounding areas have normal contractility color-coded purple. Hypocontractile areas were inferred to be either ischemic or hibernating. The follow-up maps in this patient, on the right, performed at 12 weeks after gene transfer, show no change in the unipolar voltage map (viability unchanged), while the far right panel of linear local shortening shows complete normalization of contraction in the previously hypocontractile area as indicated by the uniform purple color, following gene transfer.

EXPERIMENTAL STUDIES IN ANIMAL MODELS OF MYOCARDIAL ISCHEMIA

The most widely studied animal model of focal myocardial ischemia involves application of an ameroid constrictor to produce gradual occlusion of the left circumflex coronary artery over 10-20 days. The choice of animal is important, as species differ from one another and from humans in the number of pre-existing arteriolar connections – pigs and rabbits have few, while dogs have many. Acute coronary ligation produces transmural infarction in the pig, compared to smaller non-transmural infarcts in dogs.[55] In these models, angiogenic proteins or encoding genes have been administered successfully via a wide variety of routes. The effectiveness of angiogenesis has been documented by histologic assessment of capillary or vessel number and size, quantitation of EC markers, measures of resting or vasodilated coronary blood flow, angiography, and measures of left ventricular function at rest or during stress.

Studies with fibroblast growth factor. Most but not all of the studies have demonstrated evidence of enhanced angiogenesis after the intervention. FGF-2 increased collateral flow in the dog when given intracoronary for 2, 7 or 28 days[56-59] with effects measurable up to 5 weeks, but not at 6 months.[60] Central venous administration in the same model was ineffective,[59] presumably due to lung sequestration.[50] Beneficial effects on collateral flow and left ventricular function were also seen with FGF-2 in the pig after single doses administered perivascularly or into the pericardium.[61-63] FGF-1 recombinant protein was ineffective in the dog[64,65] probably because of rapid inactivation of this protein which can be prevented by altering its structure.[66] Experience with FGF gene transfer is more limited. Single-dose intramuscular injection of naked DNA encoding FGF-1 and intracoronary adenoviral transfer of the FGF-5 gene have each been shown to improve flow in the rabbit hindlimb[36] and porcine myocardium[37] respectively.

Studies with vascular endothelial growth factor. The effect of $VEGF_{165}$ protein has been studied in both dog and porcine models. Single intracoronary doses were effective in the pig,[46,67] as was a series of 2 local injections via a balloon catheter, 3 or 4 week peri-adventitial infusions via minipump,[67,68] and intramyocardial injection.[69] Collateral perfusion improved after VEGF and endocardial/epicardial flow ratios were improved. Intravenous administration, however, was ineffective.[69] In the dog, $VEGF_{165}$ protein injected intracoronary over 28 days was reported to improve collateral flow.[70]

Genes encoding $VEGF_{165}$ and $VEGF_{121}$ as well as VEGF-2 have been transfected in a number of animal studies using either naked plasmid DNA or adenoviral vectors. Intramyocardial injection of plasmid DNA encoding $VEGF_{165}$[71,72] (Fig. 8-2), VEGF-2,[73] or adenovirus encoding $VEGF_{121}$[74,75] via thoracotomy in a pig ameroid model improved collateral perfusion and function. Intracoronary adenoviral gene delivery produced much lower gene and VEGF levels in the myocardium with poor localization, which would favor the intramyocardial route.[75] Pericardial delivery of adenovirus encoding $VEGF_{165}$ in a dog model did not increase collateral flow.[76] Intramyocardial injection of the entire dose of plasmid $VEGF_{165}$ at a single site in a rat model of myocardial infarction induced angiogenesis with angioma formation at the injection site, without enhancing regional

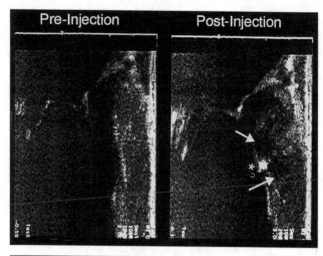

Figure 8-2. *Intramyocardial administration of VEGF DNA. Transepicardial 2D echocardiogram demonstrating distribution of VEGF DNA solution injected directly into ischemic porcine myocardium. The left panel (Pre-injection) shows the anterolateral free wall superiorly with the mitral valve plane at the left of the image. In the right panel (Post-injection), a bright needle artifact (asterisk) is seen in the anterolateral wall near two echolucent zones (arrows); the echolucency is the result of injected fluid containing the plasmid VEGF DNA.*

blood flow;[77] subsequent studies suggested that this was a dose-related event, in that a 50% reduction in dose of plasmid DNA did not induce angiomata (Kloner RA, personal communication). Similar results were observed with local, massive overexpression of VEGF achieved with transformed myoblasts.[78]

Recent studies have suggested that catheter-based intramyocardial injection of plasmid $VEGF_{165}$ is effective in the pig.[72] This less invasive approach to intramyocardial gene transfer has been shown to achieve suitable gene expression,[72,79-81] and is currently being investigated in a double-blind, randomized prospective placebo-controlled trial of VEGF-2 gene transfer[82] (Fig. 8-1).

Translation of therapeutic myocardial angiogenesis from bench to bedside. The species differences in myocardial collateralization, and the relatively small area of ischemia produced in the pig model underscore the difficulty in taking the results from animal models of myocardial ischemia directly to the clinical arena for myocardial angiogenesis. In addition, the heart is a difficult organ to access directly for either vascular or intramyocardial administration of angiogenic factors, and assessment of neovascularization and blood flow is not trivial. Consequently, to investigate therapeutic angiogenesis in human subjects, we adopted a strategy of first studying patients with peripheral artery disease, specifically critical limb ischemia. The rationale for this included consideration of two issues. First, in patients with critical limb ischemia, the risk (limb loss):benefit (limb salvage) ratio is appropriate for a novel therapeutic, due to the absence of any effective medical therapy.[83] Second, access to ischemic skeletal muscle is straightforward, requiring only a superficial, nearly painless injection with a 27 gauge needle.

We initially studied the effects of VEGF gene transfer in patients with critical limb ischemia by delivering the gene to a patent arterial site in the ischemic limb upstream from the site of occlusion.[3,84] Subsequently, however, this approach was replaced by direct intramuscular injection.[4,85] Clinical benefit, including abolition of rest pain, limb salvage, and healing of ischemic ulcers, was associated with objective findings of improved ankle/brachial index, angiographic evidence of new collaterals, and improved leg blood flow on magnetic resonance angiography. Having established proof of concept for therapeutic angiogenesis in human subjects, we then sought to extrapolate these findings to patients with myocardial ischemia.[86]

EVALUATING CLINICAL RESULTS OF MYOCARDIAL ANGIOGENESIS

There is no consensus regarding how best to evaluate the efficacy of therapeutic angiogenesis in patients with coronary heart disease. Most clinical studies have focussed on the clinical endpoints used historically to evaluate new antianginal drugs, namely angina class, exercise time, and quality of life. Each of these, however, is potentially subject to placebo and training effects, which cannot be eliminated in Phase I trials, and may limit the power of smaller Phase II studies to detect a meaningful difference. While these parameters my ultimately prove useful for establishing efficacy in larger Phase II/III trials, additional objective evaluations may help to establish evidence of biological effects attributable to therapeutic angiogenesis.

Rest and stress SPECT perfusion imaging with thallium[201] or Tc[99m]-sestamibi provide objective estimates of relative myocardial blood flow, and are used widely and routinely in clinical practice. As such, evidence of improved relative myocardial perfusion on images recorded pre- and post-gene transfer may constitute inferential evidence of angiogenesis.

Percutaneous catheter-based electromechanical mapping[87,88] is a novel technique which provides concurrent imaging of myocardial viability and endocardial wall motion (Fig. 8-1); analysis of the two resulting maps may be used to identify foci of hibernating myocardium which can be serially evaluated pre- and post-gene transfer.[89]

Positron emission tomography (PET) using $^{13}NH_3$ or $H_2^{15}O$ can quantify regional coronary blood flow at rest and during vasodilation, and has been used to demonstrate increased flow after a variety of interventions,[90] but the technique is not widely available. Novel modifications of magnetic resonance (MR) perfusion imaging to detect foci of neovascularization[91,92] may prove useful for evaluation of angiogenesis following confirmation of reproducibility, sensitivity and specificity by other centers.

Serial measures of left ventricular function have not proved consistently useful in animal or clinical studies to date. Angiographic studies have likewise failed to consistently depict reproducible evidence of neovascularization, even in animal or clinical studies with evidence of improved myocardial perfusion. This is likely due to the fact that the diameter of most collaterals formed in response to arterial occlusion, and/or therapeutic angiogenesis is <200m,[93] i.e. beyond the resolution of conventional angiography, and certainly beyond the spatial resolution of magnetic resonance angiography. Consistent with this notion is the fact that the increased resolution achieved by synchrotron radiation imaging has disclosed new collateral vessels in preclinical studies that could not be identified by conventional angiographic techniques.[94]

Initial results of therapeutic myocardial angiogenesis in patients with coronary disease.

Tables 8-2 and 8-3 list completed and ongoing clinical trials of recombinant proteins and genes employed for therapeutic angiogenesis, although data regarding the major endpoints have been published in only five, with two in press. Patients in these trials generally have severe angina unresponsive to medical therapy, and are unsuitable for conventional revascularization. Many of the studies have been small phase I trials without control groups, designed primarily to establish safety and/or evaluate dose-related effects. Nevertheless, almost all have reported encouraging reductions in angina and nitroglycerin consumption, and in certain cases, improvement in exercise time, and/or improvement in objective measures of left ventricular perfusion and/or function.

Clinical studies using recombinant proteins (Table 8-2).

The first clinical study of recombinant protein for myocardial ischemia employed intramyocardial injections of FGF-1 (aFGF) with heparin in patients undergoing left internal mammary (LIMA) bypass of the left anterior descending (LAD) coronary artery.[95,96] Twenty patients received active drug and 20 received heat denatured protein as placebo. The authors utilized a novel form of imaging to suggest improved collateralization of the distal LAD in comparison to placebo. This effect was maintained at 3-year follow-up.[97] At 3 years, 16/17 patients given FGF were in Canadian functional class I compared to 12/16 controls, and only 1/17 given FGF required nitrates compared to 12/16 controls (p<0.01). In addition, fewer patients given FGF were on calcium channel blockers (1/17 vs 10/16) or beta-blockers (5/17 vs 10/16). The same group recently completed an uncontrolled study of FGF-1 injected transepicardially via minithoracotomy in patients with severe angina unsuitable for conventional revascularization.[98] Compared to baseline preoperative values, SPECT perfusion and exercise capacity were reported to be improved at both 6 and 12 weeks.

Peri-advential implantation of FGF-2 (bFGF) administered

intra-operatively in heparin alginate beads at the site of a non-bypassable artery has been evaluated in a placebo-controlled trial of patients undergoing concomitant bypass surgery.[99] Despite a relatively high peri-operative mortality and morbidity, attributed to the advanced nature of coronary artery disease in the patient cohort, the investigators reported less angina in the active treatment group. Trends to less severe stress nuclear perfusion defects and less evidence of ischemia by MRI were noted as well in the high dose FGF-2 group.

Three uncontrolled Phase 1 studies of intravenous or intra-coronary FGF-2 or VEGF recombinant protein have been completed though not as yet published (Table 8-2). These studies overall reported less angina and improved exercise time, and improvements in either nuclear or MRI perfusion, or LV function 100-105.

Results of Phase 1 studies, designed by definition to assess safety, must be interpreted with caution. Typically, the number of patients enrolled in such trials is relatively small, and for those lacking a control group, a placebo effect cannot be excluded. For studies in which recombinant protein or gene is administered in conjunction with conventional revascularization it may be difficult to determine the relative contributions of the angiogenic agent versus bypass surgery to the symptomatic response.

VIVA study. Two larger placebo-controlled Phase II studies of intracoronary intravenous recombinant protein have recently been completed. The VIVA study compared 2 doses of VEGF-1 protein to placebo in 178 patients given a single intracoronary infusion followed by 3 separate intravenous infusions.[106-108] The primary endpoint of exercise duration was not different from placebo in the VIVA study; in each of the three groups, the increase in exercise time at 60 days, approximately 45 seconds, was similar. At 120 days, the high dose group maintained the improvement with an increase of 47 seconds over baseline, while the placebo group showed only a 14-second improvement. Although this difference was not significant, given the relatively small numbers and the large placebo effect, the possibility of a type II error cannot be excluded. There were no significant differences from placebo in angina grade or quality of life measures at 60 days though there was a significant reduction in angina grade at 120 days in the high dose group. Angiographic and nuclear perfusion studies were interpreted to show no differences between active therapy and placebo at 60 days.

Perhaps the most striking finding in the VIVA trial was that in spite of exclusion of patients with evidence of a malignancy, three patients were diagnosed and one died of cancer within the 120-day follow-up period, while one patient developed worsening retinopathy. Remarkably, all of these patients had been fortuitously randomized to the placebo group.

TABLE 8-2. CLINICAL STUDIES OF RECOMBINANT PROTEINS FOR MYOCARDIAL ANGIOGENESIS COMPLETED AND IN PROGRESS

Angiogen	Administration		Population, Phase	Nos. Active/ Placebo	Follow-up	Outcome	PI/company	Ref
	Route	Dose						
FGF-1 + heparin + fibrin glue	Intramyo near LAD at CABG	0.01 mg/Kg	3VD + distal LAD disease after LIMA insertion, Phase I	20/20	12 weeks, 3 years	New vessels bypassing distal LAD, ↑ flow (angio grey scale) vs placebo. ↓angina, ↓ anti-anginal drugs, similar angio improvement at 3 years	Stegmann	95-97
FGF 1 + heparin + fibrin glue	Intramyo at thoracotomy	0.01 mg/Kg for each involved vascular bed	Severe angina, no option, Phase I	20/0	6 & 12 weeks	SPECT perfusion and exercise capacity reported significantly improved compared to baseline	Stegmann	98
FGF-2 + heparin alginate	Peri adventitial implant at CABG	1 or 10 μg FGF-2 per implant, 10 implants/ patient	Ungraftable artery, viable myocardium Phase I	8/0	3 months	1 perioperative infarction in area of implant. All angina-free postop. Variable changes in perfusion scan	Simons	162
FGF-2 + heparin alginate	Peri adventitial implant at CABG	10 or 100 μg total dose FGF-2 or placebo divided into 10 implants	Ungraftable artery, undergoing CABG, viable myocardium Phase I	16/8	3 months, longer clinical	2 operative deaths, 3 Q MI. Less angina, reduced perfusion defect size with high dose.	Simons	99
FGF-2	14 intravenous 52 intracoronary	Incremental 0.33 - 48 μg/Kg total dose, 2 x 10 min 10ml infusions (2 distributions)	No option CAD , inducible ischemia, Phase I	66/0	1,2,6 months	↑ exercise time, ↑ angina, ↑ QOL, ↑ LV function, ↑ nuclear perfusion, ↑ MRI flow	Simons Chiron	100, 102, 103

Angiogen	Administration		Population, Phase	Nos. Active/ Placebo	Follow-up	Outcome	PI/company	Ref
	Route	Dose						
FGF-2	intracoronary	0.3, 3.0 or 30 µg/ Kg total dose, 2 x 10 min 10ml infusions (2 distributions)	No option CAD , reversible perfusion defects, Phase II FIRST multicenter study	337 total 3:1active/pla-cebo	90 days 6 months	90 day exercise time (65 s vs 45 s for placebo) and stress nuclear perfusion no different from placebo, less angina (p=0.057), trend to improved overall result in older and more symptomatic patients	Simons Chiron	109
VEGF₁₆₅	intracoronary	5-167 ng/Kg/min 10 min each artery	Angina + VUNE Phase I	15/0	30, 60 days	↓ angina 13/15. Improved rest nuclear perfusion in high dose	Henry Genentech	101, 104,105
VEGF₁₆₅	intravenous	17-100 ng/Kg/ min over 1-4 h	Angina + VUNE Phase I	28/0	60 days	Perfusion scan improved 2 grades in 40% of rest, 20% of stress. ↑ angio collats in 38%	McCluskey Gen-entech	104
VEGF₁₆₅	Intracoronary plus 3 x intravenous	17, 50 ng/Kg/min ic 20 min, + iv 4 h day 3, 6, & 9	Angina + VUNE Phase II VIVA multicenter study	115/63	60 days, 120 days, 1 year (part)	Day 60 similar ↑ exercise time for active & placebo, similar ↓ angina, QOL as placebo. Nuclear perfusion, angiography, no change day 60. Day 120 high dose ↓ angina vs placebo, trend to ↑ exercise time. Trend to ↓ angina class at 1 year	Henry Genentech	104, 106-108

PI = Principal investigator, LAD = left anterior descending coronary artery, LIMA = left internal mammary artery, CABG = coronary artery bypass graft surgery, 3VD = 3 vessel coronary artery disease, CAD = coronary artery disease, VUNE = viable underperfused myocardium in patients not eligible for revascularization, SPECT = single photon emission computed tomography, Q MI = Q-wave myocardial infarction, QOL = quality of life, LV = left ventricle , MRI = magnetic resonance imagining.

FIRST study. The FIRST study compared a single intracoronary dose of FGF-2 (bFGF) with placebo in 337 patients. The 90-day results[109] failed to show significant differences from placebo in the primary endpoint of exercise time (65 vs 45 seconds improvement, p=0.64), or in rest or stress nuclear perfusion. Angina frequency determined by the Seattle Angina Questionnaire was less in the FGF group, although this did not achieve statistical significance. In a post-hoc analysis, a significant improvement in exercise time was seen in patients older than 63 years (80 versus 40 seconds, p=0.03). The otherwise negative primary endpoint results of the VIVA and FIRST studies using intracoronary ± intravenous protein administration underscore the concern that the pharmacokinetics of recombinant protein administered into the vascular space may lead to inadequate local delivery of angiogenic growth factor within the ischemic myocardium, as suggested by studies reported previously using labeled ligand.[50,54]

Clinical studies utilizing gene transfer (Table 8-3).

Published studies of gene transfer for therapeutic angiogenesis in human subjects have thus far been limited to Phase I dose-escalating, non-randomized trials. The largest of these trials with the longest follow-up to date involved 30 patients with refractory angina unsuitable for conventional revascularization, in whom naked DNA encoding the 165 isoform of the VEGF-1 gene as sole therapy was administered intra-operatively by direct intramyocardial injection via a mini-thoracotomy.[89,110-112] A technical aspect of the procedure worthy of note was the use of intra-operative multiplane transesophageal echocardiography with test injections of agitated saline to ensure that the DNA injectate was not delivered into the left ventricular cavity.[113] Intracavitary microbubbles necessitating needle repositioning were seen in 20% of needle placements, underscoring this aspect of transepicardial gene transfer.

The patients experienced a remarkable reduction in angina frequency, with weekly nitroglycerin consumption falling from an average of 60/week to 3.5/week at 90 days. Exercise time for the group at 90 days improved by an average of 47 seconds, and exercise time to angina improved by almost 2 minutes; the improvements in symptoms were maintained at one year and there was further improvement in exercise time (increase of 98 seconds over baseline) and time to angina (increase of 2.5 minutes). There were two late deaths (4.5[111] and 28.5 months), and one patient underwent a cardiac transplant at 13 months.

An important objective evaluation in the final 13 consecutive patients was the use of electromechanical endocardial maps of left ventricular shortening before and 60 days after gene transfer.[89] Foci of electromechanical uncoupling (reduced endocardial shortening with persistent evidence of electrical viability) were identified pre-operatively in all patients, with significant improvement in these endocardial wall motion abnormalities in the repeat study at 60 days (see Fig. 8-1). These findings corresponded to improved perfusion scores calculated from SPECT-sestamibi myocardial perfusion scans recorded at rest and with pharmacological stress. Perfusion defects on the SPECT rest images were associated with ischemic characteristics on the endocardial maps. Sequential SPECT scans (Fig. 8-3) recorded before and after gene transfer demonstrated partial or complete resolution of fixed defects in 4 (33%) and 5 (43%) patients respectively in whom defects were present on the initial rest images. Partial or complete resolution of these rest defects post-gene transfer is consistent with the notion that these pre-existing defects constitute foci of hibernating viable myocardium,[114-116] which have resumed or improved contractile activity as a result of therapeutic neovascularization.

A second Phase I study of intramyocardial gene transfer was reported by Rosengart et al.[117] In that study, a first generation adenoviral vector was used to deliver the 121 isoform of the VEGF-1 gene to 15 patients undergoing bypass graft surgery, and as sole therapy to 6 patients via mini-thoracotomy. Symptoms improved in both bypass surgery and sole therapy groups, though stress-induced nuclear perfusion images remained unchanged. The same group has since injected adenoviral $VEGF_{121}$ transepicardially, using video-assisted thoracotomy or thoracoscopy in

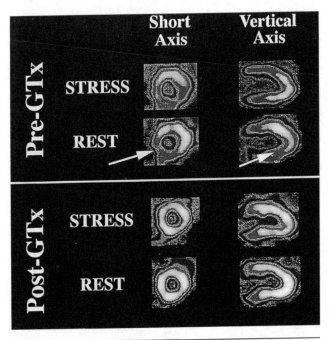

Figure 8-3. *Rest and stress nuclear perfusion images before and after VEGF-1 gene transfer. Persantin stress SPECT sestamibi myocardial perfusion scans in a patient receiving VEGF-1 gene via mini-thoracotomy. Selected short axis and horizontal axis stress and rest images before (above) and 60 days after (below) VEGF gene transfer (GTx). White/yellow colors represent maximal radionuclide uptake, and red color indicates impaired uptake. Pre-GTx scans show an essentially fixed infero-septal defect (arrows), and a reversible infero-lateral defect. After gene transfer, there is normalization of both resting perfusion and stress defects in the infero-septal and infero-lateral walls.*

TABLE 8-3. CLINICAL STUDIES OF GENE TRANSFER FOR MYOCARDIAL ANGIOGENESIS COMPLETED AND IN PROGRESS

Angiogen	Administration		Population, Phase	Nos. Active/ Placebo	Follow-up	Outcome	PI/company	Ref
	Route	Dose						
Ph VEGF$_{165}$	Intramyo: thoracotomy	125 μg – 10, 250μg – 10, 500μg - 10	No option CAD, refractory stable angina. Phase I	0/0	2 and 6 months, 1 year, longer clinical	1 late postop death (4.5 months) and 1 late death at 28.5 months. Less angina and NTG, ↑ ex time, improved rest/stress nuclear perfusion, ↑ function e.m. mapping	Isner Genentech	89, 110-112
Ad VEGF$_{121}$	Intramyo: with CABG or at thoracotomy	4x10^8 to 4x10^{10} particle units	Ischemic non bypassable region Phase I	21/0 CABG=15 Thora-cotomy=6	30 days	2 perioperative, 1 late death with CABG, ↓ angina, ↑ function sestamibi, ↑ Rentrop and collateral score	Crystal Genvec	117
Ad VEGF$_{121}$	Intramyo: video thorac – otomy, oscopy	4x10^{10} particle units	Severe angina, not ideal for revascularization Phase I	10/0 thora-cotomy 6 thoracosco-py 4	30 days	1 death at 40 days. In progress	Crystal Genvec	118
Ph VEGF-2	Intramyo: thoracotomy	200μg – 10, 800μg – 10, 2000μg - 10	No option CAD, refractory stable angina. Phase I	0/0	30,60, 90 days, longer clinical	1 perioperative death. Less angina and NTG, ↑ exercise time, improved nuclear perfusion ↓ angina class ≥ 2 in 70%. ↑ function e.m. mapping	Isner VGI	119, 120

Angiogen	Administration		Population, Phase	Nos. Active/Placebo	Follow-up	Outcome	PI/company	Ref
	Route	Dose						
Ph VEGF-2	Intramyo: via e.m. catheter in LV	200µg	No option refractory stable angina. Phase I multicenter	6 (incl 3 single blind control crossed over to active)	30, 60, and 90 days, longer clinical	Less angina and NTG at 60 & 90 days. Improved rest nuclear perfusion at 90 days. ↑ function e.m. mapping	Isner VGI	82
Ph VEGF-2	Intramyo: via e.m. catheter in LV	200µg – 6/3 800µg – 6/3 2000µg – (6/3)	No option refractory stable angina. Phase I/II multicenter	19 (2:1 active vs placebo). Total of 27 proposed	60 and 90 days, longer clinical	In progress	Isner VGI	82
Ad FGF-4	Intracoronary AG-ENT study	3×10^8 to 10^{11} virus particles, incremental	Class 2-3 angina, 1 open vessel with other options Phase I/II	67 (3:1 active vs placebo)	4 and 12 weeks	Reported to show significant improvement in treadmill time at 4 and 12 weeks vs placebo	Hammond CTI, Berlex, Schering	Personal communication

(As in Table 8-2), intramyo = intramyocardial injection, e.m. = eloctromechanical, NTG = nitroglycerin

10 patients,[118] with one late death. Symptomatic outcomes in these latter patients have not yet been reported.

Our initial experience with intramyocardial naked DNA gene transfer has been subsequently reproduced in a multi-center, consecutive series, dose escalating study of transepi-cardial VEGF-2 gene transfer in 30 patients with Class 3 or 4 angina. Once again, angina frequency, and nitroglycerin consumption were both reduced, and exercise time was increased by over 2 minutes (unpublished data); improvement in nuclear perfusion studies and NOGA maps similar to that described for naked DNA gene transfer of VEGF-1[119,120] were documented as well. Among the 30-patient cohort, 29 are alive at minimum of 12 months follow-up, and none have undergone cardiac transplantation. A single post-operative death occurred 20 hours following gene transfer.

More recently, we completed the first clinical study of per-cutaneous, catheter-based myocardial gene transfer.[82] This single-blind pilot study, designed to establish the safety and feasibility of non-surgical needle injection, involved a total of six patients randomized to gene transfer or a mock procedure; each of the three patients assigned to the mock group ultimately required crossover to gene transfer for persistent symptoms. The number of anginal episodes fell similarly in the active and control groups over the first 30 days after gene transfer, suggesting an initial placebo effect (33 ± 5 to 14 ± 5 episodes/week for active therapy vs 40 ± 5 to 15 ± 5 episodes/week for control, p=ns). Longer fol-low-up, however, disclosed that angina continued to decrease at 90 days only in the active group, while patients in the mock group regressed toward their initial sympto-matic status (3 ± 6 episodes/week vs 22 ± 4, p=0.002), sug-gesting that the late reduction in angina was not a placebo effect. The symptomatic improvement was again accompa-nied by non-invasive evidence of improved myocardial per-fusion, and electromechanical evidence of improved myocardial function.[82] This study served as the basis for a multi-center randomized, double blind, placebo-controlled trial of catheter-based VEGF-2 gene transfer that has thus far enrolled 19 patients. There have been no complications associated with a total of 150 injections among the 25 patients given either VEGF-2 or placebo in these two stu-dies.

With specific regard to mortality, it should be noted that the cumulative mortality for the 85 patients with class 3 or 4 angina, all of whom were refused for conventional revas-cularization, undergoing operative or percutaneous naked DNA gene transfer of VEGF-1 or VEGF-2 has been 3/85 or 3.5% at up to 33 months follow-up (Fig. 8-4). This compares favorably with an average 11-13% 1-year mortality for a similar group of almost 1000 patients receiving laser myo-cardial revascularization (see below) or continued medical therapy in 5 contemporary controlled studies.[121-125]

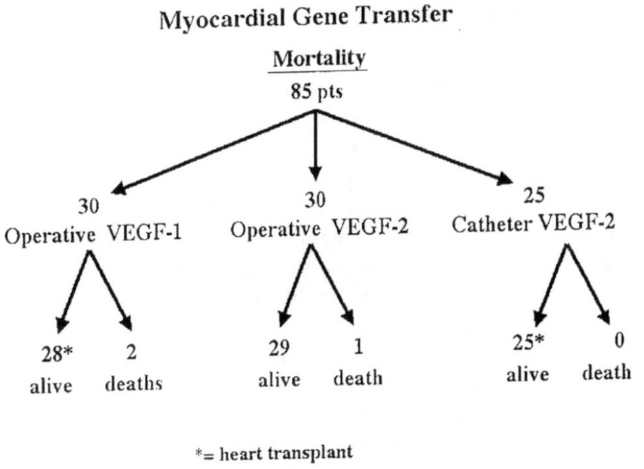

Myocardial Gene Transfer

Mortality

85 pts

30	30	25
Operative VEGF-1	Operative VEGF-2	Catheter VEGF-2
28* 2	29 1	25* 0
alive deaths	alive death	alive death

*= heart transplant

Figure 8-4. Mortality after naked DNA VEGF-1 and VEGF-2 gene transfer. Mortality outcome data for all clinical trials using plasmid human (naked DNA) VEGF-1 or VEGF-2 gene transfer in patients with disabling angina and severe coronary artery disease unsuitable for revascularization. Cumulative overall mortality in all 85 patients in the combined studies, with follow-up ranging from 10 – 33 months, was 3.5%, with 1 patient requiring cardiac transplantation at 13 months for symptoms (asterisk). There has been no mortality in the catheter-based gene transfer studies.

POTENTIAL RISKS OF INDUCING ANGIOGENESIS

The risks associated with therapeutic angiogenesis include those that are specific to the growth factor per se, and those generic to strategies of promoting angiogenesis. With regard to the former, risks thus far recognized clinically in association with VEGF depend upon the mode of administration. Administration of recombinant protein may lead to hypotension[46,126] due to the fact that VEGF upregulates nitric oxide synthesis;[127,128] this complication, however, has never been described following gene transfer in either animals or humans. While experiments performed in transgenic mice engineered to overexpress VEGF ± angiopoietin have been interpreted to suggest lethal permeability-enhancing effects of VEGF,[129] evidence of enhanced permeability in humans has been limited to transient lower extremity edema in patients with critical limb ischemia following VEGF gene transfer.[47] A third issue concerns the development of angiomata in mice[130] or rats[77] treated with transduced myoblasts or supraphysiologic doses of plasmid DNA respectively. Importantly, in the latter study, no angiomata were observed when the dose of administered plasmid DNA was reduced by 50%, (Kloner et al, unpublished data). Excepting these studies, no other preclinical or clinical reports, including those using adenoviral vectors, have described this complication. With bFGF, hypotension may also result from use of recombinant protein – again mediated via augmented nitric oxide release – but has not been described following gene transfer. Use of recombinant protein has also been associated with proteinuria.[49]

More generic safety issues concern the potential to stimulate tumor vascularity and growth in the case of occult neoplasms, as well as the potential to exacerbate proliferative and/or hemorrhagic retinopathy in patients with diabetes, in view of the high VEGF levels demonstrated in the ocular fluid of patients with active proliferative retinopathy.[131] With regard to carcinogenesis, there are neither *in vitro* nor *in vivo* data to date to suggest that VEGF increases the risk of neoplastic growth and/or metastases, although longer term follow-up will be required to address this issue in clinical trials. With regard to retinopathy, more than 100 patients receiving VEGF-1 or 2 have now been treated at our institution and undergone serial funduscopic examinations pre- and post-gene transfer by an independent group of retinal specialists; none to date (up to four-year follow-up) have shown evidence of new retinopathy, despite the fact that nearly one-third had a history of diabetes and/or remote retinopathy.[132]

Another concern stems from the recent demonstration that inhibitors of angiogenesis tested in an apolipoprotein E deficient mouse model of atherosclerosis inhibited plaque growth and intimal neovascularization.[133] It is important to underscore the fact that these experiments were designed to test the hypothesis that inhibition of plaque angiogenesis would reduce the growth of atherosclerotic lesions; the experiments were not designed to test the hypothesis that administration of agents which promote angiogenesis would enhance atherosclerosis. To this end, four separate animal studies[134-137] and two clinical studies of human subjects[138,139] fail to support the notion that accelerated atherosclerosis is a likely consequence of administering angiogenic cytokines; the outcome, in fact, is quite the opposite, in that administration of VEGF led to a statistically significant reduction in intimal thickening due to accelerated re-endothelialization. The data available to date thus do not support the notion that acceleration of atherosclerosis will be a consequence of VEGF-induced stimulation of angiogenesis.

TRANSMYOCARDIAL LASER REVASCULARIZATION

Transmyocardial laser revascularization (TMR) was investigated initially by Mirhoseini in 1982[140] as a means of augmenting blood flow to the myocardium by creating sinusoidal tracts typical of amphibian ventricles. The past decade has witnessed renewed interest in this strategy, particularly for patients who are not suitable candidates for conventional revascularization. Indeed, the U.S. Food and Drug Administration recently approved two systems for commercial use, and the costs of TMR are now coded for reimbursement by HCFA. As interest in TMR was renewed during the past decade, it was suggested that putative benefit from the procedure might be the result of angiogenesis,[141-143] as multiple pathologic studies failed to show evidence that the lased channels remained patent.[144-146] This issue remains unresolved due to the difficulty in distinguishing neovascularization associated with wound healing in response to laser injury, from nutrient angiogenesis.[147,148]

Mechanisms aside, TMR as sole therapy has now been compared to maximum medical therapy for severe angina in just under 1 000 patients with coronary artery disease not amenable to standard revascularization in five randomized trials.[121-125] One year mortality was high in this patient group (11.5% for laser and 12.7% for medical controls). The trials were concordant in showing reduced angina compared to controls, but quite variable in comparisons of treadmill time. There was no consistent pattern of change in SPECT nuclear perfusion, with three of four studies showing no improvement in reversible SPECT defects. In two uncontrolled studies in which perfusion was determined by positron emission tomography,[149,150] no increase in regional blood flow was observed in the laser irradiated regions. These findings have been interpreted by some to suggest that reduction in angina may result from either denervation or from the placebo effect of thoracotomy. Denervation as a mechanism of symptom relief is supported by the predominance of silent ischemia in the perioperative period[151] and by evidence of denervation in canine models of TMR[152,153] as well as in patients who showed reduced hydroxyephedrine uptake with positron tomography.[150]

More recently, several trials have tested the potential to perform TMR percutaneously using catheter-based fiber optic delivery of laser light to multiple left ventricular endocardial sites. The first of these trials[154] showed a significant improvement in exercise capacity and reduction in anginal symptoms at 6 months, but thallium perfusion scintigraphy was unchanged. The DIRECT trial, a stringent multicenter, double-blind, placebo-controlled study in which patients received either holmium:YAG or mock laser irradiation, failed to show improvement in anginal symptoms or exercise time compared to placebo; at 6 months, both the treated and control groups reported an almost identical reduction in angina symptoms and a similar improvement in exercise time (27 and 35 second increases in high and low dose laser respectively vs 31 seconds in placebo).[155]

CONCLUSIONS

The immediate goal of clinical research in therapeutic myocardial angiogenesis with either protein administration or gene transfer is to demonstrate efficacy in larger scale, placebo-controlled trials. To be sure, the rate at which regulatory agencies have permitted clinical trials of gene therapy, as opposed to recombinant protein or TMR, to progress, has delayed achieving this objective. In addition, it should be acknowledged that clinical evaluation of therapies designed to promote collateral development would benefit from improvements in imaging capabilities that would permit routine, high resolution imaging of vessels <200 μm in diameter, typical of synchrotron radiation,[94] but not possible with current angiographic imaging suites. Given the goal of optimizing tissue exposure to growth factor, it remains to be demonstrated that this can be achieved with single or even multiple injections of recombinant protein; recognizing this, certain groups are currently investigating sustained-release formulations of recombinant protein (N. Ferrara, personal communication). In contrast, sustained release is an inherent feature of gene transfer, at least over a period of two to four weeks in the case of naked plasmid or adenoviral gene transfer,[52,156] and thus constitutes a potential advantage for gene therapy. Subsequent studies will be required to confirm preliminary suggestions that the levels and duration of gene expression achieved with naked plasmid DNA are of sufficient magnitude to achieve therapeutic angiogenesis while avoiding adverse effects, and to optimize the choice, dose, and route of administration of angiogenic growth factor. Similarly, clinical trials will ultimately be required to test combinations of growth factors[157,158] in an attempt to reproduce the cascade evolved by nature to elaborate vascular networks.

Finally, complementary strategies that are not limited to supplying the growth factor, but instead enrich the cellular population capable of responding to the ligand may be required for optimally robust vascularity. A number of studies[15,39-41,44,159,160] have suggested that the viable population of endothelial cells capable of responding to angiogenic cytokine replacement may represent a limiting factor in trials of angiogenesis. Preliminary attempts to address this by a strategy of "supply side" angiogenesis, administering expanded populations of endothelial progenitors harvested from the patient's own circulating blood volume, have successfully augmented hindlimb[13] and myocardial[161] angiogenesis. Clinical implementation of such a strategy will require further research into techniques for harvesting and separating cells, and stimulation of their growth *ex-vivo* before re-infusion at the time of cytokine stimulation. Implicit in this approach is the development of paradigms capable of identifying which patients are likely to have inadequate cytokine[42] or cellular responses to ischemia, so that therapy can be tailored and therapeutic angiogenesis targeted appropriately.

SUMMARY

A large body of evidence has accumulated in animal models of ischemia showing that administration of angiogenic growth factors either as recombinant protein or by gene transfer can augment nutrient perfusion through neovascularization. While many cytokines have angiogenic activity, the best studied both in animal models and clinical trials are vascular endothelial growth factor (VEGF) and fibroblast growth factor (FGF). Clinical trials of therapeutic angiogenesis in patients with end-stage coronary artery disease have shown large increases in exercise time and marked reductions in anginal symptoms, as well as objective evidence of improved perfusion and left ventricular function. Larger scale placebo-controlled trials have been limited to intracoronary and intravenous administration of recombinant protein, and have not yet shown significant improvement in either exercise time or angina when compared to placebo. Larger scale placebo-controlled studies of gene transfer are in progress.

Future clinical studies will be required to determine the optimal dose, formulation, route of administration and combinations of growth factors, as well as the requirement for endothelial progenitor cell or stem cell supplementation, to provide effective and safe therapeutic myocardial angiogenesis. Determination of what growth factors or cells may be required in an individual patient so that angiogenesis could be tailored to individual needs, should be a goal of research in this area.

ACKNOWLEDGEMENTS

We would like to acknowledge the contributions of Rene Tio, M.D., James F. Symes, M.D., Peter R.Vale, M.D. Douglas W. Losordo, M.D., and Charles Milliken, B.S., M.S. to several of the studies summarized in this paper; and to Mrs. Mickey Neely for preparation of the manuscript.

REFERENCES

1. Folkman J: Tumor angiogenesis: therapeutic implications. *N Engl J Med* 1971;285:1182-1186.
2. Takeshita S, Zheng LP, Brogi E, et al: Therapeutic angiogenesis: A single intra-arterial bolus of vascular endothelial growth factor augments revascularization in a rabbit ischemic hindlimb model. *J Clin Invest* 1994;93:662-670.
3. Isner JM, Pieczek A, Schainfeld R, et al: Clinical evidence of angiogenesis following arterial gene transfer of phVEGF165. *Lancet* 1996;348:370-374.
4. Baumgartner I, Pieczek A, Manor O, et al: Constitutive expression of phVEGF165 following intramuscular gene transfer promotes collateral vessel development in patients with critical limb ischemia. *Circulation* 1998;97:1114-1123.
5. Mukherjee D, Bhatt DL, Roe MT, et al: Direct myocardial revascularization and angiogenesis - how many patients might be eligible? *Am J Cardiol* 1999;84:598-600.
6. Gilbert SF: *Developmental Biology, Fourth Edition.* Sunderland, MA , Sinauer Associates, Inc., 1997, pp 342.
7. Risau W: Differentiation of endothelium. *FASEB J* 1995;9:926-933.
8. Flamme I, Risau W: Induction of vasculogenesis and hematopoiesis in vitro. *Development* 1992;116:435-439.
9. Weiss M, Orkin SH: In vitro differentiation of murine embryonic stem cells: new approaches to old problems. *J Clin Invest* 1996;97:591-595.
10. Asahara T, Murohara T, Sullivan A, et al: Isolation of putative progenitor endothelial cells for angiogenesis. *Science* 1997;275:965-967.
11. Asahara T, Masuda H, Takahashi T, et al: Bone marrow origin of endothelial progenitor cells responsible for postnatal vasculogenesis in physiological and pathological neovascularization. *Circ Res* 1999;85:221-228.

12. Takahashi T, Kalka C, Masuda H, et al: Ischemia- and cytokine-induced mobilization of bone marrow-derived endothelial progenitor cells for neovascularization. *Nature Med* 1999;5:434-438.

13. Kalka C, Masuda H, Takahashi T, et al: Transplantation of *ex vivo* expanded endothelial progenitor cells for therapeutic neovascularization. *Proc Natl Acad Sci USA* 2000;97:3422-3427.

14. Arras M, Ito WD, Scholz D, et al: Monocyte activation in angiogenesis and collateral growth in the rabbit hindlimb. *J Clin Invest* 1998;101:40-50.

15. Isner JM: Tissue responses to ischemia: local and remote responses for preserving perfusion of ischemic muscle. *J Clin Invest* 2000;106:615-619.

16. Goldberg MA, Schneider TJ: Similarities between the oxygen-sensing mechanisms regulating the expression of vascular endothelial growth factor and erythropoietin. *J Biol Chem* 1994;269:4355-4359.

17. Shima DT, Deutsch U, D'Amore PA: Hypoxic induction of vascular endothelial growth factor (VEGF) in human epithelial cells is mediated by increases in mRNA stability. *FEBS Lett* 1995;370:203-208.

18. Forsythe JA, Jiang BH, Lyer NV, et al: Activation of vascular endothelial growth factor gene transcription by hypoxia-inducible factor 1. *Mol and Cell Biol* 1996;16:4604-4613.

19. Levy AP, Levy NS, Wegner S, et al: Transcriptional regulation of the rat vascular endothelial growth factor gene by hypoxia. *J Biol Chem* 1995;270:13333-13340.

20. Stein I, Neeman M, Shweiki D, et al: Stabilization of vascular endothelial growth factor mRNA by hypoxia and hypoglycemia and coregulation with other ischemia-induced genes. *J Mol Cell Biol* 1995;15:5363-5368.

21. Takeshita S, Weir L, Chen D, et al: Therapeutic angiogenesis following arterial gene transfer of vascular endothelial growth factor in a rabbit model of hindlimb ischemia. *Biochem Biophys Res Commun* 1996;227:628-635.

22. Shalaby F, Rossant J, Yamaguchi TP, et al: Failure of blood-island formation and vasculogenesis in Flk-1 deficient mice. *Nature* 1995;376:62-66.

23. Carmeliet P, Collen D: Molecular analysis of blood vessel formation and disease. *Am J Physiol* 1997;273:H2091-H2104.

24. Fong GH, Rossant J, Gertsenstein M, et al: Role of flt-1 receptor tyrosine kinase in regulating the assembly of vascular endothelium. *Nature* 1995;376:66-70.

25. Jeltsch M, Kaipainen A, Joukov V, et al: Hyperplasia of lymphatic vessels in VEGF-C transgenic mice. *Science* 1997;276:1423-1425.

26. Waltenberger J, Mayr U, Pentz S, et al: Functional upregulation of the vascular endothelial growth factor receptor KDR by hypoxia. *Circulation* 1996;94:1647-1654.

27. Li J, Brown LF, Hibberd MG, et al: VEGF, *flk-1*, and *flt-1* expression in a rat myocardial infarction model of angiogenesis. *Am J Physiol* 1996;270:H1803-H1811.

28. Namiki A, Brogi E, Kearney M, et al: Hypoxia induces vascular endothelial growth factor in cultured human endothelial cells. *J Biol Chem* 1995;270:31189-31195.

29. Kalka C, Masuda H, Takahashi T, et al: Vascular endothelial growth factor 165 gene transfer augments circulating endothelial progenitor cells in human subjects. *Circ Res* 2000;86:1198-1202.

30. Asahara T, Takahashi T, Masuda H, et al: VEGF contributes to postnatal neovascularization by mobilizing bone marrow-derived endothelial progenitor cells. *EMBO J* 1999;18:3964-3972.

31. Kalka C, Tehrani H, Laudenberg B, et al: Mobilization of endothelial progenitor cells following gene therapy with VEGF165 in patients with inoperable coronary disease. *Ann Thorac Surg* 2000;70:829-834.

32. Isner JM: Angiogenesis, in Topol EJ (ed): *Textbook of Cardiovascular Medicine*. Philadelphia, Lippincott-Raven Publishers, 1998, pp 2491-2518.

33. Henry TD: Therapeutic angiogenesis. *BMJ* 1999;318:1536-1539.

34. Hamawy AH, Lee LY, Crystal RG, et al: Cardiac angiogenesis and gene therapy: a strategy for myocardial revascularization. *Curr Opin Cardiol* 1999;14:515-522.

35. Carmeliet P: Mechanisms of angiogenesis and arteriogenesis. *Nature Med* 2000;6:389-395.

36. Tabata H, Silver M, Isner JM: Arterial gene transfer of acidic fibroblast growth factor for therapeutic angiogenesis in vivo: critical role of secretion signal in use of naked DNA. *Cardiovasc Res* 1997;35:470-479.

37. Giordano FJ, Ping P, McKirnan D, et al: Intracoronary gene transfer of fibroblast growth factor-5 increases blood flow and contractile function in an ischemic region of the heart. *Nature Med* 1996;2:534-539.

38. McKirnan MD, Guo X, Waldman LK, et al: Intracoronary gene transfer of fibroblast growth factor-4 increases regional contractile function and responsiveness to adrenergic stimulation in heart failure. *Cardiac and Vascular Regeneration* 2000;1:11-21.

39. Rivard A, Fabre J-E, Silver M, et al: Age-dependent impairment of angiogenesis. *Circulation* 1999;99:111-120.

40. Rivard A, Silver M, Chen D, et al: Rescue of diabetes related impairment of angiogenesis by intramuscular gene therapy with adeno-VEGF. *Am J Pathol* 1999;154:355-364.

41. Couffinhal T, Silver M, Kearney M, et al: Impaired collateral vessel development associated with reduced expression of vascular endothelial growth factor in ApoE-1- Mice. *Circulation* 1999;99:3188-3198.

42. Schultz A, Lavie L, Hochberg I, et al: Interindividual heterogeneity in the hypoxic regulation of VEGF: Significance for the development of the coronary artery collateral circulation. *Circulation* 1999;100:547-552.

43. Rohan RM, Fernandez A, Udagawa T, et al: Genetic heterogeneity of angiogenesis in mice. *FASEB J* 2000;14:871-876.

44. Isner JM, Asahara T: Angiogenesis and vasculogenesis as therapeutic strategies for postnatal neovascularization (Perspective). *J Clin Invest* 1999;103:1231-1236.

45. Asahara T, Kalka C, Isner JM: Stem cell therapy and gene transfer for regeneration. *Gene Therapy* 2000;7:451-457.

46. Hariawala M, Horowitz JR, Esakof D, et al: VEGF improves myocardial blood flow but produces EDRF-mediated hypotension in porcine hearts. *J Surg Res* 1996;63:77-82.

47. Baumgartner I, Rauh G, Pieczek A, et al: Lower-extremity edema associated with gene transfer of naked DNA vascular endothelial growth factor. *Ann Int Med* 2000;132:880-884.

48. Mazue G, Bertolero MG, Jacob F, et al: Preclinical and clinical studies with recombinant human basic fibroblast growth factor. *Ann NY Acad Sci* 1991;638:329-340.

49. Cooper LT, Hirsch AT, Regensteines JG, et al: A double-blind, placebo-controlled, phase II study of basic fibroblast growth factor in the treatment of intermittent claudication. *Circulation* 2000;102:II-373(Abstract).

50. Lazarous DF, Shou M, Stiber JA, et al: Pharmacodynamics of basic fibroblast growth factor: route of administration determines myocardial and systemic distribution. *Cardiovasc Res* 1997;36:78-85.

51. Wolff JA, Ludtke JJ, Acsadi G, et al: Long-term persistence of plasmid DNA and foreign gene expression in mouse muscle. *Human Molecular Genetics* 1992;1:363-369.

52. Tsurumi Y, Takeshita S, Chen D, et al: Direct intramuscular gene transfer of naked DNA encoding vascular endothelial growth factor augments collateral development and tissue perfusion. *Circulation* 1996;94:3281-3290.

53. Takeshita S, Isshiki T, Sato T: Increased expression of direct gene transfer into skeletal muscles observed after acute ischemic injury in rats. *Lab Invest* 1996;74:1061-1065.

54. Laham RJ, Rezaee M, Garcia L, et al: Tissue and myocardial distribution of intracoronary, intravenous, intrapericardial and intramyocardial 125I-labeled basic fibroblast growth factor (bFGF) favor intramyocardial delivery. *J Am Coll Cardiol* 2000;35:10A(Abstract).

55. Schaper W, Munoz-Chapuli R, Wolf C, Ito W: Collateral circulation of the heart, in Ware JA, Simons M (eds): *Angiogenesis and Cardiovascular Disease*. New York, Oxford University Press, 1999, pp 159-198.

56. Unger EF, Banai S, Shou M, et al: Basic fibroblast growth factor enhances myocardial collateral flow in a canine model. *Am J Physiol* 1994;266:H1588-H1595.

57. Lazarous DF, Scheinowtiz M, Shou M, et al: Effects of chronic systemic administration of basic fibroblast growth factor on collateral development in the canine heart. *Circulation* 1995;91:145-153.

58. Lazarous DF, Shou M, Scheinowitz M, et al: Comparative effects of basic fibroblast growth factor and vascular endothelial growth factor on coronary collateral development and arterial response to injury. *Circulation* 1996;94:1074-1082.

59. Rajanayagam MA, Shou M, Thirumurti V, et al: Intracoronary basic fibroblast growth factor enhances myocardial collateral perfusion in dogs. *J Am Coll Cardiol* 2000;35:519-526.

60. Shou M, Thirumurti V, rajanayagam S, et al: Effect of basic fibroblast growth factor on myocardial angiogenesis in dogs with mature collateral vessels. *J Am Coll Cardiol* 1997;29:1102-1106.

61. Harada K, Grossman W, Friedman M, et al: Basic fibroblast growth factor improves myocardial function in chronically ischemic porcine hearts. *J Clin Invest* 1994;94:623-630.

62. Lopez JJ, Edelman ER, Stamler A, et al: Basic fibroblast growth factor in a porcine model of chronic myocardial ischemia: a comparison of angiographic, echocardiographic and coronary flow parameters. *J Pharmacol Exp Ther* 1997;282:385-390.

63. Laham RJ, Rezaee M, Post M, et al: Intrapericardial delivery of fibroblast growth factor-2 induces neovascularization in a porcine model of chronic myocardial ischemia. *J Pharmacol Exp Ther* 2000;292:795-802.

64. Banai S, Jaklitsch MT, Casscells W, et al: Effects of acidic fibroblast growth factor on normal and ischemic myocardium. *Circ Res* 1991;69:76-85.

65. Unger EF, Shou M, Sheffield CD, et al: Extracardiac to coronary anastomoses support regional left ventricular function in dogs. *Am J Physiol* 1993;264:H1567-H1574.

66. Lopez JJ, Edelman ER, Stamler A, et al: Angiogenic potential of perivascularly delivered aFGF in a porcine model of chronic myocardial ischemia. *Am J Physiol* 1998;274:H930-H936.

67. Lopez JJ, Laham RJ, Stamler A, et al: VEGF administration in chronic myocardial ischemia in pigs. *Cardiovasc Res* 1998;40:272-281.

68. Harada K, Friedman M, Lopez JJ, et al: Vascular endothelial growth factor in chronic myocardial ischemia. *Am J Physiol* 1996;270:H1791-H1802.

69. Hughes CG, Biswas SS, Yin B, et al: Intramyocardial but not intravenous vascular endothelial growth factor improves regional perfusion in hibernating porcine myocardium. *Circulation* 1999;100:I-476(Abstract).

70. Banai S, Jaklitsch MT, Shou M, et al: Angiogenic-induced enhancement of collateral blood flow to ischemic myocardium by vascular endothelial growth factor in dogs. *Circulation* 1994;89:2183-2189.

71. Tio RA, Tkebuchava T, Scheuermann TH, et al: Intramyocardial gene therapy with naked DNA encoding vascular endothelial growth factor improves collateral flow to ischemic myocardium. *Human Gene Ther* 1999;10:2953-2960.

72. Vale PR, Milliken CE, Tkebuchava T, et al: Catheter-based gene transfer of VEGF utilizing electromechanical LV mapping accomplishes therapeutic angiogenesis: pre-clinical studies in swine. *Circulation* 1999;100:I-512(Abstract).

73. Vale PR, Tkebuchava T, Milliken CE, et al: Percutaneous electromechanical mapping demonstrates efficacy of pVGI.1 (VEGF2) in an animal model of chronic myocardial ischemia. *Circulation* 1999;100:I-22(Abstract).

74. Mack CA, Patel SR, Schwarz EA, et al: Biologic bypass with the use of adenovirus-mediated gene transfer of the conplementary deoxyribonucleic acid for vascular endothelial growth factor 121 improves myocardial perfusion and function in the ischemic porcine heart. *J Thorac Cardiovasc Surg* 1998;115:168-176.

75. Lee LY, Patel SR, Hackett NR, et al: Focal angiogen therapy using intramyocardial delivery of an adenovirus vector coding for vascular endotehlial growth factor 121. *Ann Thorac Surg* 2000;69:14-24.

76. Lazarous DF, Shou M, Stiber JA, et al: Adenoviral-mediated gene transfer induces sustained pericardial VEGF expression in dogs: effect on myocardial angiogenesis. *Cardiovasc Res* 1999;44:294-302.

77. Schwartz ER, Speakman MT, Patterson M, et al: Evaluation of the effects of intramyocardial injection of DNA expressing vascular endothelial growth factor (VEGF) in a myocardial infarction model in the rat - angiogenesis and angioma formation. *J Am Coll Cardiol* 2000;35:1323-1330.

78. Lee RJ, Springer ML, Blanco-Bose WE, et al: VEGF gene delivery to myocardium: deleterious effects of unregulated expression. *Circulation* 2000;102:898-901.

79. Vale PR, Losordo DW, Tkebuchava T, et al: Cather-based myocardial gene transfer utilizing nonfluoroscopic electromechanical left ventricular mapping. *J Am Coll Cardiol* 1999;34:246-254.

80. Deutsch E, Tarazona N, Sanborn TA, et al: Percutaneous endocardial gene therapy: patterns of in-vivo gene expression related to regional myocardial delivery. *J Am Coll Cardiol* 2000;35:6A(Abstract).

81. Kornowski R, Fuchs S, Vodovotz Y, et al: Catheter-based transendocardial injection of adenoviral VEGF121 offers equivalent gene delivery and protein expression compared to a surgical-based transepicardial injection approach. *J Am Coll Cardiol* 2000;35:73A(Abstract).

82. Vale PR, Losordo DW, Milliken CE, et al: Randomized, placebo-controlled clinical study of percutaneous catheter-based left ventricular endocardial gene transfer of VEGF-2 for myocardial angiogenesis in patients with chronic myocardial ischemia. *Circulation* 2000;102:II-563(Abstract).

83. Schainfeld RM, Isner JM: Critical limb ischemia: nothing to give at the office? *Ann Int Med* 1999;130:442-444.

84. Isner JM: Arterial gene transfer for naked DNA for therapeutic angiogenesis: early clinical results. *Advanced Drug Delivery* 1998;30:185-197.

85. Isner JM, Baumgartner I, Rauh G, et al: Treatment of thromboangiitis obliterans (Buerger's disease) by intramuscular gene transfer of vascular endothelial growth factor: preliminary clinical results. *J Vasc Surg* 1998;28:964-975.

86. Ben-Haim SA, Osadchy D, Schuster I, et al: Nonfluoroscopic, *in vivo* navigation and mapping technology. *Nature Med* 1996;2:1393-1395.

87. Gepstein L, Goldin A, Lessick J, et al: Electromechanical characterization of chronic myocardial infarction in the canine coronary occlusion model. *Circulation* 1998;98:2055-2064.

88. Vale PR, Losordo DW, Milliken CE, et al: Left ventricular electromechanical mapping to assess efficacy of phVEGF165 gene transfer for therapeutic angiogenesis in chronic myocardial ischemia. *Circulation* 2000;102:965-974.

89. Huggins GS, Pasternak RC, Alpert NM, et al: Effects of short-term treatment of hyperlipidemia on coronary vasodilator function and myocardial perfusion in regions having substantial impairment of baseline dilator reserve. *Circulation* 1998;98:1291-1296.

90. Pearlman JD, Hibberd MG, Chuang ML, et al: Magnetic resonance mapping demonstrates benefits of VEGF-induced myocardial angiogenesis. *Nature Med* 1995;1:1085-1089.

91. Pearlman JD, Laham RJ, Simons M: Coronary angiogenesis: detection in vivo with MR imaging sensitive to collateral neocirculation – preliminary study in pigs. *Radiol* 2000;214:801-807.

92. White FC, Carroll SM, Magnet A, et al: Coronary collateral development in swine after coronary artery occlusion. *Circ Res* 1992;71:1490-1500.

93. Takeshita S, Isshiki T, Tanaka E, et al: Use of synchrotron radiation microangiography to assess development of small collateral arteries in a rat model of hindlimb ischemia. *Circulation* 1997;95:805-808.

94. Schumacher B, Pecher P, vonSpecht BU, et al: Induction of neoangiogenesis in ischemic myocardium by human growth factors: first clinical results of a new treatment of coronary heart disease. *Circulation* 1998;97:645-650.

95. Schumacher B, Stegmann T, Pecher P: The stimulation of neoangiogenesis in the ischemic human heart by the growth factor FGF: first clinical results. *J Cardiovasc Surg* 1998;39:783-789.

96. Stegmann TJ, Hoppert T, Schlurmann W, et al: First angiogenic treatment of coronary heart disease by FGF-1: long-term results after 3 years. *Cardiac and Vascular Regeneration* 2000;1:5-10.

97. Stegmann TJ, Hoppert T, Schneider A, et al: Induction of myocardial neoangiogenesis by human growth factors. A new therapeutic option in coronary heart disease. *Herz* 2000;25:589-599.

98. Laham RJ, Sellke FW, Edelman ER, et al: Local perivascular delivery of basic fibroblast growth factor in patients undergoing coronary bypass surgery: results of a phase 1 randomized, double-blind, placebo-controlled trial. *Circulation* 1999;100:1865-1871.

99. Laham RJ, Chronos NA, Leimbach M, et al: Results of a phase 1 open label dose escalation study of intracoronary and intravenous basic fibroblast growth factor (rFGF-2) in patients (pts) with severe ischemic heart disease: 6 months follow-up. *J Am Coll Cardiol* 2000;35:73A(Abstract).

100. Henry TD, Rocha-Sing K, Isner JM, et al: Intracoronary administration of recombinant human vascular endothelial growth factor (rhVEGF) to patients with coronary artery disease. *Am Heart J* 2000;(In Press).

101. Laham RJ, Chronos NA, Pike M, et al: Intracoronary basic fibroblast growth factor (FGF-2) in patients with severe ischemic heart disease: results of a phase 1 open labe dose escalation study. *J Am Coll Cardiol* 2000;(In Press).

102. Udelson JE, Dilsizian V, Laham RJ, et al: Therapeutic angiogenesis with recombinant fibroblast growth factor-2 improves stress and rest myocardial perfusion abnormalities in patients with severe symptomatic chronic coronary artery disease. *Circulation* 2000;102:1605-1610.

103. Henry TD, Abraham JA: Review of prelcinical and clinical results with vascular endothelial growth factors for therapeutic angiogenesis. *Current Interventional Cardiology Reports* 2000;2:228-241.

104. Hendel RC, Henry TD, Rocha-Singh K, et al: Effect of intracoronary recombinant human vascular endothelial growth factor on myocardial perfusion: evidence for a dose-dependent effect. *Circulation* 2000;101:118-121.

105. Henry TD, Annex BH, Azrin MA, et al: Final results of the VIVA trial of rhVEGF for human therapeutic angiogenesis. *Circulation* 1999;100:I-476(Abstract).

106. Ferguson JJ: Meeting highlights: highlights of the 48th scientific sessions of the american college of cardiology. *Circulation* 1999;100:570-575.

107. Henry TD, McKendall GR, Azrin MA, et al: VIVA trial: one year follow up. *Circulation* 2000;102:II-309(Abstract).

108. Kleiman NS, Califf RM: Results from late-breaking clinical trials sessions at ACCIS 2000 and ACC 2000. *J Am Coll Cardiol* 2000;36:310-311.

109. Losordo DW, Vale PR, Symes J, et al: Gene therapy for myocardial angiogenesis: initial clinical results with direct myocardial injection of phVEGF165 as sole therapy for myocardial ischemia. *Circulation* 1998;98:2800-2804.

110. Symes JF, Losordo DW, Vale PR, et al: Gene therapy with vascular endothelial growth factor for inoperable coronary artery disease: preliminary clinical results. *Ann Thorac Surg* 1999;68:830-837.

111. Vale PR, Losordo DW, Dunnington C, et al: Direct myocardial injection of phVEGF165: results of complete patient cohort in phase 1/2 clinical trial. *Circulation* 1999;100:I-477(Abstract).

112. Esakof DD, Maysky M, Losordo DW, et al: Intraoperative multiplane transesophageal echocardiograpy for guiding direct myocardial gene transfer of vascular endothelial growth factor in patients with refractory angina pectoris. *Human Gene Ther* 1999;10:2315-2323.

113. Shen Y-T, Vatner SF: Mechanism of impaired myocardial function during progressive coronary stenosis in conscious pigs: hibernation versus stunning? *Circ Res* 1995;76:479-488.

114. Wijns W, Vatner SF, Camici PG: Hibernating myocardium. *N Engl J Med* 1998;3:173-181.

115. Dilsizian V, Bonow RO: Current diagnostic techniques of assessing myocardial viability in patients with hibernating and stunned myocardium. *Circulation* 1993;87:1-20.

116. Rosengart TK, Lee LY, Patel SR, et al: Angiogenesis gene therapy: Phase I assessment of direct intramyocardial administration of an adenovirus vector expression VEGF121 cDNA to individuals with clinically significant severe coronary artery disease. *Circulation* 1999;100:468-474.

117. Rosengart TK, Lee LY, Port JL, et al: Video assisted epicardial delivery of angiogenic gene therapy to the human myocardium utilizing an adenovirus vector encoding for VEGF121. *Circulation* 1999;100:I-770(Abstract).

118. Vale PR, Milliken CE, Fortuin FD, et al: Effective gene transfer of phVEGF-2 for therapeutic angiogenesis in chronic myocardial ischemia as assessed by NOGATM left ventricular electromechanical mapping (abstract). *Circulation* 2000;102:II-689.

119. Hendel RC, Vale PR, Losordo DW, et al: The effects of VEGF-2 gene therapy on rest and stress myocardial perfusion: results of serial SPECT imaging. *Circulation* 2000;102:II-769(Abstract).

120. Schofield PM, Sharples LD, Caine N, et al: Transmyocardial laser revascularisation in patients with refractory angina: a randomised controlled trial. *Lancet* 1999;353:519-524.

121. Burkhoff D, Schmidt S, Schulman SP, et al: Transmyocardial laser revascularisation compared with continued medical therapy for treatment of refractory angina pectoris: a prospective randomised trial. *Lancet* 1999;354:885-890.

122. Allen KB, Dowling RD, Fudge TL, et al: Comparison of transmyocardial revascularization with medical therapy in patients with refractory angina. *N Engl J Med* 1999;341:1029-1036.

123. Frazier OH, March RJ, Horvath KA, et al: Transmyocardial revascularization with a carbon dioxide laser in patients with end-stage coronary artery disease. *N Engl J Med* 1999;341:1021-1028.

124. Aaberge L, Nordstrand K, Dragsund M, et al: Transmyocardial revascularization with CO2 laser in patients with refractory angina pectoris: clinical results from the Norwegian randomized trial. *J Am Coll Cardiol* 2000;35:1170-1177.

125. Horowitz JR, Rivard A, van der Zee R, et al: Vascular endothelial growth factor/vascular permeability factor produces nitric oxide-dependent hypotension. *Arterioscler Thromb Vasc Biol* 1997;17:2793-2800.

126. van der Zee R, Murohara T, Luo Z, et al: Vascular endothelial growth factor (VEGF)/vascular permeability factor (VPF) augments nitric oxide release from quiescent rabbit and human vascular endothelium. *Circulation* 1997;95:1030-1037.

127. Murohara T, Asahara T, Silver M, et al: Nitric oxide synthase modulates angiogenesis in response to tissue ischemia. *J Clin Invest* 1998;101:2567-2578.

128. Thurston G, Suri C, Smith K, et al: Leakage-resistant blood vessels in mice transgenically overexpressing angiopoietin-1. *Science* 1999;286:2511-2514.

129. Springer ML, Chen AS, Kraft PE, et al: VEGF gene delivery to muscle: potential role of vasculogenesis in adults. *Mol Cell* 1998;2:549-558.

130. Aiello LP, Avery RL, Arrigg PG, et al: Vascular endothelial growth factor in ocular fluids of patients with diabetic retinopathy and other retinal disorders. *N Engl J Med* 1994;331:1480-1487.

131. Vale PR, Rauh G, Wuensch DI, et al: Influence of vascular endothelial growth factor on diabetic retinopathy. *Circulation* 1998;17:I-353(Abstract).

132. Moulton KS, Heller E, Konerding MA, et al: Angiogenesis inhibitors endostatin and TNP-470 reduce intimal neovascularization and plaque growth in apolipoprotein E-deficient mice. *Circulation* 1999;99:1726-1732.

133. Van Belle E, Tio FO, Couffinhal T, et al: Stent endothelialization: time course, impact of local catheter delivery, feasibility of recombinant protein administration, and response to cytokine expedition. *Circulation* 1997;95:438-448.

134. Van Belle E, Tio FO, Chen D, et al: Passivation of metallic stents following arterial gene transfer of phVEGF165 inhibits thrombus formation and intimal thickening. *J Am Coll Cardiol* 1997;29:1371-1379.

135. Asahara T, Bauters C, Pastore CJ, et al: Local delivery of vascular endothelial growth factor accelerates reendothelialization and attenuates

intimal hyperplasia in balloon-injured rat carotid artery. *Circulation* 1995;91:2793-2801.

136. Asahara T, Chen D, Tsurumi Y, et al: Accelerated restitution of endothelial integrity and endothelium-dependent function following phVEGF165 gene transfer. *Circulation* 1996;94:3291-3302.

137. Vale PR, Wuensch DI, Rauh GF, et al: Arterial gene therapy for inhibiting restenosis in patients with claudication undergoing superficial femoral artery angioplasty. *Circulation* 1998;98:I-66.

138. Laitinen M, Hartikainen J, Hiltunen MO, et al: Catheter-mediated vascular endothelial growth factor gene transfer to human coronary arteries after angioplasty. *Human Gene Ther* 2000;11:263-270.

139. Mirhoseini M, Muckerheide M, Cayton MM: Transventricular revascularization by lasers. *Lasers Surg Med* 1982;2:187-198.

140. Yamamoto N, Kohmoto T, Gu A, et al: Angiogenesis is enhanced in ischemic canine myocardium by transmyocardial laser revascularization. *J Am Coll Cardiol* 1998;31:1426-1433.

141. Mack CA, Patel SR, Rosengart TK: Myocardial angiogenesis as a possible mechanism for TMLR efficacy. *J Clin Laser Med Surg* 1997;15:275-279.

142. Hughes GC, Lowe JE, Kypson AP, et al: Neovascularization after transmyocardial laser revascularization in a model of chronic ischemia. *Ann Thorac Surg* 1998;66:2029-2036.

143. Burkhoff D, Fisher PE, Apfelbaum M, et al: Histologic appearance of transmyocardial laser channels after 4 1/2 weeks. *Ann Thorac Surg* 1996;61:1532-1534.

144. Fisher PE, Khomoto T, DeRosa CM, et al: Histologic analysis of transmyocardial channels: comparison of CO2 and holmium: YAG lasers. *Ann Thorac Surg* 1997;64:466-472.

145. Whittaker P, Kloner RA, Przyklenk K: Laser-mediated transmural myocardial channels do not salvage acutely ischemic myocardium. *J Am Coll Cardiol* 1993;22:302-309.

146. Isner JM: Pathology, in Isner JM, Clarke RH (eds): *Cardiovascular Laser Therapy*. New York, Raven Press, 1989, pp 63.

147. Malekan R, Reynolds C, Narula N, et al: Angiogenesis in transmyocardial laser revascularization: a nonspecific response to injury. *Circulation* 1998;98:II-62-II-66.

148. Rimoldi O, Burns SM, Rosen SD, et al: Measurement of myocardial blood flow with positron emission tomography before and after transmyocardial laser revascularization. *Circulation* 1999;100:II-134-II-138.

149. Al-Sheikh T, Allen KB, Straka SP, et al: Cardiac sympathetic denervation after transmyocardial laser revascularization. *Circulation* 1999;100:135-140.

150. Hughes GC, Landolfo KP, Lowe JE, et al: Diagnosis, incidence, and clinical significance of early postoperative ischemia after transymocardial laser revascularization. *Am Heart J* 1999;137:1163-1168.

151. Kwong KF, Kanellopoulos GK, Nickols JC, et al: Transmyocardial laser treatment denervates canine myocardium. *J Thorac Cardiovasc Surg* 1997;114:883-890.

152. Kwong KF, Schuessler RB, Kanellopoulos GK, et al: Nontransmural laser treatment incompletely denervates canine myocardium. *Circulation* 1998;98:II-67-II-72.

153. Lauer B, Junghans U, Stahl F, et al: Catheter-based percutaneous myocardial laser revascularization in patients with end-stage coronary artery disease. *J Am Coll Cardiol* 1999;34:1663-1670.

154. Leon MB, Baim DS, Moses JW, et al: A randomized blinded clinical trial comparing percutaneous laser myocardial revascularization (using Biosense LV mapping) vs placebo in patients with refractory coronary ischemia. *Circulation* 2000;102:II-565(Abstract).

155. Lemarchand P, Jones M, Yamada I, et al: In vivo gene transfer and expression in normal uninjured blood vessels using replication-deficient recombinant adenovirus vectors. *Circ Res* 1993;72:1132-1138.

156. Asahara T, Bauters C, Zheng LP, et al: Synergistic effect of vascular endothelial growth factor and basic fibroblast growth factor on angiogenesis in vivo. *Circulation* 1995;92:II-365-II-371.

157. Asahara T, Chen D,, Takahashi T, et al: Tie2 receptor ligands, angiopoietin-1 and angiopoietin-2, modulate VEGF-induced postnatal neovascularization. *Circ Res* 1998;83:233-240.

158. Van Belle E, Rivard A, Chen D, et al: Hypercholesterolemia attenuates angiogenesis but does not preclude augmentation by angiogenic cytokines. *Circulation* 1997;96:2667-2674.

159. Luscher TF, Noll G: Endothelium dysfunction in the coronary ciruclation. *J Cardiovasc Pharmacol* 1994;24:16S-26S

161. Kawamoto A, Gwon H-C, Iwaguro H, et al: Therapeutic potential of *ex vivo* expanded endothelial progenitor cells for myocardial ischemia. *Circulation* 2000;(In Press).

162. Sellke FW, Laham RJ, Edelman ER, et al: Therapeutic angiogenesis with basic fibroblast growth factor: technique and early results. *Ann Thorac Surg* 1998;65:1540-1544.

CHAPTER 9

Angiogenesis at the Limits

PD Lambiase, M Wright and MS Marber

Since the measuring device has been constructed by the observer . . . we have to remember that what we observe is not nature in itself but nature exposed to our method of questioning. WK Heisenberg (1901-1976)

Over the past decade there has been a rapid expansion in basic molecular research investigating the process of angiogenesis in the cardiovascular field. This has rekindled interest in the coronary collateral circulation as a route to promote and restore myocardial perfusion in territories unsuitable for PTCA or surgical revascularisation. This has important implications ranging from the treatment of patients with intractable angina to the optimisation of contractile function in areas of stunned or hibernating myocardium. Recent strategies have focussed upon the introduction of single angiogens in the form of recombinant peptides or cDNAs encoded within plasmid and adenoviral vectors. It is now technically possible to modulate gene transcription such that there is both spatial and temporal control of gene expression at an ischaemic site. However, although these highly sophisticated approaches appear revolutionary, there are a number of factors limiting their clinical application. In this chapter we will consider the following issues:

1. *The aims of gene therapy.*
2. *The problems of myocardial gene transfer with illustrative data from our own work.*
3. *The clinical trials of angiogenic therapies.*
4. *The philosophy of promoting coronary collateral development.*

However, before analysing the role of gene therapy in this field, the biology of therapeutic angiogenesis will be briefly reviewed.

OVERVIEW OF BIOLOGY UNDERLYING THERAPEUTIC ANGIOGENESIS

Currently, 3 specific processes are thought to contribute to the formation of new blood vessels: *angiogenesis, arteriogenesis* and *vasculogenesis*.[1,2] *Angiogenesis* describes the development of new blood vessels lacking an intact media from pre-existing vascular structures and results from the inter-play of cell-cell, cell-matrix and cell-cytokine interactions. It is tightly regulated and transient occurring in the female reproductive organs, during wound healing or along the border of myocardial infarction. *Arteriogenesis* describes the appearance of new arteries possessing fully developed tunica media. This may occur through remodelling of pre-existing vascular structures or de novo. Furthermore, it provides the most clinically desirable conduits capable of producing significant increases in coronary flow reserve. The latter differ fundamentally from *vasculogenesis*, which applies to the de novo formation of vessels in the embryo by the association of angioblasts.

The development of coronary collaterals involves both re-modelling (i.e: hypertrophy and elongation of pre-existent collateral vessels) and angiogenesis. Angiogenesis is charac-terised and modulated by the interactions between stimula-tors and inhibitors-many of which were first identified during studies of tumour development. Hypoxia, ischaemia, mechanical stretch and inflammation have all been shown to increase endothelial mitogen levels and expression of angiogen receptors. In fact, few patients exhibit continuous tissue level ischaemia, suggesting that inflammation and shear stress may also be important factors determining angiogenesis in individuals with multivessel coronary artery disease. There is a wide variation in the native myo-cardial collateral network both between and within indivi-dual animal species.

Therefore, modelling collateral development in coronary ischaemia has been difficult. However, common patterns exist between species allowing sequential studies with in situ DNA hybridisation techniques to detect angiogen expression- principally in canine and porcine models of chronic ischaemia.[3]

The process of angiogenesis is highly orchestrated with a number of peptides released from local endothelial and smooth muscle cells, platelets and macrophages inducing cellular recruitment and differentiation in a precisely ordered fashion.[4] It is beyond the scope of this review to delineate the interplay of the increasing number of ligands involved. However, as Table 9-1 demonstrates, the principal angiogenic peptides can be classified into either pro or anti-angiogenic molecules and the angiogenic milieu will depend upon their delicate balance plus the responsiveness and viability of the cellular elements recruited into this process.

As the list of angiogenic peptides grows, we are faced with an exponential increase in the theoretical range of interac-tions. Any evaluation of this increasingly complex ligand network is confounded by the limited number of in vitro assays available to assess angiogenesis. These are semi-quantitative at best and have not significantly changed over the past 20 years. Indeed, the key to delineating the indivi-dual role of these peptides lies in the development of ani-mal models where collateral development can be accurately

TABLE 9-1.   EXTRA-CELLULAR DETERMINANTS OF COLLATERAL
FORMATION

Positive	Negative
• VEGF	• Peptides
• FGF -1, -2, -5	• Angiostatin
• PDGF-BB	• Thrombospondin
• TGF-α	• Interferon-alpha
• G-CSF	• SST Platelet factor 4
• Tissue factor	• *Steroids*
• IL-8	Methoxyprogesterone
• Angiopoietins 1 & 2	2-methoxyestradiol
	• *Angiostatic retinoids*
	• *Metalloproteinase inhibitors*
	• *Other:*
	Taxol, Pentosan, Thalidomide

quantified and individual peptide expression precisely
manipulated. It is naïve to assume that the introduction of
a single angiogen should significantly modify sequences of
arterio- and angiogenesis to produce stable vessels capable
of optimising myocardial perfusion. In many instances an
angiogen may only be expressed for hours to days in a
window where synergism or antagonism of other peptides
is the key to modulating vessel formation in a co-ordinated
manner. Uncontrolled expression of the angiogens poses
the risk of haemagioma formation which may appear to
increase perfusion on scintillation scanning or PET but has
no functional significance and may be detrimental. Schwarz
demonstrated that injection of a plasmid vector expressing
VEGF alone in the peri-infarct region of a rat heart resulted
in functionally redundant angioma formation.[5] This disor-
ganised growth of vascular channels bears no resemblance
to the well characterised patterns of collateral vessels seen
in man (Figure 9-1).

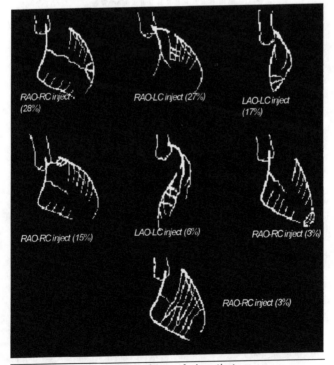

Figure 9-1. Patterns of collateral networks in patients.

Gene therapy refers to the introduction of nucleic acid into cells to achieve a therapeutic effect[6] (Figure 9-2). It offers the tantalising opportunity of creating a molecular switch that triggers and amplifies collateral vessel formation in a targeted way. This has significant advantages over peptide angiogenic therapy which is limited by short serum half life, the need for repeated treatment, the risks of systemic exposure (e.g: transient hypotension with VEGF and stimulation of occult tumours at remote sites) and high production costs.

Vector efficiency is primarily related to its ability to cross the plasma membrane and engage the transcriptional apparatus of the cell whilst avoiding lysosomal degradation. Some viral vectors may also induce an inflammatory response that destroys the host cell. This disadvantage can at least be partially overcome by deleting endogenous viral genes that encode coat proteins involved in host recognition. Through this strategy the virus avoids the host's immune response allowing prolonged gene expression. Thus the ideal gene transfer vector should satisfy the following criteria:

1. Efficient transfer of genetic material to the target cell(s).
2. Efficient transgene expression without any deleterious effects on the transfected cell.

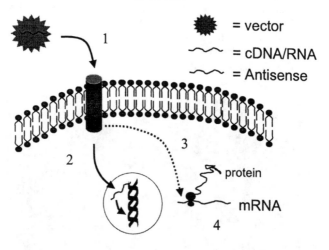

Figure 9-2. *Simplified diagram of the steps involved in DNA/RNA gene therapy. The DNA/RNA of interest is either cloned into a recombinant virus, complexed with a synthetic gene vector, or used as naked DNA. The vector enters the cell by either receptor mediated endocytosis (eg: adenovirus, integrin targeting peptides) or membrane fusion (Herpes simplex virus or cationic liposomes) (1). Once in the cell the vector enters an endosomal pathway (2) or is released in the cytoplasm (3). If the vector is taken into primary or secondary endosomes, there has to be a mechanism to release the vector and nucleic acid before lysosomal degradation. Once in the cytoplasm, the DNA has to enter the nucleus where it can express the transgene. The DNA will remain episomal (eg: recombinant adenovirus) or may integrate (eg: adeno-assoiated virus). Messenger RNA is then translated and the functional protein has its effect either within the cell or is secreted (4). If anti-sense RNA is delivered it will bind to specific complimentary mRNA and the resultant double stranded RNA will be recognised and degraded.*

3. Manufacture should be simple and cheap.
4. Gene expression in the target cell should be regulated by normal physiological stimuli i.e: hypoxia/ischaemia in the context of angiogenic therapy.
5. Expression should be self-limiting.
6. No cellular immune response should be induced.

In vivo cardiac myocyte transfection is proving to be remarkably difficult. The two most clinically applicable routes are direct intramyocardial injection and intracoronary infusion. Although intracoronary infusion is the most directly applicable, efficiency is low and the regions most needing augmented angiogen expression are those receiving the least coronary flow and therefore exposure to vector. One method to overcome this would be to use HIF-1 response elements within the angiogen promoter. These response elements would bind HIF-1, a protein that is activated by hypoxia. Similarly, it would be theoretically possible to deliver a vector into the systemic circulation providing the promoter driving angiogen expression was cardiac specific. In practice however, systemic administration results in hepatic expression. We have attempted to address some of these issues.

We have evaluated a number of vectors (Table 9-2) by both direct intramyocardial injection and intracoronary infusion in an in vivo rabbit model. Direct intramyocardial injection of plasmid DNA results in <1% myocyte transfection. Adenoviral vectors are the most effective with transfection efficiencies of up to 30% in the myocardium immediately adjacent to the needle track. However this vector is associated with a marked inflammatory response leading to a significant reduction in gene expression within 2 weeks (Figure 9-3). The primary method of assessment of gene transfer in myocardium is also prone to generate false positive data.X gal staining has traditionally been used to assess gene transfer with vectors encoding the β galactosidase reporter gene (lac Z). However, within an inflammatory infiltrate intrinsic β galactosidase activity is increased. This results in false positive staining of transfected myocardium[7]. Transfection should ideally be assessed by rt-PCR to identify the expression of specific mRNA trancripts encoded by the vector. Such data are often absent in the preliminary

TABLE 9-2.   A COMPARISON OF THE COMMON VECTORS FOR GENE TRANSFER

Vector	Manufacture	Properties
Liposomes+/- protein	Easy, cheap	Non-toxic, low efficiency
Adenovirus	High titre, labour intensive	Toxic, high efficiency
Herpes Simplex Virus	Intermediate titre, labour intensive	Toxic, low efficiency
Adeno-associated virus	Intermediate titre, labour intensive	Non-toxic, ? efficiency, ? integrates
Lentivirus	Intermediate titre, labour intensive	? toxicity, ? efficiency, ? integrates
Retroviruses	Intermediate titre, cheap	No efficiency. Integrates.

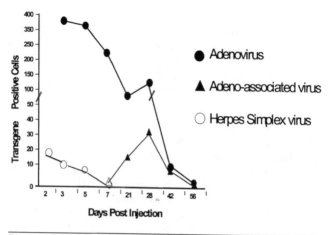

Figure 9-3. The time course of gene expression with 3 viral gene vectors.

animal studies of in vivo cardiac myocyte gene transfer. This method of assessment is far superior to ELISA which only measures protein levels. Problems with ELISA include cross reactivity with similar native proteins unless the ectopic protein contains unique epitopes. Other proteins may also interfere by binding the protein of interest or competing for the primary antibody used in detection. In summary, this technique is rarely able to confirm that the angiogen assayed originates from the transfected gene.

Intracoronary infusion offers a less invasive approach, amenable to routine percutaneous catheter techniques. However, the coronary endothelium/basement membrane is an extremely effective barrier to both plasmid and viral vectors. A number of techniques have been employed to improve transfection across the endothelium. These include administration of VEGF, adenosine or calcium free buffer to increase permeability, prolonged intracoronary dwell time and/or increasing the intracoronary pressure to increase the trans-capillary gradient allowing permeation of vector laden material.[8]

CLINICAL TRIALS OF GENE THERAPY

Vascular endothelial growth factor (VEGF) was the first angiogen utilised in phase 1 clinical trials of angiogenesis[9]. It is secreted as a polypeptide which, through alternative splicing, exists in multiple isoforms. The best-researched isoform is the 165 amino acid residue polypeptide-$VEGF_{165}$. VEGF stimulates capillary formation and increases vascular permeability. Indeed it was this latter effect which caused it to be identified in the ascitic fluid of rats which had peritoneal metastases. Its effects appear to be limited to endothelial cells since they are the only cell type to express the 2 specific tyrosine kinase receptors (flk-1 and flt-1) activated by VEGF. Hypoxia or ischaemia increase VEGF secretion, through transcriptional activation and mRNA stabilisation, but also upregulate VEGF receptor expression.[10] These characteristics give VEGF an important theoretical specificity for therapeutic angiogenesis since even if distant, non-ischaemic, sites are exposed to VEGF DNA the risk of pathological neovascularisation is minimised. The principal phase 1 & 2 clinical trials have focused upon vectors expressing VEGF and Fibroblast Growth Factor (FGF).

Baumgartner et al conducted the first clinical trial of VEGF gene therapy in man.[11,12] They injected 4000mcg of ph-$VEGF_{165}$ into 10 critically ischaemic limbs of 9 patients who were facing amputation. Haemodynamic measurements improved and there was immunohistochemical evidence of proliferation of endothelial cells in tissue specimens. This was coupled with reduced pain and enhanced ulcer healing. At 60 days post injection, 3 limbs had been salvaged and amputation thereby avoided. All patients experienced an increase in pain free walking time that was sustained at 13 weeks post gene transfer. Collateral vessels did not develop at other sites despite significantly elevated serum VEGF levels. This may reflect the short half-life of VEGF in the circulation (minutes) as well as an increase in mRNA stability in ischaemic tissue. Endogenous upregulation of VEGF expression by hypoxic endothelial cells may provide an amplifying mechanism that localizes the action of exogenous VEGF to the ischaemic limb. In this study, no ocular angiogenesis or distant tumorigenesis occurred.

This study was promptly followed by Losordo and Vale who injected 125 micrograms of ph-$VEGF_{165}$ into the myocardium of 5 patients with intractable angina.[13] Two months post gene transfer a reduction in angina frequency occurred in all patients. This was associated with an improvement in myocardial perfusion assessed semi-quantitatively by nuclear myocardial perfusion imaging (Sestamibi-spect).

The mean number of normally perfused segments per patient increased from 6 to 8 accompanied by a decrease in the number of irreversibly perfused segments from 2.4 to 1.2. All these findings were statistically significant despite the small sample size. The magnitude of this effect was greater than that seen following direct injection of an adenoviral vector encoding $VEGF_{121}$. However, the study was limited by the lack of direct evidence of gene transfer and expression. Furthermore, it was uncontrolled and lacked blinding.

The first phase 1 clinical study using a viral vector was reported by Rosengart et al.[14] They employed an E1⁻/E3⁻ adenoviral vector encoding the 121 residue splice variant of human VEGF (Ad $_{GV}$VEGF 121.10). Treatment was administered to 2 groups of patients:

Group A underwent intramyocardial injection of vector to a site unsuitable for conventional grafting (Left anterior descending or circumflex territory) as an adjunct to conventional CABG (n=15).

Group B underwent intramyocardial injection via a mini-thoracotomy as the only therapy (n=6).

Although the numbers of subjects were too small for statistical comparison, most patients exhibited an improvement in both angina class and treadmill exercise time. There was also a trend towards an increased Rentrop score, a semiquantative measure of collateral quality, in both groups. Importantly, there was no evidence of any dose related adverse trend in blood parameters ie: FBC, creatine kinase, renal and liver function or adverse effect at the time of intramyocardial injection ie: arrhythmia, myocardial infarction or ischaemia. No adenoviral particles capable of replication in complimenting cells were recovered from urine, blood, nose and throat swabs. Coronary angiography and echocardiography did not demonstrate haemangioma formation or deterioration in regional wall motion at the injection sites. There was no evidence of tumorigenesis or retinal vessel proliferation.

Following these promising but uncontrolled phase 1 trials, attempts are now being made to quantify any changes in myocardial perfusion by objective means. This is proving to be a challenging task.[15] Hendel assessed 14 patients with single photon emission CT (SPECT) at baseline, 30 days and 60 days post intracoronary administration of plasmid VEGF (rhVEGF) to ischaemic myocardium. Employing a visual, semi quantitative 20-segment scoring method, he demonstrated that summed stress scores failed to improve over 0-30 days. Conversely, there was an improvement in the qualitative summed rest score after rhVEGF (13.2 vs 10.4; $p < 0.05$). However, quantitative analysis of these scans failed to demonstrate statistical significance. The improvement in perfusion score was most clearly shown in the high dose subgroup of patients.

Udelson has published the first myocardial perfusion results of intracoronary and intravenous recombinant fibroblast growth factor-2 therapy in 59 patients with intractable angina.[16] The pooled data, from this unblinded dose response study, demonstrated a reduction in the segmental reversibility score (reflecting the magnitude of inducible ischaemia) from 1.7 ± 0.4 at baseline to 1.1 ± 0.6 at day 29 ($p < 0.001$), 1.2 ± 0.7 at day 57 and 1.1 ± 0.7 at day 180 ($p < 0.001$). There was also a significant improvement in resting perfusion in the 37 patients with resting hypoperfusion. This improvement persisted until day 57. The SPECT scans were analysed by blinded observers using a similar semi-quantitative scoring system to Hendel.[15] No quantitative scan analysis was undertaken and patients did not undergo serial pharmacological testing or imaging at matched exercise levels.

The VIVA trial of VEGF peptide therapy is the first therapeutic angiogenesis clinical trial to be conducted employing a double blind placebo-controlled design.[17] The main clinical end-points were exercise ECG time to ischaemia and exercise duration. 150 patients were randomised into 3 treatment groups receiving a 10 minute intracoronary infusion of placebo or 17 or 50 ng/kg/min of $VEGF_{165}$. This was followed by three 4 hour sessions of intravenous VEGF infusion (placebo or 17 or 50 ng/kg/min on days 3, 6 and

9). There was a 20% improvement in exercise duration in *both* the patients receiving VEGF and placebo! Indeed even SPECT perfusion was similarly enhanced in both groups. This trial highlights the key problems of measuring any clinical benefit in this population of patients and emphasises the fundamental requirement that ongoing or future clinical trials must incorporate objective measures of ischaemia coupled with a double blind study design.

The principal problem with the current clinical trials is that there is no definitive evidence that transgene expression occurs in the target myocardial tissue. To achieve this the myocardial tissue at the site of intramyocardial injection would have to be excised and analysed by rt-PCR to prove that the angiogen induced arises from the transgene and not the native gene. This means that most of the trials to date have been forced to use changes in systemic growth factor levels, myocardial perfusion or exercise tolerance as surrogate markers of efficacy. Currently we have no robust evidence that transgene expression has occurred in human myocardium and that any improvement in perfusion we observe is not simply due to a placebo effect or a non-specific inflammatory response to injury.

These issues have been carefully evaluated and are the subject of an Expert Panel Summary published in *Circulation* designed to guide the planning of future angiogenesis trials.[18] This has highlighted the limitations of the end points available to cardiologists in evaluating angiogenic therapies and warrants more detailed discussion, as these issues are fundamental to the planning of future therapeutic strategies in this field.

THE LIMITATIONS OF CURRENT ASSESSMENT MODALITIES

1) Exercise Testing. Exercise tolerance testing is highly variable. Performance can change from day to day due to factors unrelated to angina such as claudication, pulmonary disease, deconditioning and patient motivation. The adoption of exercise tolerance testing as a primary end point should be carefully considered since the original anti-anginal drug trials that produced consistent exercise tolerance data were conducted in patients with mild angina and normal left ventricular function. Any study should ensure that blinded observers perform the exercise tests and that patients are excluded if they demonstrate greater than 30% variability in exercise duration between 2 consecutive screening exercise tests.

2) Perfusion Imaging. The problems of exercise testing are compounded by the limitations of perfusion imaging. SPECT myocardial perfusion imaging with 201 Thallium or 99m Technetium is a well-validated clinical tool in the *diagnosis* of ischaemic heart disease and demonstration of improved perfusion post revascularisation. The main problems are related to the resolution of SPECT in detecting improved perfusion of collateral dependant myocardium and distinguishing improved perfusion in the subendocardium where angiogenesis is most likely to optimise flow. There are also problems with the consistency of pharmacological stress eg: adenosine or dipyridamole. Collateral dependant myocardium has a significantly reduced flow reserve when compared to normal myocardial tissue and the potential of coronary steal occuring during maximal hyperaemia can result in an apparent reduction in relative perfusion of collateral dependant regions when absolute collateral support may have increased. Furthermore, as the study above illustrates,[15] objective scores of perfusion require computer algorithms that currently lack the sensitivity of trained blinded observers assessing serial scans.

A number of these difficulties can be addressed by positron emission tomography (PET) which can objectively measure absolute myocardial blood flow (MBF) and has the sensitivity to detect the even more subtle alterations in MBF that may be more clinically relevant. However, there is still limited data describing the degree of change in transmural MBF required to achieve clinical benefit, whilst techniques to quantitate subendocardial perfusion are only just beginning to develop.

These limitations to the objective clinical assessment of a potential angiogenic response mean that the results of past uncontrolled trials are greeted with scepticism. Furthermore increasing concerns over the safety of gene therapy have caused professional and public disquiet which can only be addressed through the generation of robust evidence to support the continued application of these techniques.

SAFETY CONCERNS

The main concerns of angiogenic gene and peptide therapy centre upon the potentiation of pathological processes which depend on angiogenesis such as tumour growth, retinopathy, and expansion of atheromatous plaque. Other concerns relate to the specific properties of the vector. The exposure of atheromatous plaque to angiogens can promote the expansion of cellular elements within the plaque and consequent destabilisation. This is further supported by a number of clinical observations demonstrating upregulation of VEGF and its receptors in plaques with a marked inflammatory cellular infiltrate. Since VEGF is a chemoattractant it may cause, rather than simply be associated with, the rupture-prone plaque.[19] Similarly, coronary atherectomy specimens from unstable plaques show elevated levels of acidic and basic FGF. FGF transgene transfer into the porcine arterial wall induces marked intimal hyperplasia and neocapillary formation.[20]

In addition to the risks of the transgene encoded by the vector, the vector itself may have inherent properties that are unattractive. These include the induction of local inflammation with destruction of transfected cells that limits the duration and increases the toxicity of gene transfer. Furthermore some vectors have the inherent ability to integrate into the genome and although under certain circumstances this may carry the advantage of prolonged transgene expression, it carries the disadvantage of insertional mutagenesis. In addition if integration occurs in cells within the germline there is the potential to alter the human gene pool.

These concerns have been brought into sharp focus with the occurrence of 6 deaths in recent clinical cardiac angiogenesis trials conducted in 2 centres in America.[21] There is currently no evidence to suggest that these patients died as a direct result of angiogenic gene therapy. Nevertheless, the whole field has been forced to re-evaluate its position and face the reality that a return to the laboratory bench is mandatory if public confidence is to be maintained in the application of these techniques.

As angiogenic gene therapy stands at a crossroads we should carefully consider the rationale of this approach and evaluate its clinical role.[22]

QUESTIONING THE PHILOSOPHY OF ANGIOGENESIS

The greater the ignorance the greater the dogmatism.
Sir William Osler 1902

The protective role of coronary collaterals. We have firm evidence that coronary collaterals are very effective in limiting infarct size, incidence of cardiogenic shock, arrhythmia and mortality during and following acute MI. Futhermore there are many examples of a mature collateral network preventing resting ischaemia in the context of chronic occlusion and maybe even supplying sufficient flow to preserve normal resting wall motion.

However, the capacity of collaterals to achieve adequate perfusion during exercise is questionable. Studies addressing this have been confounded by the fact that patients were often not matched for the extent of coronary artery disease and had variable patterns of collateral growth. This is fundamental to any developments in the field since the native collateral network may have already reached its full potential and any further effects of therapy may only be of marginal benefit. Vanoevershelde has demonstrated the capacity of collaterals to maintain resting perfusion and viability in an elegant clinical study employing PET.[23]

He investigated 26 angina patients with chronic occlusion of a major epicardial coronary artery but without previous infarction. In 9 patients the wall motion was normal in the region of coronary occlusion. In these patients the regional myocardial blood flow, oxidative metabolism and glucose uptake were similar in the collateral dependant and remote myocardial segments. However, in the 17 patients with regional dysfunction, the collateral-dependant segments had lower myocardial blood flow (77 ± 25 versus 95 ± 27 mL/min/100g tissue) and higher glucose uptake versus remote segments. The myocardial blood flow at rest was similar in the collateral dependant segments of patients with and without regional dysfunction. Following intravenous dipyridamole, collateral dependant myocardial blood flow increased 3 fold in 3 patients with normal wall motion and by only 27% in 8 patients with regional dysfunction. Angina symptoms were less severe in those patients with normal function and high collateral flow reserve supporting the concept that the collateral network has the capacity to not only maintain normal LV function following coronary occlusion but also reduce ischaemic symptoms. However, these collaterals could not fully protect against angina during hyperaemic stress even in the patients with normal wall motion and significantly greater collateral flow reserve. A further difficulty with the interpretation of studies of this type is that it is only the symptomatic patients that present for angiography.

As we have already implied, we also do not have any convincing evidence that exercise tolerance is any better in those patients with a well-developed collateral supply when matched for the extent of native coronary artery disease. At St Thomas' Hospital, we have precisely characterised a population of patients with single vessel LAD coronary artery disease by measuring collateral support to the distal myocardium during 2, 180 second intracoronary balloon occlusions. This was done using the pressure wire technique developed by Pijls[24] (Figure 9-4a and 9-4b).

There are no differences in exercise time to ischaemia on treadmill testing (Figure 9-5) in those patients with significant recruitable collateral flow (Collateral Flow Index ≥ 0.25) during PTCA and those without (CFI<0.25). Therefore, in patients with no recruitable collaterals, we may not objectively improve exercise tolerance even by increasing the collateral contribution to anterior wall blood flow.

Despite an increased understanding of the processes involved in collateral vessel formation and angiogenesis, we

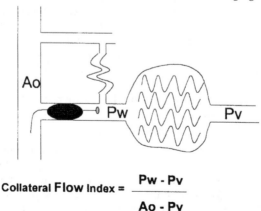

$$\text{Collateral Flow Index} = \frac{Pw - Pv}{Ao - Pv}$$

Figure 9-4a. Model of coronary circulation at total occlusion.

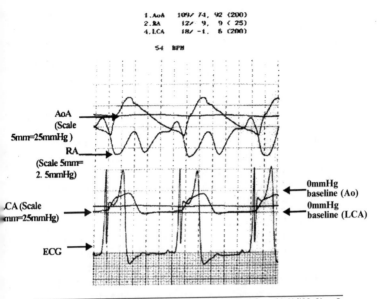

Figure 9-4b. The CFI in this patient was calculated as (6-9)/(92-9) ≈0. The scale for each pressure measurement is described above with the baseline marked 0mmHg. LCA = coronary occlusion pressure.

have very poor knowledge of the factors that maintain a collateral network and prevent its regression. The effects of collateral regression are suggested by data from the TOTAL study.[25] The TOTAL study involved 305 patients undergoing PTCA to open chronic total occlusions proximal to collateral dependant myocardium. Although it was designed to compare the efficacy of laser wires versus conventional mechanical wires in crossing total occlusions, the outcome of the patients provides an interesting insight into the plasticity and rate of regression of the collateral supply. The incidence of CABG was 32% in patients where occlusions were not successfully re-opened versus only 6% in the open group at 6 months. There was a trend to increased incidence of both MI and death in those patients who had successful recanalisation of the occluded coronary artery. This suggests that once normal perfusion is achieved, these patients lose native protection possibly through the regres-

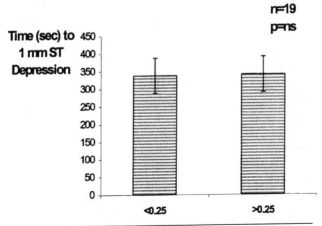

Figure 9-5. Ischaemic thresholds in high and low CFI patient groups.

sion of collateral support and perhaps preconditioning. The former has been confirmed by Werner who used measurements of CFI immediately on opening a chronic total occlusion and then 24 hours later by balloon occlusion within the stented segment, to show that collaterals regress by at least 50% in 24h.[26]

Therefore, although it may appear desirable to optimise myocardial perfusion by enhancing collateral growth, when growth factor levels fall the collaterals are likely to regress. Thus the presence of collaterals is probably synonymous with ischaemia. This paradox may limit the development of a fully mature collateral network which would be capable of ischaemic protection during exercise stress.

The current paradigm which forms the basis of the clinical trials in angiogenic therapy is that neovascularisation fails to occur because the balance of pro and anti angiogenic factors favours inhibition. However, this concept takes no account of the fact that the substrate ie: the existing cellular components of vessels and pericytes are already maximally stimulated and may indeed be resistant to angiogens. This may be due to a number of factors including receptor down regulation, position in the growth cycle or cellular – viability. Perhaps there is a resistance to growth factors in the myocardium that prevents further collateral development. Data from our group suggests that this may be an issue in a proportion of patients.

We have been able to identify two groups of patients with single vessel LAD disease classified according to the degree of collateral development measured by the pressure wire technique developed by Pijls. There are no significant differences in the arteriovenous gradients of VEGF or FGF across the coronary bed. However, coronary sinus serum from patients with impaired collateral development is able to induce endothelial cell proliferation at a 2 fold higher rate than in patients with well developed collaterals (Figure 9-6). This was quantified with an in-vitro culture-based assay

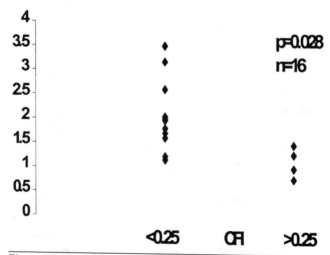

Figure 9.6: *Relative Mitogenicity of Coronary Sinus serum (versus control pooled human serum) in patients with high and low CFI.*

measuring the rate of ^3H thymidine incorporation into DNA compared to control pooled human serum in the 2 groups. These 2 populations of patients are well matched for age, risk factors and duration of symptoms. The increased serum mitogenicity may reflect the fact that although there is an upregulation in local angiogen production, there is an inadequate response. The stimulus may be be due to tissue ischaemia. This data suggests that one should closely consider the cellular elements in the myocardial bed as myocardial resistance to stimulation maybe a key limiting step.

The discordant results of therapy in the transition from animal models to man is leading to the investigation of alternative angiogenic strategies to optimise myocardial perfusion.

ALTERNATIVES TO ANGIOGENIC PEPTIDE AND GENE THERAPY

Recent attention has focussed upon a limited number of peptides and little attention has been paid to pathways which may act as key downstream modulators of the process. One such candidate is the tissue angiotensin converting enzyme (ACE) system.

The tissue ACE system has been implicated in angiogenesis in a number of studies. Angiotensin II is known to augment rat cremaster muscle microvascular density (via the AT-1 receptor) and to promote angiogenesis in pre and post capillary vessels in the chick embryo chorioallantoic membrane.[27] Even though captopril inhibits neovascularisation in the rat cornea and microvascular development in hypertensive and normotensive rats, other ACE inhibitors have been shown to promote capillary formation in other tissues, including rat limb muscle. One agent, spirapril, has demonstrated this activity in cardiac tissue. Angiotensin II blockade in sciatic nerve also has angiogenic effects.[28]

In this context, perhaps the most convincing study to date was performed in the rabbit model of hindlimb ischaemia.[29] Quinaprilat (a nonsulphhydryl ACE-I with high tissue affinity), administered subcutaneously, was compared with a) captopril (lower efficacy of tissue bound ACE-I) and b) intra arterial recombinant human $VEGF_{165}$ therapy. At day 40, both functional and morphological markers of angiogenesis were significantly elevated in the quinaprilat and recombinant VEGF treated animals versus captopril treatment or controls. Capillary density in quinaprilat treated limbs was 50% greater than captopril or controls ($214/mm^2$ vs $140.5/mm^2$). This effect was sustained at 5 days after cessation of quinaprilat indicating that these findings were not the result of a transient pharmacologically mediated improvement in endothelium dependant blood flow. The results indicated a persistent modification of the hindlimb vasculature which was also demonstrated histologically by increased capillary density. The failure of captopril to induce an angiogenic effect was thought to be due to its lower affinity for tissue ACE. The drug doses were selected so that the same level of plasma ACE inhibition was achieved with both agents. It is possible that mobilisation of endothelial cells, which typically occurs during angiogenesis, was opposed by the metalloproteinase inhibition associated with the sulphydryl group of captopril.

The mechanisms responsible for these effects of tissue ACE inhibition remain to be fully elucidated. Upregulation of angiogenic cytokines is unlikely to be responsible; since Ang II promotes VEGF expression by endothelial and smooth muscle cells, ACE-I should be anti-angiogenic. However, upregulation of local nitric oxide (NO) production could explain the phenomenon. NO is an important regulatory molecule in angiogenesis. Knock-out mice homozygous for disrupted eNOS alleles have an impaired angiogenic response to hindlimb ischaemia.[30] Rabbits fed a diet supplemented with L-arginine improve local neovascularisation in the same model. VEGF directly upregulates endothelial NO production and may be crucial for VEGF induced angiogenesis – eNOS deficient mice are unresponsive to VEGF. Therefore, the angiogenic effects of ACE-I may occur by increasing NO bioavailability. At least 2 possible mechanisms have been proposed: 1) increased bradykinin levels which can activate the L-arginine-NO pathway or 2) prevention of accumulated Ang II from stimulating NADH oxidase to produce superoxide anions which can scavenge NO.[25]

These findings have important implications for the promotion of myocardial perfusion and could explain some of the positive effects of ACE-I on cardiovascular mortality, left ventricular remodelling post MI and coronary event rates. This may be significant in determining future approaches in therapeutic angiogenesis research.

CONCLUSION

The clinical demand for solutions to the problem of persistent myocardial ischaemia in those with patterns of coronary artery disease unsuitable for revascularisation are increasing. Currently 15 000 CABG operations are performed in the UK per annum. However, 20-35% of bypass grafts fail between 1 and 24 months leaving over 4000 patients per annum in this country alone with a suboptimal result of surgical myocardial revascularisation. There are no national statistics describing the size of the population where PTCA or surgery are considered too high risk or unattractive. This number is set to increase with a National Service Framework to expand cardiac diagnostic and surgical services. Therefore, non-invasive strategies to optimise myocardial perfusion, particularly in these patients, must be rigorously investigated.

Targeted modulation of angiogenesis in ischaemic myocardium offers a potential treatment for such patients with intractable angina. The peptide and gene therapy trials in progress have highlighted the fact that our knowledge base needs improvement and the techniques currently available to assess the success of therapy lack sensitivity and specificity.

We are at a crossroads which demands that we take stock of the present data and carefully evaluate the design of future trials. This means that pharmacological agents targeted to specific modulators of the process should be assessed. Furthermore, the cellular elements fundamental to angiogenesis should not be ignored since these are the key effectors determining the stability and functional capacity of collateral vessels in the human heart. Future approaches may involve the introduction of endothelial progenitor cells to participate in the formation of new myocardial vessels aswell as agents to modulate local angiogen levels in the heart. It is only with such a methodical approach that these strategies will be able to pass safely from the laboratory bench to the clinic.

REFERENCES

1. Carmeliet P. Mechanisms of angiogenesis and arteriogenesis. Nat Medicine 2000: 6, 389-395.
2. Carmeliet, P. and Collen, D. Molecular analysis of blood vessel formation and disease. Am.J.Physiol 273(5 Pt 2) H2091-104, 1997.
3. Banai S, Shureihi D, Pinson A, Chandra M, Lazarovici G, Keshet E. Upregulation of vascular endothelial growth factor induced by myocardial ischemia. Implications for coronary angiogenesis. Cardiovasc Res 28:1176-79,1994.
4. Folkman, J. and D'Amore, P.A. Blood vessel formation: what is its molecular basis? [comment]. Cell 87:1153-1155, 1996.
5. Schwarz ER, Speakman MT, Patterson M, Hale SS, Isner JM, Kedes LH, Kloner RA. Evaluation of the effcts of ntramyocardial injection of DNA expressing VEGF in a myocardial infarction model in the rat-angiogenesis and angioma formation. JACC 2000;35:1323-30.
6. Yla-Herttuala S, Martin JF. Cardiovascular gene therapy. Lancet 2000 355:213-22. [Review.].
7. Wright MJ, Rosenthal E, Stewart L, Wightman LML, Miller AD, Latchman DS, Marber MS. ß-galactosidase staining following intracoronary infusion of cationic liposomes in the in vivo rabbit heart is produced by microinfarction rather than effective gene transfer. A cautionary tale. Gene Therapy 1998;5:301-308.
8. Donahue A, Heldman AW, Fraser H, McDonald AD, Miller JM, Rade JJ, Eschenhagen A, and Marbán E. Focal modulation of electrical conduction in the heart by viral gene transfer. Nat Medicine 2000:6;1395-1398.
9. Thomas FA.VEGF–A potent and selective angiogenic agent. J Biol Chem 1996;271:603-606.
10. Brogi E, Schatteman G, Wu T, et al. Hypoxia-induced paracrine regulation of vascular endothelial growth factor receptor expression. J Clin Invest 1996; 97: 469-476.
11. Baumgartner, I., Pieczek, A., Manor, O., Blair, R., Kearney, M., Walsh, K., and Isner, J.M. Constitutive expression of phVEGF165 after intramuscular gene transfer promotes collateral vessel development in patients with critical limb ischemia [see comments]. Circulation 97:1114-1123, 1998.
12. Baumgartner, I. and Isner, J.M. Stimulation of peripheral angiogenesis by vascular endothelial growth factor (VEGF). Vasa 27:201-206, 1998.
13. Losordo, D.W., Vale, P.R., Symes, J.F., Dunnington, C.H., Esakof, D.D., Maysky, M., Ashare, A.B., Lathi, K., and Isner, J.M. Gene therapy for myocardial angiogenesis: initial clinical results with direct myocardial injection of phVEGF165 as sole therapy for myocardial ischemia. Circulation 98 :2800-2804, 1998.
14. Rosengart TK, Lee LY, Patel SR, Sanborn TA, Parikh M, Bergman GW, Hachamovitch R, Szulc M, Kligfield PD, Okin PM, Hahn RT, Devereux RB, Post MR, Hackett NR, Foster T, Grasso TM, Lesser ML, Isom W, Crystal RG: Phase 1 assessment of direct intramyocardial administration

of an adenovirus vector expressing VEGF 121 cDNA to individuals with clinically significant severe coronary artery disease. Circulation 1999, 100:468-477.

15. Hendel RC, Henry TD, Rocha-Singh K, Isner JM, Kereiakes DJ, Giordano FJ, Simons M, Bonow RO . Effect of intracoronary recombinant human vascular endothelial growth factor on myocardial perfusion: evidence for a dose-dependent effect. Circulation 2000;101:118-21.

16. Udelson JE, Dilsizian, V, Laham, RJ; Chronos, N; Vansant J, Blais M, Galt JR; Pike M, Yoshizawa C; Simons M . Therapeutic Angiogenesis With Recombinant Fibroblast Growth Factor-2 Improves Stress and Rest Myocardial Perfusion Abnormalities in Patients With Severe Symptomatic Chronic Coronary Artery Disease Circulation. 2000;102:1605.

17. Henry TD, Annex BH, Azrin MA, Mc Kendall GR, Willerson JT, Hendel RC, Giordano FJ, Klein R, Gibdon M, Berman DS, Luce CA, Mc Cluskey ER. Double blind placebo controlled trial of recombinant human VEGF: The VIVA Trial: JACC 1999;33(suppl A):384A. Abstract.

18. Michael Simons, Robert O. Bonow, Nicolas A. Chronos, David J. Cohen, Frank J. Giordano, H. Kirk Hammond, Roger J. Laham, William Li, Marylin Pike, Frank W. Sellke, Thomas J. Stegmann, James E. Udelson, and Todd K. Rosengart. Clinical Trials in Coronary Angiogenesis: Issues, Problems, Consensus: An Expert Panel Summary Circulation 2000, 102: e73-e86.

19. Inoue, Hiroshi Itoh, Makiko Ueda, Takahiko Naruko, Akiko Kojima, Ryushi Komatsu, Kentaro Doi, Yoshihiro Ogawa, Naohisa Tamura, Kazuhiko Takaya, Toshio Igaki, Jun Yamashita, Tae-Hwa Chun, Ken Masatsugu, Anton E. Becker, and Kazuwa Nakao Vascular Endothelial Growth Factor (VEGF) Expression in Human Coronary Atherosclerotic Lesions: Possible Pathophysiological Significance of VEGF in Progression of Atherosclerosis . Circulation 1998; 98: 2108-2116.

20. Flugelman MY, Virmani R, Correa R, Yu ZX, Leon MB, Elami A, Fu YM, Cscalls W, Epstein SE. Smooth muscle cell abundance and fibroblast growth fators in coronary lesions of patients with non-fatal unstable angina: a clue to the mechanism of transformation from the stable to the unstable clinical state. Circulation 1993;88:2493-2500.

21. The increasing opacity of gene therapy. Nature 1999 402 Issue no 6758.

22. SoRelle,R. Gene therapy at the crossroads. Circulation 2000;101, 107:e9001.

23. Vanoverschelde JJ, Wijns W, Depre C, Essamri B, Heyndrickx GR, Borgers M, Bol A, Melin JA: Mechanisms of chronic regional postischemic dysfunction in humans. Circulation 1993;87:1513-1523.

24. Pijls NHJ, van Son JAM, Kirkeeide RL, de Bruyne B, Gould KL. Experimental basis of determining maximum coronary, myocardial, and collateral blood flow by pressure measurements for assessing functional stenosis severity before and after percutaneous transluminal coronary angioplasty. Circulation 1993;87:1354-1367.

25. Serruys PW, Hamburger JN, Fajadet J, Haude M, Klues H, Seabra-Gomes R, Corcos T, Hamm C, Pizzuli L, Meier B, Fleck E, Taeymans Y, Melkert R, Teunissen S, Simon R.Total occlusion trial with angioplasty by using laser guidewire. The TOTAL trial. Eur Heart J. 2000 21:1797-1805.

26. Werner GS, Richartz BM, Gastmann O, Ferrari M, Lang K, Figulla. Recruitable and non-recruitable collateral circulation after successful recanalisation of chronic total coronary occlusions. JACC 2000;25: Suppl A,64A.

27. Le Noble FA, Schreurs NH, van Straaten HW, Slaaf DW, Smits JF, Rogg H, Struijker-Boudier HA. Evidence for a novel angiotensin II receptor involved in angiogenesis in chick embryo chorioallantoic membrane. Am J Physiol. 1993;264:R460R465.

28. Cameron NE, Cotter MA, Robertson S. Angiotensin Converting Enzyme inhibition prevents development of muscle and nerve dysfunction and stimulates angiogenesis in streptozotocin diabetic rats. Diabetologia 1992, 35:12-18.

29. Chua CC, Hamdy RC, Chua BH. Upregulation of vascular endothelial growth factor by angiotensin II in rat heart endothelial cells. Biochim Biophys Acta 1998; 1401: 187-194.

30. Murohara T, Asahara T, Silver M, Bauters C, Masuda H, Kalka C, Kearney M, Chen D, Symes JF, Fishman MC, Huang PL, Isner JM. Nitric oxide synthase modulates angiogenesis in response to tissue ischemia. J Clin Invest. 1998;101:25672578.

31. Gibbons GH. Cardioprotective mechanisms of ACE inhibition. The angiotensin II-nitric oxide balance. [Review] [74 refs]. Drugs 1997; 54 Suppl 5: 1-11.